BASIC
With Business
Applications

BASIC With Business Applications

Richard W. Lott, CDP, CMA
Bentley College
Waltham, Massachusetts

JOHN WILEY & SONS
New York • Chichester • Brisbane • Toronto

Library of Congress Cataloging in Publication Data:

Lott, Richard W.
    BASIC with business applications.

    Bibliography: p.
    Includes index.
    1. Basic (Computer program language) I. Title.

HF5548.5.B3L67   001.6'424   77-8320
ISBN 0-471-02341-8

Printed in the United States of America
10 9 8 7 6

PREFACE

This textbook deals with three closely related topics.

1. An introduction to interactive computing through the use of the BASIC programming language.

2. Instruction in program flowcharting and other methods to help design the logical part of problem solution.

3. Tying together a program flowchart and BASIC instructions to solve numerous problems in a variety of business situations.

The various equipment manufacturers and BASIC users have not yet adopted a set of standards to surround the language. Thus, many differences exist in how BASIC may be used. I have, therefore, covered certain aspects of BASIC in a general way; you may pick up the specifics at your own site of operations. Appendix B shows common system commands available at the Bentley College Computer Center.

Most of the instruction in BASIC and in program flowcharting is covered in Part I. Each new instruction is immediately illustrated in a working program. Several topics are introduced in Part II, where it is apparent that the need for a certain variation exists. All of the instructions presented are summarized in Appendix A.

My coverage of BASIC largely bypasses the "mathematical" approach. While every application program does call on the computer to perform mathematical functions, most of the formulas are relatively simple. The derivation of the formulas can be found in accounting and finance references. More of the mathematical capability of BASIC may be obtained from other books named in Appendix F.

Each of the applications in Part II starts with a verbal statement of a common business problem. Then there is a discussion of how the problem will be solved. The application is completed by the writing and the execution of an appropriate BASIC program.

The end-of-chapter exercises are of four major types.

1. Recall from instructional topics.

2. Questions about your understanding of the sample programs.

3. Requests for you to make certain changes to programs in the text.

4. Situations that require you to develop a complete program to solve a specific problem.

Part I is designed for any person who wants to learn the major elements of the BASIC language. No prior knowledge of any phase of computers or programming is assumed.

Part II has been written so that you can see practical uses of the language. Even students whose major interest is the applications in Part II will find that a minimum of time is needed to cover Part I well enough to understand the applications.

Other educators who helped in writing this book are John Homeister, Molly Lovelock, and Ed Wondolowski. Students who either helped to write programs or to serve as reviewers are John Homeister, Jr., Gerry McCue, Steve Robinson, Susan Woodard, and Joan Zanger.

R. W. Lott

CONTENTS

BASIC
With Business
Applications

Part 1

Instruction in The BASIC Language

1 CHAPTER
INTRODUCTION TO TIME-SHARING

The word BASIC is an acronym for "*B*eginners *A*ll-purpose *S*ymbolic *In*struction *C*ode." This language was developed to make computer programming and computer use relatively easy for millions of people who want to solve certain types of problems. BASIC is referred to as a high-level language since one does not need to learn many technical aspects of the computer to use it.

BASIC is most often used in a time-sharing mode. "Time-sharing" means that a particular computer is set up in a special way to process the individual, unrelated programs of dozens or even hundreds of people at any one time. Generally, each user is served quickly enough to be unaware of any other users.

Time-sharing operates in an interactive mode between the user and the computer. That is, the user directly submits a program and some data to the computer. The computer executes the program and furnishes the results back to the user immediately. This process is in contrast to a batch-type of computer operation where the user submits the data to Computer Center personnel who then input the data to the computer. The user may not get any results from the Computer Center for several days.

Getting immediate feedback has at least two major advantages. First, you find out if your program is working properly. If it is not, you can change your program on the spot and try again while everything is still fresh in your mind. Second, once your program is working properly, you get the answers to problems in seconds and minutes rather than in hours and days.

Using the computer in this fashion is often called conversational computing. The user enters data, and the computer immediately responds with results.

The link between the person and the computer is most often some form of teletypewriter. This is a specially designed typewriter that is either wired directly to the computer or is tied into the computer over a telephone line. See an example of a teletypewriter in Fig. 1-1.

Thus the computer itself can physically be located anywhere provided that the Computer Center and the user are served by a telephone company. Programs and data going to and from the computer obviously move over the telephone line or over some similar arrangement in a di-

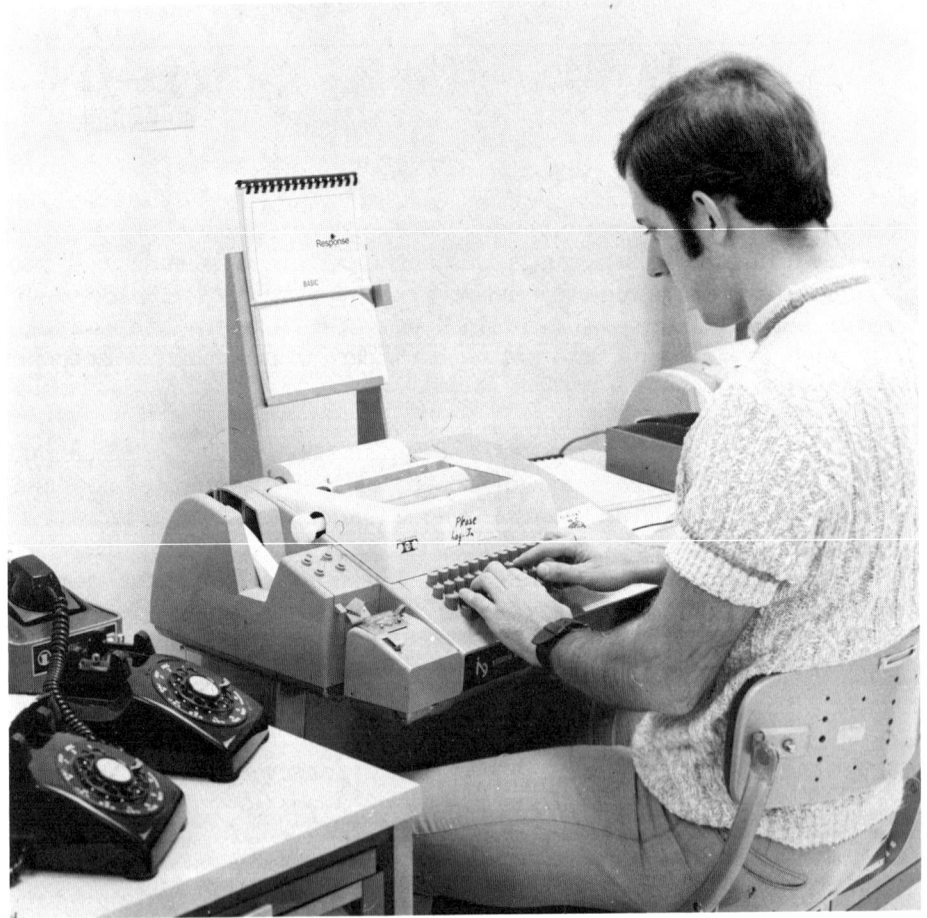

Fig. 1-1. Picture of a teletypewriter.

4   INSTRUCTION IN THE BASIC LANGUAGE

rectly wired system. The transmission could also take place through air waves.

The time-sharing service itself is provided by an institution such as a computer manufacturer, a college, a service bureau, or an organization providing services for its own employees. Whether the vendor of the service is a profit-seeking or a nonprofit organization, some control must be exercised over those who use the service. This control is normally carried out by issuing special codes and passwords to authorized users.

When one wants to use the service, he or she "calls" the computer as if he or she were making a regular phone call. The computer responds by typing back certain statements to the person on the teletypewriter.

The person is expected to type a special code and a password back to the computer. If the person can do so, the computer accepts that person as a user and allocates a portion of its available resources to him or her. The user is then able to write and/or run programs on the computer, controlling the computer to do what he or she wants within the capability of the machine and the BASIC language.

A part of this "signing on" process generally allows the user to assign a name to the program that will be used. Both the computer and the user can keep better track of all programs if they have been assigned names.

Each time-sharing service has established the procedures that must be used to sign on and to sign off its computer. Instead of providing only a general statement about these requirements here, I feel that you can best learn them directly from the center that you will use. You should be able to do so in a few minutes.

You might then try the procedures on your own to make sure that you understand how to sign on and sign off. The procedures that are appropriate to my use of the Bentley College time-sharing service are shown in Appendix B.

2 CHAPTER
GETTING STARTED
IN TIME-SHARING

Generally, computer programming involves the preparation of instructions that:

1. Put certain data into the computer (by one of several methods).

2. Perform certain steps upon that data (such as arithmetic).

3. Present the results by one of several methods (which, in our case, will be from a teletypewriter).

In order to prepare instructions that will do the above things, it is necessary to keep track of the data. In BASIC, we keep track of the different units of data by assigning each of them a unique data or variable name. A variable name can be either one alphabetic character (A, B, C, ... Z) or one alphabetic character and one digit (A1, B4, C7, Z0, etc.).

It is usually helpful if the variable names are assigned in a way that will help us to easily remember what we are doing. The first sample program will illustrate this idea.

Let us use as a sample program, one that will accept two values, add them, and print the total. A BASIC program requires only a few steps to accomplish this. I will assign specific amounts to both the first value and the second value (to which I will assign variable names V1 and V2); I will add the two values to get a total (to which I will assign the variable name T); and then I will print the total (T).

7

Suppose that we want V1 (the first value) to be equal to 4. We can cause the machine to accept that fact by typing a line number and the word LET followed by V1 = 4.

A "line number" is required for each instruction. The number must be within the range of 1 through 9999 (99999 in some computers). A line number provides a convenient means for both the computer and the user to refer to any particular instruction.

The numbers must be assigned sequentially (not necessarily consecutively), with no duplication of numbers. It is better if the numbers are not consecutive (1, 2, 3, 4, 5, etc.) because if they are, it becomes more difficult to go back and insert additional instructions later.

Some computers require the word LET in all instructions that involve the equal (=) symbol. The word LET will be used in this way in Chapters 2 and 3, but it will not be used in subsequent chapters.

I will arbitrarily choose number 10 as the first line number. The first instruction would then look like this:

```
10 LET V1 = 4
```

You can space between the various characters as you wish in order to provide readability. However, the computer ignores all spaces within instructions; you could have prepared the above instruction in either of the following ways, among others.

```
10 L E T V1    =    4

10LETV1=4
```

With a little practice, you will probably decide not to do much spacing within instructions because you will find that you don't need it to keep track of what you are doing. Furthermore, you can save time if you are not too precise on spacing within instructions. Proper spacing of output results is discussed later.

Now, let's set V2 equal to 7. This instruction can be entered by choosing a line number higher than 10 and by putting it into the computer in the same way. I have chosen line number 20 because that will allow plenty of room for more instructions to be inserted later, if necessary. At this point, we have:

```
10 LET V1 = 4
20 LET V2 = 7
```

Next, we want to add V1 and V2 to product T. The required addition step will be composed as follows.

1. As in all BASIC instructions, there must be a line number.

2. The word LET must follow the line number.

3. A variable name must be assigned to the answer. Then, later, when we want to do something to the answer, we simply refer to its variable name.

4. Following the name assigned to the answer there must be an equal (=) symbol.

5. The units of data to be added must be shown separated by a plus (+) symbol (BASIC requires the + symbol to cause addition).

Based on the above five points and the discussion preceding them, I will prepare the addition instruction this way:

```
30 LET T = V1 + V2
```

Next, we need an instruction to print the answer. The instruction itself requires a line number and the word PRINT, followed by the name(s) of the values that you want printed. This instruction will be set as:

```
40 PRINT T
```

The four instructions just described represent everything that we wanted the program to do. But there must be one additional instruction. It is an END statement that tells the computer where the physical "end" of the program is to be. Its use will be more meaningful in a later example. For our purposes, we will merely write:

```
50 END
```

Once you have typed in the program, as above, and you are ready to have the computer execute the program, it is only necessary to type the word RUN on the line following the END statement and push the RE-TURN key. This is the signal to the computer that it is to convert your instructions in BASIC to its own internal language and that it is to perform the steps as you directed. The complete program and its execution are shown in Fig. 2-1.

When the command RUN is used on the computer available to me, the machine prints the program name (SIMPLE, which was assigned when

```
10 LET V1 = 4
20 LET V2 = 7
30 LET T = V1 + V2
40 PRINT T
50 END

READY
RUN

SIMPLE            14:07         21-NOV-76


    11



TIME:  0.04 SECS.

READY
```

Fig. 2-1. Listing and execution of SIMPLE.

signing on), the time of day, and the date. On completion of execution, it prints the elapsed computer time. Note that what is provided at the beginning of, and just after, execution will vary among computer centers. (For our purposes, the time of day and the date are not relevant.)

The output of the number 11, sitting by itself, certainly looks barren, but that is exactly what we told the computer to do. Rarely does the computer "anticipate" our needs and do anything more than what we tell it to do.

Suppose that we want the computer to print the values of V1 and V2 as well as their total. How hard will this be? Do we have to type in a whole new program?

Making the change is a simple process, since the computer will keep our program as long as we wish. It is only the PRINT step that needs to be changed. We only need to alter it so that V1 and V2 will be printed from it as well as T. It can be done like this (see how commas are used to separate the data names):

```
40 PRINT V1, V2, T
```

A change can be made to any existing instruction by merely typing the same line number and the rest of the instruction the way that you want it. This causes the computer to "forget" the instruction that was there before. After changing line 40 as above, you only need to type RUN. The output of the program will then look like this:

```
RUN

SIMPLE          16:52         02-NOV-76


4               7             11


TIME:  0.06 SECS.
```

READY

The output is still bare. Suppose you would like to see some identification above the three values. Let's instruct the computer to print the words VALUE 1, VALUE 2, and TOTAL above their respective values. BASIC permits the printing of any combination of letters and/or numbers that you wish by enclosing them in quotation marks. This is known as a "nonnumeric literal" or a "character string."

Where is a logical place to put the instruction? We want the heading above the data on our printout, so let's put the instruction for printing the literal value ahead of the instruction at line number 10. I will arbitrarily assign line number five and set it up this way:

```
5 PRINT "VALUE 1", "VALUE 2", "TOTAL"
```

The quotation marks tell the computer to print exactly what is between quotations in the order shown. Merely typing the additional instruction as shown and then typing RUN will cause the new instruction to be inserted in its proper sequence and the program will then be executed as in Fig. 2-2.

Very often a user would like to see a list of answers coming from data whose values vary according to some plan. Suppose you want to see how the answer T would change if you were to vary the value of V1. Let's make V1 larger by adding a value of 1 to it and execute the program in that way.

Where is a convenient place to put an instruction that will make V1 larger? Figure 2-2 shows that we might add this instruction at line 45. Let's do it:

```
45 LET V1 = V1 + 1
```

In computer programming, this step makes sense, since it says "make V1 one more than it was before." Variable names (such as V1, V2, and T) are so-called because they refer to data that can vary during run-

```
5 PRINT "VALUE 1", "VALUE 2", "TOTAL"
10 LET V1 = 4
20 LET V2 = 7
30 LET T = V1 + V2
40 PRINT V1, V2, T
50 END

READY
RUN

SIMPLE          14:04          21-NOV-76


VALUE 1         VALUE 2        TOTAL
4               7              11


TIME:  0.05 SECS.

READY
```

Fig. 2-2. Listing and execution of SIMPLE with headings.

ning of the program. The one (1) in line 45 is called a constant, since it obviously cannot change during running of the program.

After V1 has been made one larger than it was before, do we want the program to go on to the END step as it has done each previous time? The answer is "No," because if it did, the computer would only perform as it did in Fig. 2-3.

```
5 PRINT "VALUE 1", "VALUE 2", "TOTAL"
10 LET V1 = 4
20 LET V2 = 7
30 LET T = V1 + V2
40 PRINT V1, V2 , T
45 LET V1 = V1 + 1
50 END

READY
RUN

SIMPLE          14:02          21-NOV-76


VALUE 1         VALUE 2        TOTAL
4               7              11


TIME:  0.06 SECS.

READY
```

Fig. 2-3. SIMPLE with an error.

12   INSTRUCTION IN THE BASIC LANGUAGE

What we need is a way to cause the computer to go back to a prior step and go through a segment of the program again. This can be accomplished through the use of the GO TO instruction. GO TO is used when you want the computer to go to an instruction other than the next one in sequence.

Do you want the computer to go back to line 5 and execute that step again? Not really, unless you want it to print a heading, a line of data, a heading, a line of data, and so on, as in Fig. 2-4.

By inserting the instruction as we did at line 47, we have created an "endless loop." The program cycles down through line 47 and then back to line 5. It never reaches END. Even though the instruction at 45 makes V1 larger by 1, line 10 makes V1 equal to 4 again and, therefore, V1 and T do not increase in value. Also, the heading prints on each cycle. An "endless loop" is stopped either by pushing the "BREAK" key or by pushing the "CONTROL" key and "C" simultaneously.

We will solve the "heading" problem and the "V1" problem by

```
5 PRINT "VALUE 1", "VALUE 2", "TOTAL"
10 LET V1 = 4
20 LET V2 = 7
30 LET T = V1 + V2
40 PRINT V1, V2, T
45 LET V1 = V1 + 1
47 GO TO 5
50 END

READY
RUN

SIMPLE          17:06          02-NOV-76


VALUE 1         VALUE 2        TOTAL
   4               7             11
VALUE 1         VALUE 2        TOTAL
   4               7             11
VALUE 1         VALUE 2        TOTAL
   4               7             11
VALUE 1         VALUE 2        TOTAL
   4               7             11
VALUE 1         VALUE 2        TOTAL
   4               7             11
VALUE 1         VALUE 2        TOTAL
   4               7             11
VALUE 1         VALUE 2        TOTAL
   4               7            ^C
VALUE 2         TOTAL

READY
```

Fig. 2-4. *SIMPLE with several errors.*

```
 5 PRINT "VALUE 1", "VALUE 2", "TOTAL"
10 LET V1 = 4
20 LET V2 = 7
30 LET T = V1 + V2
40 PRINT V1, V2, T
45 LET V1 = V1 + 1
47 GO TO 30
50 END

READY
RUN

SIMPLE          17:09          02-NOV-76


VALUE 1          VALUE 2          TOTAL
   4                7               11
   5                7               12
   6                7               13
   7                7               14
   8                7               15
   9                7               16
  10                7               17
  11                7               18
  12                7               19
  13          ^C
                  7                        23


READY
```

Fig. 2-5. SIMPLE with an endless loop.

changing line 47 to GO TO 30. That change will produce the result shown in Fig. 2-5.

We are not yet getting acceptable results because we still had to stop the computer from executing an endless loop. Let's make the change required to make our program quit by itself at some logical point. On what condition do we want the program to stop? Let us arbitrarily say that we want the computer to stop when T is greater than 14.

Any numerical value in the computer can be tested by an IF instruction. If T is greater than 14, then we want the computer to stop (proceed to END). If T is not greater than 14, we want the computer to continue with the next sequential step. Where is a good place to put this test? Let's make it number 43 and show it like this:

```
43 IF T > 14 THEN 50
```

This step means that if T is greater than 14, then the computer will branch to line 50 where it is instructed to stop. The symbol used in arithmetic to signify greater than (>) is the same symbol used to signify

14   INSTRUCTION IN THE BASIC LANGUAGE

"greater than" in BASIC. If T is not greater than 14, the computer will go on to the next sequential step, which is line 45. Executing line 45 and then 47 will cause an unconditional branch back to line 30. The complete program listing and its execution are shown in Fig. 2-6.

```
5 PRINT "VALUE 1", "VALUE 2", "TOTAL"
10 LET V1 = 4
20 LET V2 = 7
30 LET T = V1 + V2
40 PRINT V1, V2, T
43 IF T > 14 THEN 50
45 LET V1 = V1 + 1
47 GO TO 30
50 END

READY
RUN

SIMPLE          17:10          02-NOV-76


VALUE 1         VALUE 2        TOTAL
   4               7             11
   5               7             12
   6               7             13
   7               7             14
   8               7             15


TIME:   0.11 SECS.

READY
```

Fig. 2-6. Listing and execution of SIMPLE free of errors.

EXERCISES

1. Which of the following are correctly assigned variable names? Describe why each is or is not correct.

A	S	B1	DN	1C
DATA	B*	L24	R 2	1ST
C#	-V	18R	(A)	$T

2. What is the purpose(s) of a line number?

3. What is a limitation of assigning line numbers 1, 2, 3, 4, etc. in consecutive fashion?

4. From a logical standpoint, why do line numbers have to be assigned in sequence?

5. In the following statement, why doesn't the computer consider B+5 to be a variable name since there is no spacing among the latter three characters?

```
30 LET A = B+5
```

6. Is it possible to type the instructions into the computer in any order you wish (assume the line numbers that are used would be logical if they were in sequence)? What happens if you do? Why?

7. Does the = (equal sign) always mean "equal to" in BASIC? Explain why. Refer to appropriate statements in Fig. 2-6 to illustrate.

8. How do you insert another instruction between existing ones? How do you replace a single instruction?

9. What is the purpose of a literal? How is it used?

10. What is the difference between PRINT A and PRINT "A"?

11. How can you stop the computer when it is executing in a way that is obviously not what you intended?

12. Make a verbal statement explaining how careful you have to be to make the computer do what you want it to do. Does the computer actually guide you into preparing those steps correctly or does it just show you when you are wrong?

13. The following questions refer to the program in Fig. 2-6. The parts are independent of each other.
    (a) What would the printed results have been if line 40 had been PRINT T, V1, V2?
    (b) What would the results have been if line 45 had been LET V2 = V2+1? Explain.
    (c) Change the program so that it would end when the total was 20. Try to do this by altering only one item in the existing program (not a completely changed instruction).
    (d) What would have happened if line 43 had been IF V1>8 THEN 50? Why?
    (e) Make the necessary changes in the program so that it would print "T IS NOW > 14" below the fifth line of numeric output, that is, just before the computer signals "TIME".

14. What would be the printed results of the program in Fig. 2-7?

```
10 PRINT "ABLE", "BAKER", "CHARLIE"
20 LET A = 20
30 LET B = 8
50 LET C = A + B
60 IF B > A THEN 100
70 PRINT A, B, C
80 LET B = B + 2
90 GO TO 50
100 PRINT "THATS ALL"
110 END

READY
```

Fig. 2-7. A program exercise.

15. Write a program that will set up units of data called A and B, with each unit initially set equal to 1. Add A and B to obtain C, and print C. Then add a 1 to both A and to B. Next, have a step that branches back to the add step where A and B are accumulated into C. What would happen if you program to branch to END "IF C = 15"? How can you correct the situation?

16.   A program certainly is not very effective if it does not provide for output, which, in our case, is a PRINT step. Do you think that the computer considers it an error if a program contains no PRINT step? Write a short program that has no PRINT step and RUN it— did the computer signal an error?

17.   Write a BASIC program that would produce the following results.

```
BONUS              13:14           28-NOV-76


REG. PAY          BONUS           TOT. PAY
  100               10              110
  100               20              120
  100               30              130
  100               40              140
  100               50              150


TIME:   0.09 SECS.

READY
```

18.   Write a program that assigns beginning values to R and to S. Print both R and S, then add 2 to R, and print both again. Continue this process until R is larger than S. (*Hint.* Since the beginning values could be any amounts that you wish, do you want to place the IF before or after the PRINT?)

3 CHAPTER
BASIC
PROGRAMMING
TECHNIQUES

The purpose of this chapter is threefold.

1. I will intentionally make some of the errors that beginning and even experienced programmers are likely to make. I will show what the computer does to indicate an error and describe what you can do to recover from the error.

2. Several programming techniques will be presented. Mainly, these will be ideas that you can use to help make the task of programming easier.

3. I will introduce some optional methods of performing certain BASIC steps. Quite often one method of performing a given step will be more appealing to a certain programmer than an alternate method.

Error Detection

All computer languages are designed with rather strict rules to be followed in a precise manner. The computer detects certain types of programmer errors, and it lets you know about them in one of several ways.

Figure 3-1 includes six programmer mistakes with a list of errors or "diagnostics" at the bottom. Notice that the error in example 1 is difficult to detect. Actually, the word PRINT was spelled PR1NT. A digit one and the letter I are quite similar in shape, and the eye often "sees" what it is expecting rather than what is actually there. However, the com-

```
5 PRINT V1

47 GO TO 5

15 "T"

35 PRINT AB, "C"

GO TO 30

? WHAT?
READY
RUN

FIG3.1        14:00        21-NOV-76

? INITIAL PART OF STATEMENT NEITHER MATCHES A STATEMENT KEYWORD NOR HAS A FO
RM LEGAL FOR AN IMPLIED LET--CHECK FOR MISSPELLING IN LINE 5
? INITIAL PART OF STATEMENT NEITHER MATCHES A STATEMENT KEYWORD NOR HAS A FO
RM LEGAL FOR AN IMPLIED LET--CHECK FOR MISSPELLING IN LINE 15
? ILLEGAL VARIABLE IN LINE 35
? T WAS SEEN WHERE = WAS EXPECTED IN LINE 47

? NO END INSTRUCTION

TIME:  0.21 SECS.

READY
```

Fig. 3-1. Common programming errors.

puter has spotted the error and diligently given an error message. The message suggests an error in spelling. (Note that this particular error would not be caused by a slip of the typing finger, given the relative keyboard placements of the letter I and the digit 1.)

The second error, while being slightly easier to visually detect than the previous one, is more likely to occur. The second character in G0 was a zero rather than the alphabetic O. Notice the difference in the shapes provided by this teletypewriter. (Some teletypewriters make a much more distinctive difference between a zero and an "O" by placing a slash (/) through the numeric 0.)

Example 3 is an error because the attempted statement did not contain a valid verb. A "verb" tells the computer what to do. Examples are PRINT, LET, GO TO, and IF.

In Example 4, the variable name AB is invalid; a variable name can be only one letter or one letter followed by a digit.

The fifth error was caused by the lack of a line number. The computer immediately responded to that error by typing "?WHAT?". That attempted statement did not become a part of the program and, therefore, it was not commented on in the error diagnosis that was produced when the program was run.

Finally, the program did not contain an END statement. Most versions of BASIC require END as the highest numbered line for a program to be valid.

All of the examples in Fig. 3-2 show steps that, while they may or may not be what was desired, were not invalid to the computer. Example

```
5 PRINT "ABC"
6 LET A = 2
7 LET B = 9
8 LET C = 3
10 END

READY
RUN

FIG3.2A        18:01         02-NOV-76


ABC


TIME:  0.04 SECS.

READY
```

(A)

Fig. 3-2. Variations in the use of PRINT.

```
25 PRINT "A", "B", "C",
30 PRINT "D"
35 END

READY
RUN

FIG3.2B          18:02          02-NOV-76


A               B               C               D


TIME:  0.04 SECS.

READY
```

(B)

```
15 PRINT A, "B", "C"
25 END

READY
RUN

FIG3.2C          18:03          02-NOV-76


 0              B               C


TIME:  0.05 SECS.

READY
```

(C)

```
100 PRINT "A" "B", "C"
200 END

READY
RUN

FIG3.2D          18:03          02-NOV-76


AB              C


TIME:  0.03 SECS.

READY
```

(D)

Fig. 3-2. cont.

22   INSTRUCTION IN THE BASIC LANGUAGE

A prints the letters ABC as a group rather than spreading them across the page. The numerical values assigned to the variable names A, B, and C were not instructed to print.

Placing a comma after literal C in example B is acceptable. The printer simply does not automatically space up one line when there is a comma as the last character in a PRINT statement.

In example C, the computer printed the value of variable name A as a zero. The reason is that BASIC automatically sets all computer storage containers to zero at the beginning of a program. Since nothing has been done to assign a value to A, it still contained a zero at the time of printing. The literals B and C were printed on the same line.

In example D, there was no comma between literals A and B. Notice how they were printed next to each other in the execution of the program.

Thus you can see that the comma in a PRINT instruction is a signal to the computer to automatically space between literals and/or data fields. Further comments will be found under Programming and Printing Variations later in this chapter.

There is a different type of error illustrated in Fig. 3-3. A line number was improperly assigned to RUN. The word RUN is not a part of your program; it is a command to the computer to do something to your program. Thus RUN does not require (and it actually deplores) the inclusion of a line number.

Error Correction

The means needed to correct an error depends upon the nature of the error. If the simple insertion of an additional instruction is required, determine the proper place to put the instruction by assigning a logical line number. Several examples were shown in Chapter 2.

If an entire instruction is to be deleted, just type that instruction's line number and push RETURN.

When an instruction is to be altered, type the same line number followed by the instruction as you want it.

```
30 LET C = A PLUS B
30 LET C = A + B
```

Suppose that you personally detect an error as soon as you have made it—before you have typed the next character. How can you correct it before proceeding?

Assume that you meant to type 47 GO TO 5 but typed a digit zero as the second character in GO. The problem then is how to make the computer "backspace." That is, you want to wipe out that last character

```
10 LET A = 4
20 LET B = 7
30 LET C = A + B
40 PRINT C
50 END
60 RUN

READY
RUN

FIG3.3        13:56        21-NOV-76

? END IS NOT LAST IN LINE 50
? INITIAL PART OF STATEMENT NEITHER MATCHES A STATEMENT KEYWORD NOR HAS A FO
RM LEGAL FOR AN IMPLIED LET--CHECK FOR MISSPELLING IN LINE 60

? NO END INSTRUCTION

TIME:  0.10 SECS.

READY
```

Fig. 3-3. A programming error.

so you can put the correct one in. On the computer used in this book, we merely push the DELETE key. That causes a backward slash (\) to print, followed by the character being wiped out, followed by another backward slash. Then the computer is ready for you to type in the correct character. For instance:

```
47 GO\0\O TO 5
```

Some programming systems require a different approach to correct such an error. A common version is the use of a different keyboard char-

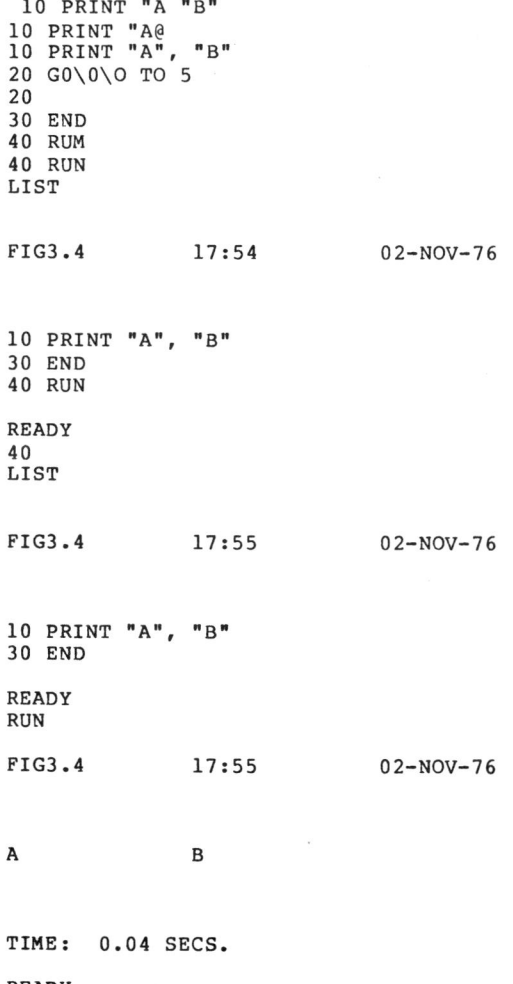

```
10 PRINT "A "B"
10 PRINT "A@
10 PRINT "A", "B"
20 GO\0\O TO 5
20
30 END
40 RUM
40 RUN
LIST


FIG3.4          17:54          02-NOV-76



10 PRINT "A", "B"
30 END
40 RUN

READY
40
LIST


FIG3.4          17:55          02-NOV-76



10 PRINT "A", "B"
30 END

READY
RUN

FIG3.4          17:55          02-NOV-76



A               B



TIME:  0.04 SECS.

READY
```

Fig. 3-4. Use of LIST.

acter. The upper case character of the letter O contains a leftward pointing arrow. Holding the CONTROL key and depressing the letter O key at the same time causes the last typed character to be wiped out. Please check with your Computer Center to determine which method is appropriate for you.

It is always desirable to have a list of the instructions as they now exist in the computer. They can be obtained through the use of the LIST command.

Assume a situation such as the one shown at the top of Fig. 3-4. So many attempts have been made to prepare those few instructions, that it is desirable to determine exactly what is in the computer. That determination is done by typing LIST; the results are shown below the original typing.

Once you have a current list of the instructions, you can determine what changes have to be made. In this case we just delete line 40, get another list to make sure that the program is correct, and then type RUN.

Programming and Printing Variations

It is often helpful in writing a program to include one or more statements whose purpose is to explain something about the program. These statements are for documentation purposes only and are not meant to be executed. This can be done with the use of REM (REMARKS) steps. Use a line number, the word REM, and then whatever you want to say. Everything about the statement is ignored at execution time, but the statement is printed when you list a program (see Fig. 3-5).

```
5    REM THIS PROGRAM ILLUSTRATES A REMARK STATEMENT.
10 LET A = 4
20 LET B = 7
25   REM THE NEXT STEP ADDS A & B TO FORM C.
30 LET C = A + B
40 PRINT C
50 END

READY
RUN

FIG3.5         17:52           02-NOV-76


     11


TIME:   0.03 SECS.

READY
```

Fig. 3-5. Use of REM.

In Chapter 2 we saw several versions of a simple program that added two values and printed the total. BASIC also permits the same output results without the need for a separate add step. Arithmetic can just as easily be performed in a PRINT statement.

```
100 LET V1 = 4
150 LET V2 = 7
200 PRINT V1 + V2
250 END

READY
RUN

SIMPLE        17:20         02-NOV-76


     11



TIME:   0.04 SECS.

READY
```

Notice where addition was taking place; in this case, we did not develop the total of V1 and V2 in a separate place called T. It is largely a matter of personal preference as to whether you use the approach above or the one in Chapter 2.

When we type RUN for the purpose of executing a program, the computer will furnish the name of the program and other timely data as it has done in each program executed so far. If you don't want this reference material, just place the letters NH (*No H*eading) after the word RUN:

```
RUN NH


     11



TIME:   0.05 SECS.

READY
```

Also, when you use LIST to list out your program statements, the computer will give you similar information at the front of the list. If you don't want any of that, just type the letters NH after the word LIST:

```
LIST NH
100 LET V1 = 4
150 LET V2 = 7
200 PRINT V1 + V2
250 END

READY
```

```
LIST NH
5 PRINT "VALUE 1", "VALUE 2", "TOTAL"
10 LET V1 = 4
20 LET V2 = 7
30 LET T = V1 + V2
40 PRINT V1, V2 , T
43 IF T > 14 THEN 50
45 LET V1 = V1 + 1
47 GO TO 30
50 END

READY
LIST NH 5
5 PRINT "VALUE 1", "VALUE 2", "TOTAL"

READY
LIST NH 10 - 40
10 LET V1 = 4
20 LET V2 = 7
30 LET T = V1 + V2
40 PRINT V1, V2 , T

READY
LIST NH 47
47 GO TO 30

READY
```

Fig. 3-6. Using LIST NH to print selected line numbers.

On short programs such as the ones that we have seen thus far, it obviously does not take much time for the computer to LIST the entire program. But in a long program, you may want the computer to LIST a particular instruction or, perhaps, only those instructions within certain bounds. Using the program instructions from Fig. 2-6, either situation may be handled as in Fig. 3-6.

We have seen that an instruction is wiped out of the computer when you type the same line number followed by different coding or when you type only the line number. When you want to delete the entire program, type the word SCRATCH. The results of that action are like this:

```
SCRATCH

READY
LIST NH

READY
```

In Fig. 2-6, we saw how the computer could be used to print headings above the columns of output data. While in many situations the following point is of minor importance, there may be cases where the heading should be centered somewhat differently over the column to which it applies. That has been accomplished in the changes made to the program

```
5 PRINT " V1", "V2", "   T"
10 LET V1 = 4
20 LET V2 = 7
30 LET T = V1 + V2
40 PRINT V1, V2, T
43 IF T > 14 THEN 50
45 LET V1 = V1 + 1
47 GO TO 30
50 END

READY
RUN NH
```

V1	V2	T
4	7	11
5	7	12
6	7	13
7	7	14
8	7	15

```
TIME:   0.10 SECS.

READY
```

Fig. 3-7.   Centering of columnar headings.

in Fig. 3-7. Notice how the placement of the headings varied. In line number 5, space was left between the beginning quote sign and the first printable character within the literal.

The BASIC language has been set up so that there are automatically a maximum of five columns of printed output with a preestablished format. You will get that format by simply separating the names of the units of data with commas. This situation is illustrated in Fig. 3-8.

The same results can be obtained by using individual PRINT steps where each variable name is followed by a comma (see Fig. 3-9). As you can see, the computer does not treat a comma after the last variable name as an error, but merely as an instruction that causes no vertical spacing.

We have now seen, in several instances, that a comma between variable names causes standard columnar spacing. If we want some other spacing, we have two ways of obtaining it.

One option is to use the semicolon (;) as a variable name separator instead of using a comma. The results of such use are shown in Fig. 3-10.

A second option is to use the TAB function, which works in a way that is similar to TAB stops on a typewriter. This method is shown in Fig. 3-11. Visualize a print line being composed of 72 possible printing positions across the page. You merely determine the specific print positions that you want the values to be printed in. Use the TAB function followed by the desired print position in parenthesis, the name of the variable field, a semicolon, etc.

BASIC PROGRAMMING TECHNIQUES   29

```
3     REM FIG. 3-8.
5 LET A = 1
10 LET B = 2
15 LET C = 3
20 LET D = 4
25 LET E = 5
30 LET F = 6
35 LET G = 7
40 PRINT A, B, C, D, E, F, G
55 END

READY
RUN NH


 1              2              3              4              5
 6              7


TIME:   0.06 SECS.

READY
```

Fig. 3-8. Using the preestablished column spacing format.

```
3     REM FIG. 3-9.
5 LET A = 1
10 LET B = 2
15 LET C = 3
20 LET D = 4
25 LET E = 5
30 LET F = 6
35 LET G = 7
38    REM COMMA AT END OF PRINT STEP
39    REM CAUSES NO LINE SPACING.
40 PRINT A,
41 PRINT B,
42 PRINT C,
43 PRINT D,
44 PRINT E,
45 PRINT F,
46 PRINT G,
55 END

READY
RUN

FIG3.9          17:37          02-NOV-76


 1              2              3              4              5
 6              7
TIME:   0.07 SECS.

READY
```

Fig. 3-9. Using the comma to nullify regular vertical spacing.

30 INSTRUCTION IN THE BASIC LANGUAGE

```
3     REM FIG. 3-10.
5 LET A = 1
10 LET B = 2
15 LET C = 3
20 LET D = 4
25 LET E = 5
30 LET F = 6
35 LET G = 7
38    REM REGULAR COLUMN SPACING NULLIFIED.
40 PRINT A; B; C; D; E; F; G
55 END

READY
RUN

FIG3.10         17:35           02-NOV-76


   1  2  3  4  5  6  7


TIME:  0.06 SECS.

READY
```

Fig. 3-10.   Using the semicolon to nullify regular spacing.

```
3     REM FIG. 3-11
5 LET A = 1
10 LET B = 2
15 LET C = 3
20 LET D = 4
25 LET E = 5
30 LET F = 6
35 LET G = 7
36 LET H = 95
38    REM TAB CAUSES PRINTING INTO SPECIFIC POSITIONS.
40 PRINT TAB(5)A; TAB(10)B; TAB(16)C; TAB(25)D;
42 PRINT TAB(32)E; TAB(36)F; TAB(55)G
43    REM CAUSES 1 BLANK LINE
44 PRINT
46 PRINT H
55 END

READY
RUN

FIG3.11        17:33           02-NOV-76


       1     2      3        4      5    6                   7
 95


TIME:  0.07 SECS.

READY
```

Fig. 3-11.   Using TAB to cause horizontal spacing.

If you should have a point in the execution of a program where you want the printer to skip a line (leaving one line clear of printing), you can do this by using a PRINT statement that contains neither variable names nor literals (see line 44). In effect, the computer prints nothing and it moves the paper up one line.

You may now find it desirable to study the systems commands in Appendix B.

EXERCISES

1. Why does every instruction require a line number? What does the computer do if you fail to precede an instruction with a line number?

2. Generally, how does the "computer" detect errors? What broad category of error can the computer detect?

3. What is wrong with the following statement?
   20 PRINT HOURS, AMOUNT

4. Why doesn't RUN require a line number? What happens if you try to assign a line number to RUN?

5. Describe two methods by which you can delete a character that you have just typed incorrectly. Which is the preferable way? Does that depend on the circumstances? Why?

6. What is the purpose of REM? Can a REM appear anywhere in the program or must it be only the first coding line? Why does REM need a line number?

7. What does the computer do if you type LIST when there is no program in the computer area assigned to you? What happens if you type RUN under the same conditions? Please try to do each of these to see what would happen.

8. Why would you use either RUNNH or LISTNH instead of their alternate styles?

9. Why would you ever want to LIST only part of a program? How can you do that?

10. Assume that a program contains 10 instructions, with the instructions numbered 10, 20, 30, . . . 100. What would happen if you typed RUN 10-60? Try this at your Computer Center.

11. What different results would you get from the following?
50 PRINT A, B, C
60 PRINT A; B; C

12. How can you nullify the automatic horizontal spacing from a PRINT instruction and get exactly the print spacing of your choice?

13. Is the following valid as a segment of a program? Explain why.
100 PRINT
150 PRINT
200 PRINT

14. Alter the program in Fig. 2-6 so that V1 prints from position 10, V2 from 48, and T from 62. Also, center the column headings above their respective fields.

15. What would be the printed results of the following program (the – means to subtract)?

```
5 PRINT "ABLE", "BAKER", "CHARLIE"
10 LET A = 5
20 LET B = 18
30 LET C = B - A
40 PRINT A, B, C
50 IF C < 6 THEN 80
60 LET B = B - 1
70 GO TO 30
80 END

READY
```

16. Carefully study the following attempt at preparing a program. Visualize the error listing that would result when it was run. Correct the errors so that the program can be properly executed.

```
10    REM PRINTS 3 AMOUNTS
20 PRINT "AMT.1 AMT. 2", "AMT. 3"
30 LET A1 = 20
40 LET A2 = 40
50 LET A3 = A1 PLUS A2
60 PRINT A1, A2, 3A
70 LIST "THATS ALL"
80 EMD

READY
```

17. Write a program that will print the digits zero through nine (0, 1, 2, etc.) on one line of output. Use the following as the only print statement:

"PRINT N;"

18. Write a program whose only purpose is to find out how many characters your teletypewriter can print on one line. (*Hint.* Write a PRINT instruction that will print so many characters that the printer will eventually space up one line. Then count the number of characters, including any blanks.)

19. Write a program that would produce the following results. Use REM statements to describe several of the steps.

N	A	B	C	A + B	A - B	A + B + C
1	18	3	9	21	15	30
2	17	5	10	22	12	32
3	16	7	11	23	9	34
4	15	9	12	24	6	36
5	14	11	13	25	3	38

TIME: 0.18 SECS.

READY

4 CHAPTER
METHODS OF
ENTERING DATA

The method that was introduced in Chapter 2 to enter raw data into the computer for processing is known as the assignment method. The format of the assignment method is a line number, the word LET, a variable name, the equal sign, and the value that you want to be assigned to the variable name. Examples shown in Chapter 2 were 10 LET V1 = 4 and 20 LET V2 = 7.

The word LET has also been the verb used to signify an arithmetic step, such as 30 LET T = V1 + V2.

In both assignment and arithmetic steps, the use of LET is optional. The word LET will not be used in the remainder of the book. Instead, forms such as 10 V1 = 4 and 30 T = V1 + V2 will be used.

READ and DATA

In another method of providing data to the computer, the words READ and DATA are used. The first example will involve a situation in which we want to multiply certain values by the digit 2.

The method requires a READ statement followed by the variable name into which we want the value to be stored. Additionally, a DATA statement within the program must contain the individual values that are to be read by the READ statement. The individual values in the DATA statement must be separated by commas. A sample program is as follows:

```
3     REM USE OF READ & DATA.
5 PRINT "VALUE", "PRODUCT"
10 READ A
20 B = A * 2
30 PRINT A, B
35 GO TO 10
40 DATA 5, 9, 18, 12
50 END

READY
RUN NH


VALUE              PRODUCT
  5                  10
  9                  18
 18                  36
 12                  24

? OUT OF DATA IN LINE 10


TIME:   0.12 SECS.

READY
```

The function of each of the coding lines is explained in this manner:

3   A remark about the program.

5   Prints a literal (heading) above each output column.

10 Reads one value from the DATA statement each time that the READ step is executed. Stores the value in a variable field called A.

20 Multiplies (*) the value in A by 2 and puts the result in B.

30 Prints the values of A and of B (the product of 2 times A).

35 Causes a branch back to line 10.

40 A DATA statement that contains four values to be processed.

50 An END statement is required as the last step of every BASIC program.

The nature of the use of READ and DATA is that processing will continue until the last value in the DATA statement has been processed. When the READ statement tries to go beyond the last value in the DATA statement, the computer gives the OUT OF DATA message, as shown in the example above and stops. (A way of avoiding the OUT OF DATA message is shown in Chapter 7.)

```
3     REM FIG. 4-1, ILLUSTRATING READ & DATA.
5 PRINT "A", "B", "C", "D"
10 READ A, B, C
20 D = A + B + C
30 PRINT A, B, C, D
40 GO TO 10
45     REM A DATA STATEMENT CONTAINS THE RAW DATA.
50 DATA 7, 12, 43, 72, 19, 34, 21, 92, 46, 28
70 END

READY
RUN NH


A               B               C               D
 7              12              43              62
72              19              34              125
21              92              46              159

? OUT OF DATA IN LINE 10

TIME:   0.16 SECS.

READY
```

Fig. 4-1. Use of READ-DATA.

With this method you are not restricted to reading only one unit of data in the READ step. The example in Fig. 4-1 shows three values being read in each READ step. Notice that since READ was handling three values at a time and there were not three more available for a fourth cycle, the last item (28) did not get processed.

INPUT Method

The third major way of getting raw data into a BASIC program is through the use of an INPUT step. Suppose that you have a series of two values in which you want the computer to divide the first value by the second. The program in Fig. 4-2 will perform that function.

Another feature of this program is that it will stop when the first value in any series in INPUT is 99. Recall from Chapter 2 that some method must be used to make the machine halt, and the method there was to test to see when a calculated value reached some limit.

Line numbers 20, 22, 25, 30, and 45 in Fig. 4-2 are explained this way:

20 Once the program is in the execution phase (after you type RUN and the computer prints the column headings), it comes to the INPUT step, where the computer types a "?" and waits for you to type the

```
5    REM FIG. 4-2
10 PRINT "FIRST",  "SECOND",  "QUOTIENT"
20 INPUT A, B
22 PRINT
25 IF A = 99 THEN 60
30 C = A / B
40 PRINT A, B, C
45 PRINT
50 GO TO 20
60 END

READY
RUN NH


FIRST            SECOND          QUOTIENT
  ?24, 3

  24               3              8

  ?45, 2

  45               2              22.5

  ?80, 3

  80               3              26.6667

  ?25784, 869

  25784            869            29.6709

  ?10, 3

  10               3              3.33333

  ?99, 7


TIME:   0.22 SECS.

READY
```

Fig. 4-2. Use of the INPUT statement.

input values. Once you type in two values, separated by a comma, and then press RETURN, the computer goes on to line 22.

22 Causes the printer to space up one line.

25 When A = 99, the program branches to line 60 and halts. In Chapter 2, the computer tested for a greater than (>) condition; here it is testing for an equal (=) condition.

30 The computer divides (/) A by B and stores the quotient in data name C.

45 Causes the printer to space up one line.

40   INSTRUCTION IN THE BASIC LANGUAGE

As you can see from the results, five pairs of values were typed in for processing. The sixth set of data was a 99 for A and a 7 for B. An INPUT value of 99 for A was the signal to the machine that we were through processing.

Note in the program in Fig. 4-2 that although line 20 called for the INPUT of two values, A and B, only one ? was printed when the machine asked for our INPUT. The same program is RUN again in Fig. 4-3, and two additional points are made.

1. If you type in only one value when the machine expects two, it prints another "?".

2. If you should type in more values than the INPUT statement calls for, the excess values are ignored.   (Some computers give an EXCESS DATA message.)

```
RUN NH


FIRST            SECOND        QUOTIENT
?12
?4

12               4             3

?18
?3

18               3             6

?90, 2, 67

90               2             45

?100, 25, 9867, 56, 438

100              25            4

?12, 5

12               5             2.4

?99
?56


TIME:   0.24 SECS.

READY
```

Fig. 4-3. Additional features of the INPUT statement.

The results of this method of providing data are not always artistic since the ? keeps showing up. However, this situation is not normally bad, since BASIC at this time is more of a problem-solving language than a data processing language. Quite often, the results of a BASIC program are for one's own use and not for an output report that is to be directly distributed to another user.

Each of the three methods of entering raw data has its advantages, its disadvantages, and its appropriate usage. Based upon the nature of the program to be written at any point, I will use the method appropriate to the job.

EXERCISES

1. What does the computer do when it "runs out of data" as a result of using the READ and DATA instructions?

2. What is a limitation of using READ and DATA as a means of getting raw data into the computer?

3. In BASIC, how do you separate one numerical value from another numerical value? What problem does that cause?

4. What is a limitation of the INPUT method?

5. Suppose you have written a program that contains the statement 10 INPUT A, B. When you are executing the program after the machine has typed ?, you make a mistake and type in three values instead of two. What does the computer do about this? Try a brief program and determine what the message is, if any, in your own Computer Center.

6. To date, what different methods have been used to cause our programs to go to the END step?

7. Carefully review the program shown below. What would be the output of that program when it was RUN? Try to determine the appropriate spacing.

```
 5 PRINT "    A"; "  B"; "    A+B", "A-B", "A*B", "A/B"
10 A = 12
15 B = 6
20 C = A + B
25 D = A - B
30 E = A * B
35 F = A/B
40 PRINT A; B; C, D, E, F
45 END

READY
```

8. Of the three methods used to enter data into the computer, which one would be most appropriate in each of the following cases:
   (a) A tax rate that is not likely to change often?
   (b) A tax rate that the user wants to change often?

(c) A lengthy program that is going to be used by a salesperson to illustrate many features of a product to potential customers?

(d) Using the computer to calculate the maximum amount of credit to allow any particular credit applicant?

(e) Where there is a high volume of raw data that you want to carefully proofread prior to processing?

9. What symbol is appropriate for each of the four forms of arithmetic? Why were those particular symbols chosen?

10. The following questions refer to the program in Fig. 4-2.

(a) How many digits to the right of a decimal point does BASIC provide (this will vary among computers)?

(b) What does the computer do about printing commas in values involving thousands?

(c) Does the computer automatically round its answers?

(d) What change should be made to cause the program to END when the second value in any series is 100?

(e) Make the change that would cause the computer to skip one line between the printing of the heading and the first request for INPUT.

11. Assume that a program is to contain the DATA statement shown in Fig. 4-1. Write the program steps that would multiply every other value in the DATA statement (7, 43, 19, etc.) by 5 and print the resulting product of each multiplication. (*Hint.* READ, but do not process, the unwanted values in DATA.)

12. In the following, what would happen when you depressed the RETURN key?

```
10 INPUT R, S, T
20 PRINT R+S, R-S, R*T, R+S+T, U
30 END

READY
RUN NH


?2, 4, 6, 8, 10
```

13. What would be the output of the following program if the respective values for INPUT were to be 9, 3, 7, and 4?

```
10 INPUT A
2) READ B
30 PRINT A, B, A+B
40 IF A = 4 THEN 70
50 GO TO 10
60 DATA 5, 12, 19, 6
70 END
```

READY

14. Each of the values in a DATA statement is to be divided by either
     2, 3, or 4. The user will input the divisor of his or her choice. The
     results of the execution of the program using a divisor of 2 are
     shown below. Prepare the BASIC coding which would provide re-
     sults as shown; also, include the means to permit the divisor to be a
     3 or 4.

VALUE	DIVISOR	ANSWER
48	2	24
24	2	12
12	2	6

? OUT OF DATA IN LINE 20

TIME: 0.10 SECS.

READY

15. What would be the results of the following program when it was
     run?

```
10 READ A, B, C, \D, E, F, G, H, I, J, K, L, M, N, O, P, Q, R, S
20 PRINT S;I;M;G
30 DATA 1, 2, 3, 4, 5, 6, 7, 8, 9, 10, 9, 8, 7, 6, 5, 4, 3, 2, 1
40 END
```

READY

16. In the following, what would happen when you push carriage
     return?

```
100 INPUT A, B
200 PRINT B, A
300 END
```

READY
RUN NH

?5

17. Describe the coding errors in the following program. Do not try to determine exactly what the program was intended to do.

```
10 AB = 10
20 B = 20
30 C14 = A PLUS B
40 C14 = A - B
50 PRINT D
60 END.

READY
```

5 CHAPTER
PROGRAM
FLOWCHARTING

The few programs that we have examined so far are simple enough that we can plan them in our heads and directly prepare the BASIC instructions. But as soon as programs get a little more complicated, it is wise to do some program planning prior to writing specific instructions.

It is theoretically possible to go to the computer and compose the program on an interactive basis, using the computer itself to keep testing the program until you develop the coding that seems to work. But this method is a waste of computer time in addition to usually taking more programmer time than an alternate method requires.

A program flowchart can be prepared by the programmer prior to attempting any coding of the program in the BASIC language. The program flowchart shows the steps that are to be performed and the sequence in which they are to be executed.

For our purposes, I will use five flowcharting symbols; they are shown in Fig. 5-1. In addition to the symbols shown, a straight line will be used to connect the symbols.

The symbols can be drawn freehand or prepared through the use of a plastic template. Furthermore, program flowcharts can be put on plain (blank) paper or on a form especially designed for flowcharting. I will use a template and place all flowcharts on plain paper.

If you compare the symbols shown in Fig. 5-1 with the kinds of instructions that a computer can perform, you find there is a symbol for every major function of a computer. In reality, a computer cannot do

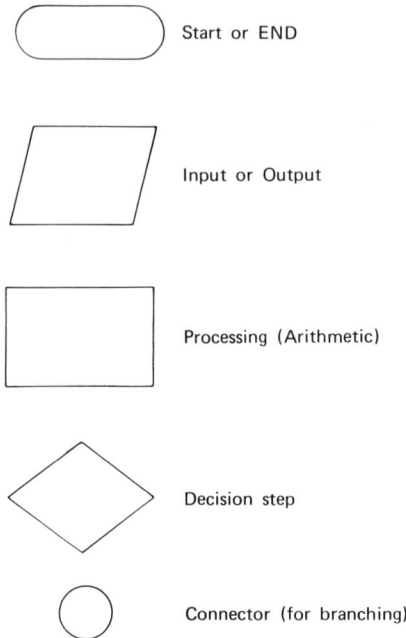

Start or END

Input or Output

Processing (Arithmetic)

Decision step

Connector (for branching)

Fig. 5-1. Program flowcharting symbols.

more than start; perform input, output, and arithmetic; make decisions and branch; and stop.

Flowcharting is a matter of planning what the computer is to do and the sequence in which to do it. Both "what" and "sequence" are necessary in order to end up with a correct solution to a problem.

Our first program flowchart will be for the following situation: data is to enter the computer through an INPUT step. The data is to be a student number followed by the numerical grades (on a scale of 100) that the student received on each of three tests. Any individual grade over 100 is to be rejected. The three numerical grades are to be averaged (simple average) and printed. The program is to provide for stopping when student number 999 is entered. Number 999 is not a valid student.

An appropriate program flowchart is shown in Fig. 5-2. Each step is described as follows:

A. The ellipse symbol containing the word START indicates where the program begins.

B. A connector symbol contains the digit 1. The purpose of the connector is to provide a place to branch back to for the next student's

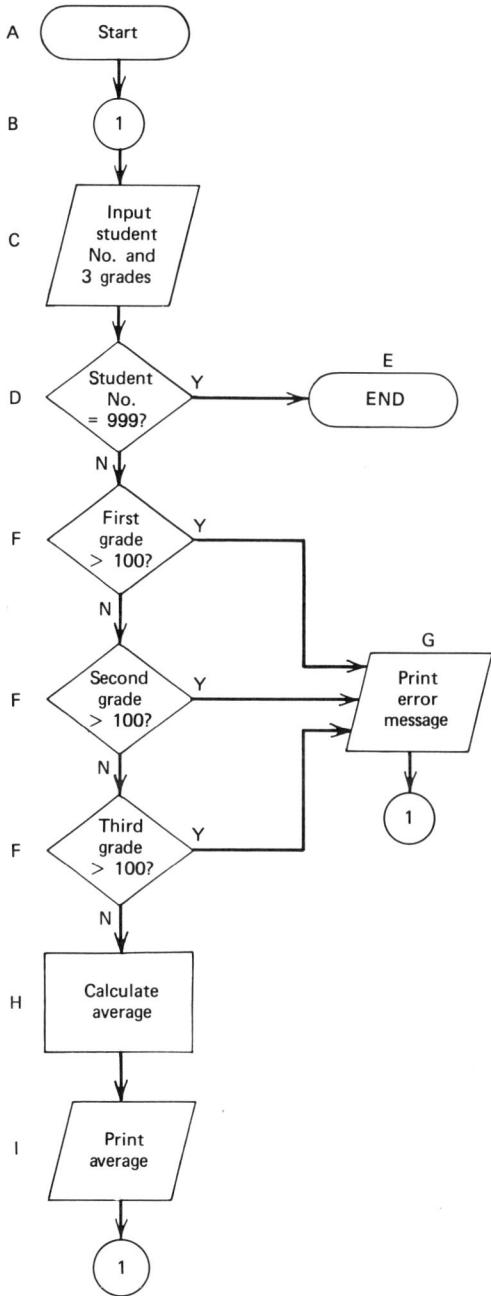

Fig. 5-2. A program flowchart for the "Grade" problem.

data, when a prior one has been completed. (Other points to be branched to could be numbered 2, 3, etc.)

C. An INPUT step provides for entering the four data fields for each student.

D. A decision step tests to see if student number 999 has entered. [A question is usually asked within a decision step so that the possible answers are Yes (Y) or No (N).] If it has entered, the program is to END (E).

   If number 999 has not entered, the data is for a valid student and must be processed.

F. Three decision steps test the respective grades. If any of the three is in excess of 100, the program is to go to a step that prints an error message, G, and then branches back to the INPUT to try again.

H. When a valid student has three valid grades (of 100 or less), the computer calculates the average.

I. The average is printed, and a connector shows that the program is to branch back to the INPUT step.

Thus the program has four decision steps and two points that branch back to the INPUT step.

The next phase in preparing the program is the coding itself, and it is shown in Fig. 5-3.

When a program flowchart has been prepared in detail (for example, the one above), there is generally one line of BASIC coding required for each symbol on the diagram.

```
5     REM FIG. 5-3.
10 INPUT A, B, C, D
20 IF A = 999 THEN 500
30 IF B > 100 THEN 100
40 IF C > 100 THEN 100
50 IF D > 100 THEN 100
55    REM CALCULATES AVERAGE.
60 E = (B + C + D) / 3
70 PRINT "AVERAGE IS"; E
75 PRINT
80 GO TO 10
100    REM HERE IS THE ERROR MESSAGE.
200 PRINT "GRADE > 100"
205 PRINT
210 GO TO 10
500 END

READY
```

Fig. 5-3. Program listing of the "Grade" problem.

The only step in the coding that is new is line 60. The purpose of this step is to calculate the student average. The reason for the parentheses is to get a total of all three grades; the computer can then divide the total by 3. Otherwise, the computer would divide only the last grade by 3 if it were written $E = B + C + D / 3$.

Once a program has been written, it is desirable to test it with all possible combinations of data. Note that Fig. 5-4 does this. There are examples in which the data is all valid (A); there are three situations where one of the test scores entered is in excess of 100 (B); and the second execution (at the bottom of the figure) was used to see what would happen if the initial data were for student number 999.

```
     RUN NH


  A   ?21, 75, 75, 75
      AVERAGE IS 75

  A   ?33, 100, 100, 100
      AVERAGE IS 100

  A   ?46, 100, 76, 88
      AVERAGE IS 88

  A   ?57, 56, 49, 72
      AVERAGE IS 59

  B   ?63, 101, 87, 89
      GRADE > 100

  B   ?63, 87, 101, 89
      GRADE > 100

  B   ?63, 87, 63, 101
      GRADE > 100

  A   ?63, 89, 87, 100
      AVERAGE IS 92

      ?999, 9, 9
      ?9


      TIME:   0.31 SECS.

      READY
      RUN NH


      ?999, 87, 56, 74

      TIME:   0.07 SECS.

      READY
```

Fig. 5-4. Two executions of the "Grade" program.

PROGRAM FLOWCHARTING   51

There is no simple statement anyone can make that will make the flowcharting process easy. I believe that the most helpful process is first, to determine how you would solve the problem by using a pencil and paper. Then perhaps it is helpful to sketch it that way. The same logic is usually the one that will work with the computer.

To help you more easily relate program coding to flowcharts, I will place relevant line numbers on future flowcharts.

EXERCISES

1. What is the purpose of a program flowchart?

2. How is it possible to spend time preparing a flowchart but to then end up taking less total time to get the whole job done?

3. In Fig. 5-2:
   (a) Suggest a reason for splitting the INPUT step into four separate steps rather than the way it appears now.
   (b) Explain why the PRINT AVERAGE step at the bottom of the diagram is not immediately followed by END?
   (c) Does the PRINT ERROR MESSAGE indicate which of the three grades is invalid? Why?

4. In Fig. 5-2:
   (a) Alter the logic so that the program would print "PROGRAM COMPLETE" when student 999 was detected.
   (b) Alter the logic so that the ERROR MESSAGE would clearly indicate which grade was greater than 100. (Use three error messages.)
   (c) Alter the logic so that it will handle the situation where there is a valid student number 999. Student number 999 is the last one to be completely processed whenever the program is run. (Test for 999 after a student has been processed.)

5. In Fig. 5-3:
   (a) Change the coding so that it agrees with the change in 4a above.
   (b) Change the coding so that it agrees with the change in 4b above.
   (c) Change the coding so that it agrees with the change in 4c above.

6. As Fig. 5-3 exists in the text:
   (a) What prevents the computer from printing "GRADE > 100" on both students with valid and those with invalid grades?
   (b) Is it necessary to type in 3 grades for the dummy student number 999? Why?

7. Prepare a program flowchart for the program in Fig. 2-6.

8. Fig. 5-5 contains a program flowchart. Prepare the BASIC instructions appropriate to that logic.

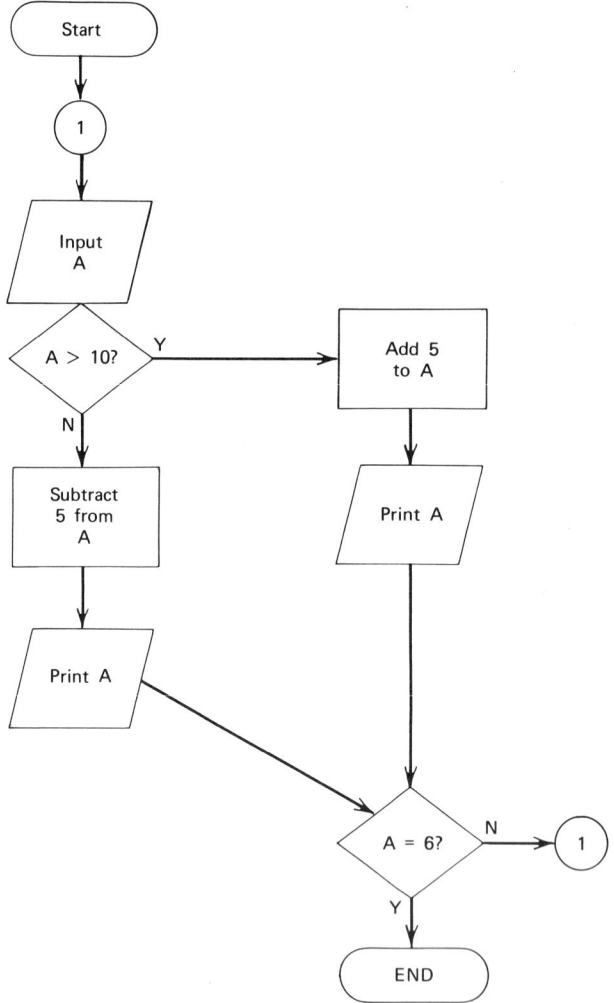

Fig. 5-5. *Program flowchart problem.*

9. Prepare both a program flowchart and the BASIC coding for a program as follows: two numeric values are to be typed into the computer (through INPUT). If they are equal, the computer is to type EQUAL. If the first is larger than the second, the computer is to type FIRST LARGER. And if the second value is larger than the first, the computer is to type SECOND LARGER.

10. Prepare a program flowchart that would handle the following situation. Students in a certain course take two exams. If students get less than 40 on either exam, they FAIL. If their average is below 60, they FAIL. An average of 60 to 80 is PASSING; an average above 80 is DEAN'S LIST. Evaluate each student in the course and then stop. No student has a student number of 99.

11. Do the BASIC coding for your diagram in Exercise 10. Test all aspects of the program to make sure that it works.

12. (a) Write (both a program flowchart and the coding) and test a program whose results would be as follows:

R	S	SUM	DIFF
5	14	19	− 9
4	16	20	−12
3	18	21	−15
2	20	22	−18
1	22	23	−21

Generate the beginning values by whatever method you wish. (The − sign will automatically print in front of negative numbers.)

(b) Assuming your program will furnish results exactly as those shown, show how many different formats the IF instruction may take. (*Hint.* The purpose of IF is to stop execution. You could test IF R = 1, IF S = 22, etc.)

13. Prepare a program flowchart for the coding in Exercise 13, Chapter 4.

14. Prepare a program flowchart that would be appropriate for the following coding.

```
5 INPUT X
10 INPUT A, B
20 C = A + B
30 D = A - B
40 PRINT A, B, C, D
50 IF D > X THEN 70
60 GO TO 5
70 END

READY
```

6 CHAPTER
ARITHMETIC
OPERATIONS

It is the computer's ability to do arithmetic so rapidly and accurately that makes it stand out as a problem-solving device. The purpose of this chapter is to consider a number of topics related to arithmetic processes.

In previous chapters, we have seen introductions to the methods of performing arithmetic. We must indicate a valid variable name to the left of an equal sign. The calculated answer will eventually appear in that storage location in the computer. Then the arithmetic itself is performed to the right of the equal sign (that part of the instruction called the "expression").

The proper symbols for the four basic forms of arithmetic are:

+	addition	−	subtraction
*	multiplication	/	division

Another form of arithmetic, the one that raises to a power (exponentiation), is performed in one of several ways. Each of the following will cube A.

1. B = A ** 3. The double asterisk signifies exponentiation, with the desired power appearing after the asterisks.

2. B = A ↑ 3. Some teletypewriters contain the upward pointing arrow. Its use is the same as the use of double asterisks.

3. B = A * A * A. This cubes A and stores the result in B. Obviously, this approach becomes cumbersome when you want to go beyond the third or fourth power.

Order of Operations

As you often do in pencil-and-paper arithmetic, you might want to prepare a long arithmetic expression in BASIC in order to save working time and amount of paper used. A natural question which arises is "How will the computer handle an expression containing different operations in relation to the regular rules of arithmetic?" The answer is that BASIC follows the same rules.

Assume that you want variable (data field) A to contain the calculated value of:

1. B.

2. Plus C divided by 4.

3. Plus 2 times D.

4. Minus E.

5. Plus F squared.

The coding for that problem would look like this:

$$A = B + C/4 + 2 * D - E + F ** 2$$

How would the computer solve this expression? According to the rules of computer arithmetic, the computer first goes through the expression and does exponentiation (in this case raising F to the second power).

Then the computer goes through the expression again and performs any multiplication and division in the order that it finds the steps (C/4 and 2 * D). Next, the computer goes through the expression a third time and does any adding and subtracting in the order that it finds the steps (in this example there are three adds and one subtract), each add step using an intermediate answer calculated on one of the previous passes.

In the event that there is some form of arithmetic you want the computer to perform before it is to do some other form (in effect, to override the rules described above), you can force the machine to do it by putting parentheses around the involved part. For example, if you want the machine to add B and C and divide their sum by 4, the above expression would be rewritten like this:

$$A = (B + C) \; / \; 4 + 2 * D - E + F ** 2$$

In effect, anything inside parentheses will be performed first, according to the rules quoted above. Then anything outside parentheses will be performed next according to those rules.

If you have any doubts about what will happen in using the computer, you should solve the problem manually, following the above rules, and then solve it on the computer. If the results aren't identical, then you know that you need to check both processes.

You may occasionally need to use parentheses within parentheses, that is, to "nest" them. This is acceptable; the machine merely goes to the inner ones first and works toward the outer ones.

Assume that A = 4, B = 2, and C = 8. The following examples illustrate most of the points presented above.

Expression	Value of D
D = (A + B + C) /2	7
D = A + B + C/2	10
D = A + B/C	4.25
D = (A + B) /C	.75
D = A/B + C	10
D = A/(B + C)	.4
D = A * B + C	16
D = A * (B + C)	40
D = (A + B) * C * 2	96
D = ((A - B) * C) ** 2	256

An important point to keep in mind is that BASIC does not provide for "implied" arithmetic operations. Whereas in arithmetic the expression 2 (A + B) means two times the total of A and B, this step in BASIC is not acceptable. It must be written with a specific multiplication code: 2 * (A + B).

Need for Intermediate Answers

We have just seen how a lengthy arithmetic expression may be set up. As a practical example of this, suppose that in a payroll program the only calculated output desired was a person's net pay. If a person's net pay is to be calculated by deducting certain items from gross pay, one instruction may develop that value as follows (the .85 is explained below):

$$N = .85 * (H * X + O * X * 1.5) - U - D$$

The variable names in the instruction have been assigned to mean:

N	Net pay	O	Overtime hours
H	Regular hours	U	Union dues
X	Regular rate	D	Other deductions

The person's gross pay is being developed within the parentheses. Gross pay is the total of regular pay (regular hours times regular rate) plus overtime pay (overtime hours times one and a half of the regular rate).

Federal income tax is calculated as 10% of gross pay, and social security tax is calculated as 5% of gross pay. These two taxes can be deducted from gross pay by either multiplying gross pay by 85% or by subtracting 15% of gross pay from gross pay. The former method was used in the expression above. Union dues and other deductions, which are fixed amounts, are then subtracted to determine net "take home" pay.

Repeating the point made earlier, one lengthy instruction can calculate net pay. Suppose, however, that the printed output is to be regular pay, overtime pay, total gross pay, federal income tax, social security, total deductions, and net pay. To accomplish this, instructions must be written so that intermediate values (as they are calculated) are held available for later output. The individual instructions could be written this way, with line numbers included for reference purposes:

Meaning of New Variable Names

400 R = H * X	R = Regular pay
410 P = O * X * 1.5	P = Premium (Overtime) pay
420 G = R + P	G = Gross pay
430 F = .10 * G	F = Federal income tax
440 S = .05 * G	S = Social security tax
450 T = F + S + U + D	T = Total deductions
460 N = G - T	N = Net pay (same as "N" above)

In effect, you need to obtain a clear-cut idea as to what problem you are trying to solve. Preparing the format of the required printout in addition to preparing a program flowchart should make it clear how the coding is to proceed.

Negative Values

In computing, there is a need to handle negative numbers as well as positive numbers. Whether you are using the assignment, READ and DATA, or INPUT methods to enter raw data into the machine, you simply precede any negative numerical value with a minus sign (-). Arithmetic is performed algebraically; that is, answers to arithmetic expressions take on a positive or a negative sign, as in the usual rules of arithmetic.

When the computer is printing a negative value, it automatically prints a minus sign in front of the value.

Use of Counters

Quite often it is necessary to set up counters so that numerical data can be accumulated during the running of a program. A "counter" is merely a storage location for which a variable (or data) name has been assigned.

Assume that you have a list of values for which you want the computer to accumulate a total, divide that total by the number of values entered, and print the simple average (arithmetic mean). The program flowchart in Fig. 6-1 will provide that logic.

The program flowchart first provides for setting up two counters, one to be used to accumulate the values and the other to count how many values there are. You may choose to show the previous in two steps instead of one as Fig. 6-1 does.

The logic provides for inputting the value of 99999 as a signal that there will be no more data. When that value is entered, the computer will calculate the average, print both totals, print the average, and end.

The program listing and two executions with some sample transactions are shown in Fig. 6-2. Counters are set up simply by giving a name and assigning a beginning value, which in most cases would be zero but could logically be any numerical value that you want. (Some BASIC systems require that you establish counters as has been done in lines 10 and 20. Those that don't require this setup would assume beginning values of zero in each counter when lines 50 and 60 were first executed.)

Remember, from the discussion in Chapter 2 that the equal sign (=) in BASIC does not mean "equal to" mathematically; it means to "replace with" the material that follows. When line 50 is first executed, the counter T has zero in it and is replaced by the value of V. Subsequent execution of line 50 keeps making T get larger by the value of the latest V.

By the same reasoning, the counter N grows by 1 at a time as each INPUT value is processed.

Since the value of 99999 is being used only as a signal to indicate that there is no more data, the processing that is appropriate when that value enters is to branch around line 50. Thus 99999 does not become a part of the final answers.

A new feature shown in Fig. 6-2 is the variable name legend in the upper right-hand corner. A legend such as this will appear in all of the future programs where there are several variables to keep track of.

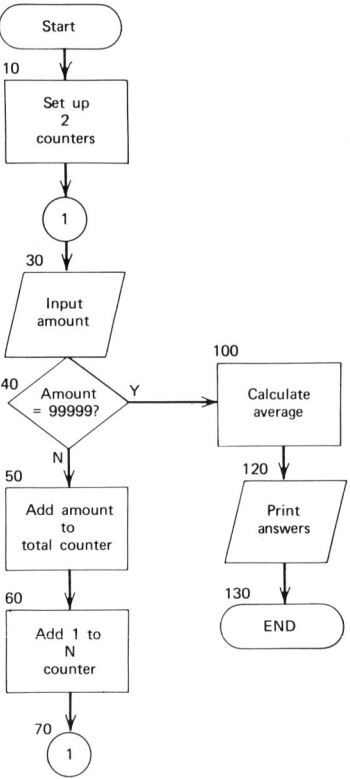

Fig. 6-1. Program flowchart to calculate an average.

This particular program creates one major problem during its execution—if you make a mistake typing in a value, you may be faced with ceasing execution and starting over from the very beginning. That problem will be overcome by placing an error-checking procedure into the program.

The program flowchart in Fig. 6-3 includes a step that permits you to review a value just entered. If you want to accept the value, just type a one, and the program continues on to add the value and to count one.

If you don't want to accept the value, just type a two, and the program branches back to the original INPUT step. Therefore, any bad values do not get added to the T counter, and 1 does not get added into the N counter.

```
5     REM FIG. 6-2.
10  T = 0
20  N = 0
30  INPUT V
40  IF V = 99999 THEN 80
50  T = T + V
60  N = N + 1
70  GO TO 30
80  PRINT
90  PRINT
95      REM    CALCULATES AVERAGE
100  A = T/N
105     REM PRINTS ALL ANSWERS.
110  PRINT "SUM", "# OF ITEMS", "AVERAGE"
120  PRINT T, N, A
130  END

READY
RUN NH


  ?78
  ?45
  ?965
  ?23
  ?48
  ?99999


SUM               # OF ITEMS      AVERAGE
  1159                5             231.8



TIME:  0.14 SECS.

READY



RUN NH


  ?-45
  ?-32
  ?-63
  ?-29
  ?99999


SUM               # OF ITEMS      AVERAGE
  -169                4            -42.25



TIME:  0.13 SECS.

READY
```

Variable Name Legend

T	Total counter
N	Occurrence (number of input values) counter
V	Input value
A	Average

Fig. 6-2. Program that calculates an average.

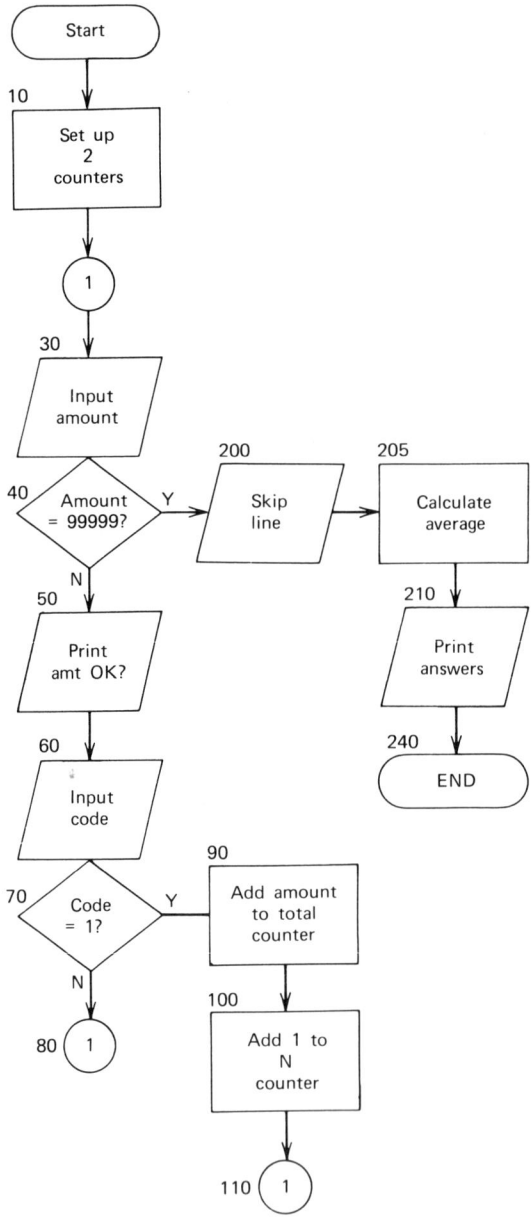

Fig. 6-3. Program flowchart includes a method to recover from an INPUT error.

```
5     REM FIG. 6-4
10 T = 0
20 N = 0
30 INPUT V
40 IF V = 99999 THEN 200
50 PRINT "AMT OK?"
60 INPUT D
70 IF D = 1 THEN 90
80 GO TO 30
90 T = T + V
100 N = N + 1
110 GO TO 30
200 PRINT
201    REM ANSWERS ON SEPARATE LINE FOR EACH.
205 A = T/N
210 PRINT "TOTAL = ", T
220 PRINT "NO OF ITEMS", N
230 PRINT "AVERAGE IS", A
240 END

READY
RUN NH


?45
AMT OK?
?1
?76
AMT OK?
?1
?72
AMT OK?
?1
?99999

TOTAL =        193
NO OF ITEMS    3
AVERAGE IS     64.3333


TIME:  0.18 SECS.

READY
RUN NH


?45
AMT OK?
?2
?54
AMT OK?
?1
?99999

TOTAL =        54
NO OF ITEMS    1
AVERAGE IS     54


TIME:  0.14 SECS.
```

Variable Name Legend

T	Total counter
N	Occurrence (number of input values) counter
V	Input value
D	Code to permit a check of input accuracy
A	Average

Fig. 6-4. Includes a method to recover from an INPUT error.

The program listing and two executions are shown in Fig. 6-4. Notice how the computer prints the message "AMT OK?" when it is time to signify approval of the INPUT. Instead of printing the final output on one line, in this case it has been placed on three separate lines. Appropriate words are printed before the numerical value in each case.

EXERCISES

1. Is the following expression the proper way to raise R to the 4th power? Why?

    $$B = R **** 4$$

2. A programmer wanted to code a step that would multiply two times the sum of A and B and store the results in C. Would C = 2 (A + B) be correct? Why?

3. What would be the result of the following?

    $$X = (\ (2*4) + 4)\ /\ 4$$

4. What does the * mean in the following: PRINT A*B?

5. What does the computer do about high-order zeroes—those to the left of significant whole numbers? Is this desirable?

6. Based upon the following narratives, prepare the appropriate BASIC coding (place each answer in A):
    (a) Take one half of the square of B.
    (b) Divide one fourth by one half.
    (c) Calculate the simple average (mean) of B, C, D, and E.
    (d) Square one half of B.
    (e) Get the sum of 1 times B, 2 times C, and 3 times D.

7. Assume that R = 50 and S = 60. How does the value of T differ if you type T = R + S/2 instead of T = (R+S) /2?

8. In Fig. 6-2:
    (a) What steps in the program made it unnecessary to manually count and then enter the number of INPUT values?
    (b) Eliminate lines 10 and 20, run the program, and review the results. Does your computer automatically zero counters at the beginning?
    (c) When executing the program, enter one negative value and several positive values. How does the computer handle this? Would you have predicted those results?

(d) Will the following method permit recovery from making an error? Explain.

When an input error is recognized, just type that same value with the opposite numerical sign on the next INPUT cycle so that the original value is "backed out."

9. In Fig. 6-4:
(a) What prevented the "errors" from entering and being counted?
(b) When executing the program, enter an alphabetic character (such as A or B) when the machine types AMT OK? What happens? What does this tell you about variable D?

10. Some companies pay overtime for any day in which work hours exceed eight. In other companies, overtime is paid for any week in which work hours exceed 40. Assume a regular pay rate of $4.00 per hour. Input to a program is a series of hours worked per day (which, for a whole week, will exceed 40 for some employees). Calculate a person's gross pay for the week based on each of the two methods.

Prepare the necessary program flowchart and the BASIC coding. Use a signal value of 999 to indicate the end of the INPUT data.

11. What would be the results of the following program when it was run?

```
10 READ A, B, C, D, E, F, G, H, I, J
20 PRINT J; A*B; C-D; E*F; G/H; I**(A+B)
30 DATA 1, 2, 3, 4, 5, 6, 7, 8, 9, 10
40 END

READY
```

12. Write a program that will raise all whole numbers from 1 through 10 to the second, third, fourth, and fifth powers.

13. What is a simple way to test if a numerical value is positive or negative?

14. A DATA statement in a program contains five one-digit numbers. The numbers are supposed to be one through five, respectively. Write the program steps that will determine if the numbers are or are not in the proper order.

15. Carefully review the program results below. Then make a statement about the intended use of fractions in DATA statements.

```
10 READ A
20 PRINT A
30 DATA 5, 1/3, 477
40 END

READY
RUN NH

? DATA NOT IN CORRECT FORM IN LINE 30

TIME:   0.04 SECS.

READY
```

16. Convert the following formula to an appropriate BASIC statement.

$$A = \frac{5(A+B+C) - R}{N^2} + 6$$

7 CHAPTER
BUILT-IN
FUNCTIONS

In addition to the arithmetic operations described in Chapter 6, BASIC also has a number of built-in arithmetic functions. Those functions appropriate to this text are explained here. The other built-in functions are summarized in Appendix E.

Decimal Versus Whole Numbers

We have previously seen how a comma is used to separate adjacent data values. This point has been illustrated in DATA, INPUT, and PRINT statements. Consequently, a comma is not used in BASIC to separate hundreds from thousands, thousands from millions, etc.

However, BASIC does use the decimal point in the standard way as the separation between the decimal and whole (or integer) portion of a numeric value. This standard use of a decimal point applies whether you are using any of the three ways of entering data into the machine, or whether it is printing results at output time.

When a numeric value is about to be printed, the computer will automatically truncate (chop off and not print) any right-hand (nonsignificant) zeroes in the printed part of the decimal. Some examples are:

Operation	Printed Value of A
A = 2 * 5	10
A = .2 * 5	1

A = .2 * .5	.1
A = .02 * .5	.01
A = .02 * .05	.001

There may be times when you want the decimal part of an answer to print, and there may be other times when just the whole number part will suit your output purposes. BASIC makes it relatively easy to get the printed output whichever way you want.

The following program is designed to create both whole and decimal number quotients; the program then rounds the quotients on two bases. The program will provide a printed format:

			A/B ROUNDED	A/B ROUNDED
A	B	A/B	2 DEC.	INTEGER

In effect, what we want printed are the following five fields.

1. A, an assigned value.

2. B, an assigned value.

3. A divided by B, including any decimal positions calculated in the quotient.

4. A divided by B, rounding the quotient to two decimal positions.

5. A divided by B, rounding the quotient to a whole number.

A program flowchart of the required logic is shown in Fig. 7-1. Values for A and B will be entered into the computer by means of assignment steps, with B being smaller than A. The value of B will increase by 1 during each program cycle; when B is equal to A, the program will end. This particular logic and the specific beginning values of A and B were chosen to create a variety of quotients that will be rounded.

The program listing and execution are shown in Fig. 7-2. Prior to the portion that does any rounding, there·are two noteworthy features. First, observe the method used in line 7 to print the first heading line (the words A/B ROUNDED in two places). Since nothing was to appear in the first three columns of that heading line, no literals were shown between the first three commas.

Second, the slash (/) between A and B in line numbers 7 and 10 did not make the computer try to divide at that time because the computer

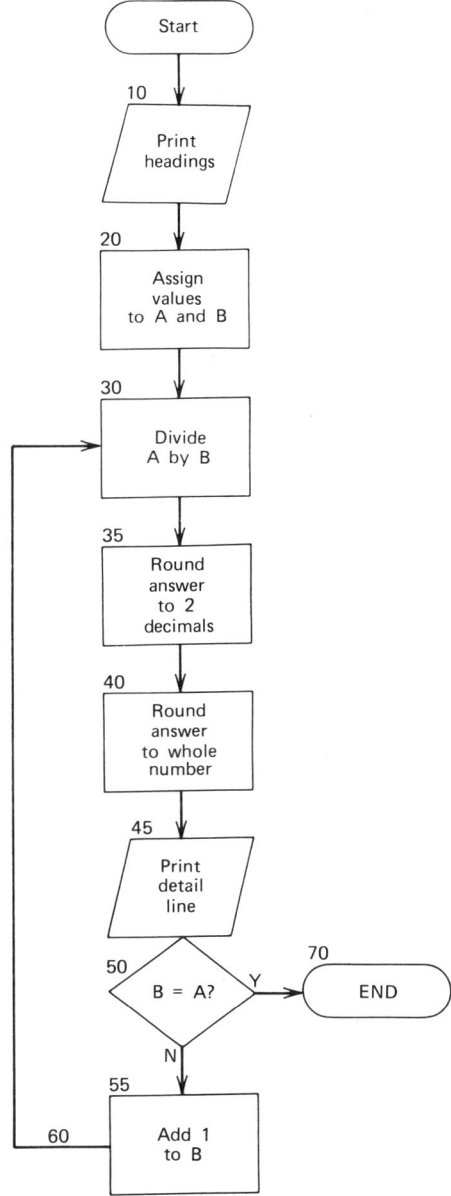

Fig. 7-1. Program flowchart to round numbers.

was working with a nonnumeric literal—a value surrounded by quote symbols—not an arithmetic instruction.

The rounding itself was aided by the built-in function INT (short for INTEGER). The purpose of INT is to truncate (chop off) all the posi-

```
5    REM FIG. 7-2
7 PRINT , , , "A/B ROUNDED", "A/B ROUNDED"
10 PRINT "  A", " B", "A/B", " 2 DEC.", "INTEGER"
15 PRINT
20 A = 11
25 B = 1
30 C = A/B
33   REM INT FUNCTION USED TO ROUND TO 2 DECIMALS.
35 D = INT (C* 100 + .5) / 100
38   REM INT FUNCTION USED TO ROUND TO 2 DECIMALS.
40 E = INT ( C + .5)
45 PRINT A, B, C, D, E
50 IF B = A THEN 70
55 B = B + 1
60 GO TO 30
70 END

READY
RUN NH
```

A	B	A/B	A/B ROUNDED 2 DEC.	A/B ROUNDED INTEGER
11	1	11	11	11
11	2	5.5	5.5	6
11	3	3.66667	3.67	4
11	4	2.75	2.75	3
11	5	2.2	2.2	2
11	6	1.83333	1.83	2
11	7	1.57143	1.57	2
11	8	1.375	1.38	1
11	9	1.22222	1.22	1
11	10	1.1	1.1	1
11	11	1	1	1

```
TIME:  0.27 SECS.

READY
```

Variable Name Legend

A   Dividend (remains constant)
B   Divisor (increments by 1 each
       cycle)
C   Quotient of A/B
D   Quotient rounded to 2 decimals
E   Quotient rounded to a whole
       number

Fig. 7-2. Using INT to help rounding.

INSTRUCTION IN THE BASIC LANGUAGE

tions to the right of the decimal point of the numerical value to which it applies. For instance, see the following examples:

ARITHMETIC INSTRUCTION	PRINT INSTRUCTION	VALUE PRINTED
F = INT (10.4)	PRINT F	10
G = INT (106.543)	PRINT G	106
H = INT (.999)	PRINT H	0

The numeric value (of which you want the computer to obtain its integer portion) must be enclosed within parentheses. The value within parentheses could be any valid arithmetic expression such as INT (I + J).

Notice that INT itself merely truncates decimal positions; it does not round in the process. If we want the machine to "raise a five or higher to the next higher number and drop anything with a four or less," we have to use an extra technique.

Assume that we want an answer such as 106.543, rounded properly and printed with two decimal positions. First we can multiply the number by 100. That multiplication would give us 10654.3. Then we add .5 to the number (10654.8). If the original decimal part is .5 or more, adding .5 to it will cause an overflow of 1 into the whole number part. If the original decimal part is .4 or less, there will be no carry of 1 into the whole number part. Then, using INT will truncate the decimal (10654). Dividing the result by 100 will convert the answer back to a value with two decimal positions, properly rounded (106.54). A sequence of instructions that will accomplish the previous are:

Line Number	Instruction
250	L = L * 100
251	L = L + .5
252	L = INT (L)
253	L = L/100

All four instructions above can be consolidated into one instruction in this manner:

250   L = INT (L * 100 + .5) / 100

Thus, if you want to round to one decimal point, you would multiply and, eventually, divide by 10 instead of 100; for three decimals, use 1000; etc. If you want just an integer that is properly rounded, use the instruction in line 40 of the program in Fig. 7-2.

The INT function can also be used to test to see if a numeric value is an integer. This is particularly helpful when you want to know if one number "divides evenly" into another. Note how such a test is made in the following program; in line 40, C is tested to see if it is equal to the INT portion of C. If it is equal, this means that C, as calculated, was an integer, and an appropriate action results.

```
10 A = 10
20 B = 15
30 C = A/3
40 IF C = INT (C) THEN 60
45 PRINT C; "IS NOT AN INTEGER"
50 GO TO 70
60 PRINT C; "IS AN INTEGER"
70 D = B/3
80 IF D = INT (D) THEN 100
85 PRINT D; "IS NOT AN INTEGER"
95 GO TO 110
100 PRINT D; "IS AN INTEGER"
110 END

READY
RUN NH


   3.33333 IS NOT AN INTEGER
   5 IS AN INTEGER


TIME:   0.08 SECS.

READY
```

Taking a Square Root

In BASIC, the SQR function takes the square root of the value or expression appearing after it in parentheses. Observe the use of SQR in the following program.

```
10 A = 10000
20 B = SQR (A)
30 C = SQR (625)
40 D = SQR (A/C)
45 PRINT "B", "C", "D"
50 PRINT B, C, D
60 END

READY
RUN NH


B                 C                 D
 100              25                20


TIME:   0.06 SECS.

READY
```

Absolute Value

A special function called ABS (short for absolute value) has been built into the BASIC language. Its purpose is to obtain the absolute value of a numeric field. In essence, the function strips the negative sign from a negative value and does nothing to a positive value. It thus reduces a number to its pure magnitude and then makes the resulting value available for any further processing.

A practical use of ABS in a business application follows. Suppose you do not want a minus sign to print in front of a negative value. Instead, you want the minus sign or a CR (credit) symbol to print immediately to the right of any negative value.

An appropriate flowchart showing this appears in Fig. 7-3. One value at a time is read from a DATA statement. If the value is negative (less than zero), the logic branches to a step that obtains the absolute value and then prints the raw data, the minus sign after the value, and the CR after the value. If a value is positive, normal printing of a positive value occurs.

Another significant feature of the program flowchart is the manner in which it handles the READ and DATA statements. Recall from the program on page 38 that an "OUT OF DATA" message prints when there is no more data and the program abruptly terminates. In this program, the last value in the DATA statement will be 999. When that dummy value is READ, it is time to END.

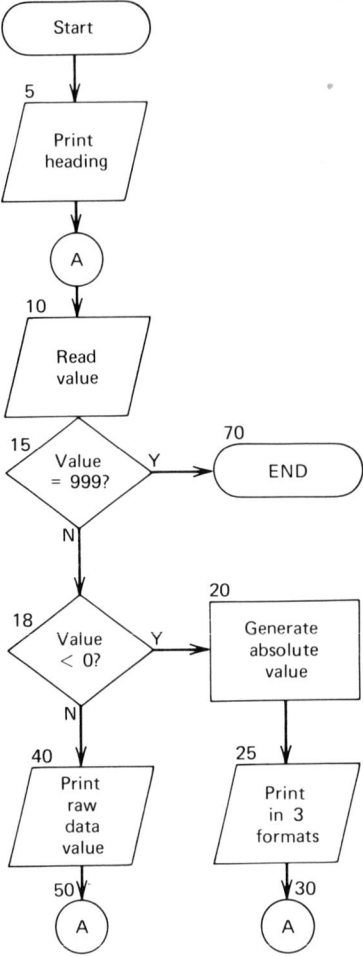

Fig. 7-3. Program flowchart to generate absolute value.

The coding and execution are shown in Fig. 7-4. Only when V is a negative number does the computer branch to line number 20, where the absolute value is obtained (the negative sign is removed). Line number 25 then causes the value to be printed in its usual form, the minus sign to the right of the value, and a CR sign to the right of the value. Note how the semicolon was used to force the signs to print right next to the values instead of in the next normal column position, as would happen if a comma had been used as a separator.

V   Original DATA value

B   Absolute value of V

```
3     REM FIG. 7-4.
5 PRINT "RAW DATA", "- SIGN AFTER", "CR SYM. AFTER"
8 PRINT
10 READ V
15 IF V = 999 THEN 70
18 IF V < 0 THEN 20
19 GO TO 40
20 B = ABS (V)
22    REM REMOVES ANY MINUS SIGN
25 PRINT V, B; "-", B; "CR"
27    REM PRINTS IN ALL 3 VERSIONS.
30 GO TO 10
40 PRINT V, V, V
50 GO TO 10
60 DATA 10,-8,-27.4,41.8,-832,21,999
70 END

READY
RUN NH
```

RAW DATA	- SIGN AFTER	CR SYM. AFTER
10	10	10
-8	8 -	8 CR
-27.4	27.4 -	27.4 CR
41.8	41.8	41.8
-832	832 -	832 CR
21	21	21

```
TIME:  0.13 SECS.

READY
```

Fig. 7-4. Using the ABS function.

Random Numbers

During the execution of a computer program, it is often desirable to generate a random number. A random number, by definition, is any value whose chance of being chosen is equal to the chance of any other value being chosen.

In BASIC, the method of doing this uses the RND (random number) function. The specific method varies among computer systems. In my case, a random number is obtained in either of the following ways:

```
10 A = RND              10 PRINT RND
20 PRINT A              30 END
30 END
                        READY
READY                   RUN NH
RUN NH

                        0.217873
     0.217873


                        TIME:   0.03 SECS.
     TIME:   0.03 SECS.
                        READY
READY
```

As you can see, the use of a variable data name (in this case A) to hold the number that is generated is an optional method. A third possible alternative (a requirement to some) is to place a specific expression inside parentheses to the right of RND.

When used in the manner shown above, repeated executions of the program produce the same "random" value for A (see Fig. 7-5). Repeated development of the same value will likely destroy the concept of a random number. This limitation can be overcome by use of the RANDOMIZE function, as seen in Fig. 7-6. (Please make careful note of the RANDOMIZE function where line 5 of Fig. 7-9 is explained below.)

Any given number of randomly generated values can be developed in the manner shown in Fig. 7-7. (Any generated value containing E-2 represents a number to the ten minus two power, a rather small number. This use of E-2 is referred to as scientific notation.)

The number that is generated is always greater than zero and always smaller than one, although the difference between zero or one, in some cases, will be slight. If a decimal answer is not acceptable but a whole number is required instead, that requirement can be met by use of the INT function (see the upper portion (A) of Fig. 7-8).

Since the INT function generates a decimal value, multiplying it by 10 will create a maximum whole number value of nine, with a string of decimal positions. Using the INT function then truncates the decimal positions, leaving an integer in the range of zero through nine.

If you should require random numbers between one and ten, the program in the lower portion (B) of Fig. 7-8 accomplishes that. Adding a value of one (in line 20) to a previously generated range of zero through nine will obviously create a range of one through ten.

In the same vein, review the following instructions and the range of random numbers generated.

```
3    REM FIG. 7-6.
5 RANDOMIZE
10 A = RND
20 PRINT A
30 END

READY
RUN NH


   0.605618



TIME:  0.04 SECS.

READY
RUN NH


   0.22461



TIME:  0.05 SECS.

READY
RUN NH


   0.898943



TIME:  0.03 SECS.

READY
RUN NH


   0.168836



TIME:  0.03 SECS.

READY
```

```
10 A = RND
20 PRINT A
30 END

READY
RUN NH


   0.217873



TIME:  0.03 SECS.

READY
RUN NH


   0.217873



TIME:  0.03 SECS.

READY
RUN NH


   0.217873



TIME:  0.05 SECS.

READY
RUN NH


   0.217873



TIME:  0.04 SECS.

READY
```

Fig. 7-5. Using the RND function to develop a repeating random number.

Fig. 7-6. Use of RANDOMIZE to develop a nonrepeating random number.

Instruction	*Range of A*
A = INT (2 * RND)	0 – 1
A = INT (3 * RND)	0 – 2
A = INT (4 * RND)	0 – 3
A = INT (26 * RND)	0 – 25

Instruction	Range of A
A = INT (2 * RND) + 1	1 - 2
A = INT (3 * RND) + 2	2 - 4
A = INT (6 * RND) + 1	1 - 6
A = INT (7 * RND)	0 - 6

Although the random-number generator can be used to simulate such games as coin flipping, dice throwing, and poker, the illustration shown here will relate to an auditing function.

Assume that auditors are reviewing a sample of the documents that support 100 transactions. The auditors do not want any personal bias to

```
3      REM FIG. 7-7.
5 RANDOMIZE
10 I = 1
20 A = RND
30 PRINT A,
40 IF I = 10 THEN 50
43 I = I + 1
47 GO TO 20
50 END

READY
RUN NH


   0.267321       0.257427       0.588417       0.270671       0.965085
   0.733782       0.882963       0.537992       0.222513       0.322199

TIME:   0.07 SECS.

READY
RUN NH


   0.812392       0.135312       0.728745       0.683522       0.695621
   0.979218       0.922329       0.495914       0.830933       0.707964

TIME:   0.06 SECS.

READY
RUN NH


   0.870597       0.893485       5.51011E-2     0.836173       0.980812
   0.458472       0.26038        0.70677        0.874297       0.513573

TIME:   0.07 SECS.

READY
```

Fig. 7-7. *Generating 10 random numbers three times.*

```
3     REM FIG. 7-8.
5 RANDOMIZE
10 I = 1
20 A = INT ( 10 * RND)
24    REM PREVIOUS STEP CAUSES EVERY
25    REM RANDOM NUMBER TO BE AN INTEGER
26    REM WITHIN THE RANGE OF 0 TO 9.
30 PRINT A,
40 IF I = 10 THEN 50
43 I = I + 1
47 GO TO 20
50 END

READY
RUN NH


2                 0              7              3              4
6                 2              5              4              4

TIME:   0.06 SECS.

READY
RUN NH


3                 2              5              4              5
0                 4              7              8              5

TIME:   0.06 SECS.

READY
```

(A)

Fig. 7-8.   Generating integer random numbers (completed on page 84).

affect their selection process.   They have decided, however, that they want to review 10%, or 10, of the items. Furthermore, they want to pick one account from each group of 10 transactions.

The program in Fig. 7-9 prints out the numbers of the accounts that should be reviewed. Various lines in the program are explained as follows:

LINE NUMBER	EXPLANATION
5	Causes the RND function to generate a different series of numbers each time the program is run. Since the use of RANDOMIZE causes differing values to be generated each time, its use prior to complete debugging may create a problem. It is better to write and debug, and then include RANDOMIZE.

```
3     REM FIG. 7-8.
5 RANDOMIZE
10 I = 1
20 A = INT (10 * RND) + 1
24     REM PREVIOUS STEP CAUSES EVERY
25     REM RANDOM NUMBER TO BE AN INTEGER
26     REM WITHIN THE RANGE OF 1 TO 10.
30 PRINT A,
40 IF I = 10 THEN 50
43 I = I + 1
47 GO TO 20
50 END

READY
RUN NH


1              5              7              8              1
6              7              8              6              3

TIME:   0.06 SECS.

READY
RUN NH


8              7              1              10             6
4              9              7              3              5

TIME:   0.06 SECS.

READY
```

                              (B)
                    Fig. 7-8. cont.

10	Sets the variable N equal to 1. N is being used to eventually stop execution.
20	Calculates a random number. Since N is 1 the first time this line is executed, the first random number will be within the range 1 through 10. Since N will be 11 the next time this line is executed, the second random number will be within 11 through 20, etc.
40	Will cause a branch to END when 10 cycles are completed.
50	Adds 10 to the factor N so that the next random number will be in the next group of 10.

84   INSTRUCTION IN THE BASIC LANGUAGE

```
3     REM FIG. 7-9.
5 RANDOMIZE
10 N = 1
20 R = INT (10 * RND) + N
30 PRINT R
40 IF N = 91 THEN 70
50 N = N + 10
60 GO TO 20
70 END

READY
RUN NH


    4
   16
   24
   31
   49
   58
   64
   75
   84
   91



TIME:   0.06 SECS.

READY
RUN NH


    3
   14
   23
   33
   48
   55
   67
   75
   82
   98



TIME:   0.06 SECS.

READY
```

Fig. 7-9. Generating random numbers in an auditing application.

Thus one account number will be selected from each group (or "decade") of 10 transactions.

EXERCISES

1. True or False? The use of the INT function alone automatically rounds a value to the nearest whole number. Explain.

2. Suppose the computer is to print a heading above only the fifth column of output data. How do you code so that a heading will print there only?

3. Examine the two styles of desired format below. What must be done differently to produce the format in Style 2?

Style 1		Style 2	
A	B	A	B
XXX.XXXXX	XXX.XXXXX	XXX.X	XXX.XX
XXX.XXXXX	XXX.XXXXX	XXX.X	XXX.XX

4. Closely examine the results produced by the following program. Explain why the results came out as they did.

```
10 A = .999
20 B = 9.9
30 C = -5.9
40 PRINT INT (A), INT (B), INT (C)
50 END

READY
RUN NH


0               9               -6


TIME:   0.04 SECS.

READY
```

5. In Fig. 7-2:
   (a) Describe how the headings were centered.
   (b) What would have been the results if line 55 had been B = B + 3?
   (c) What is a simple way to prevent the problem noted in (b) above?

6. Write a program that would take the following values and print them out rounded to thousands: 1000, 100000, 999, 9999, 10499, 10500, 111111. Use whatever method you wish to enter the values into the computer.

7. What is wrong with the following: A = SQR B?

8. Explain the principle that is illustrated in the following program. Try the program on your own and see what error message you get.

```
10 A = SQR (-9)
20 PRINT A
30 END

READY
RUN NH


% SQRT OF NEGATIVE NUMBER IN LINE 10
 3


TIME:   0.05 SECS.

READY
```

9. What is a random number? What has to be done to cause the computer to generate a different random number every time it starts with the RND function?

10. How can you test a numerical value to see if it is negative?

11. In Fig. 7-8:
    (a) How many rows of random numbers would be printed if the comma in line number 30 were replaced by a semicolon?
    (b) Why were all random numbers in the range of zero to nine in the (a) example?
    (c) Change the program so that all random numbers are in the range of three to 12.

12. In Fig. 7-9:
    (a) Why was there only one random number from each "decade" of accounts?

(b) Change the program so that there would be two random numbers for each "decade" of account numbers.

13. Shown below are the desired results of a program. Prepare the necessary program flowchart and BASIC coding. Enter the data however you wish, and round MPG to tenths.

Car Number	MILES	GALLONS	MPG
1	100	10	10
2	500	125	4
3	XXX	XXX	XX.X
4	XXX	XXX	XX.X
TOTALS	XXXX	XXXX	
WEIGHTED AVERAGE			XX.X

14. Prepare a program flowchart and the required BASIC coding to produce results as follows:

Student Number	Exam 1	Exam 2	Exam 3	Average
15	100	100	100	100
27	60	90	81	77
XX	XXX	XXX	XXX	XXX

Class Average = XXX

Exams 1 and 2 are given equal weight; exam 3 is to receive as much weight as exams 1 and 2 combined. Each average is to be printed as a properly rounded whole number.

15. Write a program that will divide one number by another and make the quotient a whole number. Do not round according to normal rules; any quotients with fractional positions are to be raised to the next whole number.

16. Write a program (using the INT function) that will determine if a numerical value is odd or even.

17. Write the program steps that will take a square root of any given INPUT numerical value. Print the letter I (for imaginary) to the right of the root of any negative values.

18. An accounting entry is to consist of a debit (generally a positive dollar amount) to one account and a credit (generally a negative dollar amount) to another account. In an INPUT of such an entry, the data may appear on a line as follows:

? 174, 500.50, 683, - 500.50

Write those BASIC steps that provide for such INPUT. Then provide for steps that will check the INPUT to see if the credit amount is equal to the debit amount, but with a negative sign instead of no (an implied positive) sign. Use the ABS function in your solution. Then test the program to see if it works properly.

19. Write a program that will print 10 one-digit random numbers on one line (no vertical paper spacing).

20. Write a program that will take the square root of all of the positive even numbers smaller than 100. But print only the square roots that are integers. Make sure you use the capabilities built into BASIC.

8 CHAPTER
DECISION
PROCESSES I

The value in using a computer, in most cases, stems from its ability to perform arithmetic and to make decisions. To make a decision in a computer sense is not quite the same as in the human sense. To the computer, a decision involves a test of the conditions encountered in the data; the program itself must then contain all of the possible alternate paths to follow based on those conditions.

What kinds of decisions can be programmed into a computer? In a general sense, computers can make decisions in the following categories:

1. When to stop executing the program (that is, when to proceed to the last or the END step).

2. How many times to repeatedly go through a series of steps before proceeding on to other steps.

3. Whether or not to apply certain steps to a particular transaction.

4. Whether a special code or specific amount exists in the input data.

5. Whether a special code or specific amount exists in the output data.

We have seen that decisions are made in the BASIC language through the use of the IF statement. One unit or field of data is compared to another field of data. If the two fields being compared are equal, the program is directed to a particular step to be executed next. If the two fields are not equal, the computer executes other steps instead.

There are six different ways to test for a relationship between data fields. The six "relational operators" are:

=	equal to	<>	not equal to
>	greater than	>=	greater than or equal to
<	less than	<=	less than or equal to

Although all tests for relations between fields could be performed through the use of just the equal to (=) and the greater than (>), the other variations are provided to make some tests easier. Also, some people logically think of a situation differently (however correctly) as compared to other people. Some of the variations possible are:

<table>
<tr><td>Situation</td><td>Possible Versions of
BASIC Coding</td></tr>
<tr><td>A. If A is equal to B, go to 50. Otherwise, go to 60.</td><td>1. 20 IF A = B THEN 50
   30 GO TO 60</td></tr>
<tr><td></td><td>2. 20 IF A<>B THEN 60
   30 GO TO 50</td></tr>
<tr><td></td><td>3. 20 IF A > B THEN 60
   30 IF A < B THEN 60
   40 GO TO 50</td></tr>
<tr><td>B. If C is greater than D, go to 100. If not, go to 500.</td><td>1. 70 IF C > D THEN 100
   80 GO TO 500</td></tr>
<tr><td></td><td>2. 70 IF D<C THEN 100
   80 GO TO 500</td></tr>
<tr><td></td><td>3. 70 IF C <= D THEN 500
   80 GO TO 100</td></tr>
<tr><td>C. If E is less than or equal to F, go to 600. Otherwise, go to 700.</td><td>1. 550 IF E <= F THEN 600
   560 GO TO 700</td></tr>
<tr><td></td><td>2. 500 IF E < F THEN 600
   560 IF E = F THEN 600
   570 GO TO 700</td></tr>
<tr><td></td><td>3. 550 IF F > E THEN 600
   560 IF F = E THEN 600
   570 GO TO 700</td></tr>
</table>

4. 550 IF E<>F THEN 570
   560 GO TO 600
   570 IF F < E THEN 700
   580 GO TO 600

You can see that several of the examples begin to get somewhat complicated. However, if that is the type of reasoning process that some people use to reach a certain goal, perhaps it was easier to design so many variations into the language rather than to try to force people to think in a particular pattern.

Arithmetic in an IF Statement

It is possible to do more than to just compare one field to another field in an IF statement.

Suppose you want to branch to line 300 if A + B + C - D is greater than 75. You could cause this to happen in a routine way:

30   E = A + B + C - D

40   IF E > 75 THEN 300

Or you could combine both of the previous statements into one instruction in this manner:

30   IF A + B + C - D > 75 THEN 300

In the latter case, the computer merely develops A + B + C - D first and then proceeds to compare that value to 75 in the usual manner. Remember that, in this approach, the total of A + B + C - D is not available as it is in the prior example where it is held in a variable named E.

RESTORE Statement

We have seen several examples of the general use of the READ and DATA statements. In Fig. 7-4 we also saw how to avoid an "OUT OF DATA" message by testing for the last item in the DATA statement.

If you have a situation where you want the computer to be able to READ the fields in the DATA statement again, that can be accomplished through use of the RESTORE statement. Figure 8-1 shows a program flowchart whose purpose is to multiply each item in the DATA statement by two and to then go through the DATA statement again and divide each item by two. Note that the signal for the last DATA item, number 99, is to be processed as a regular item.

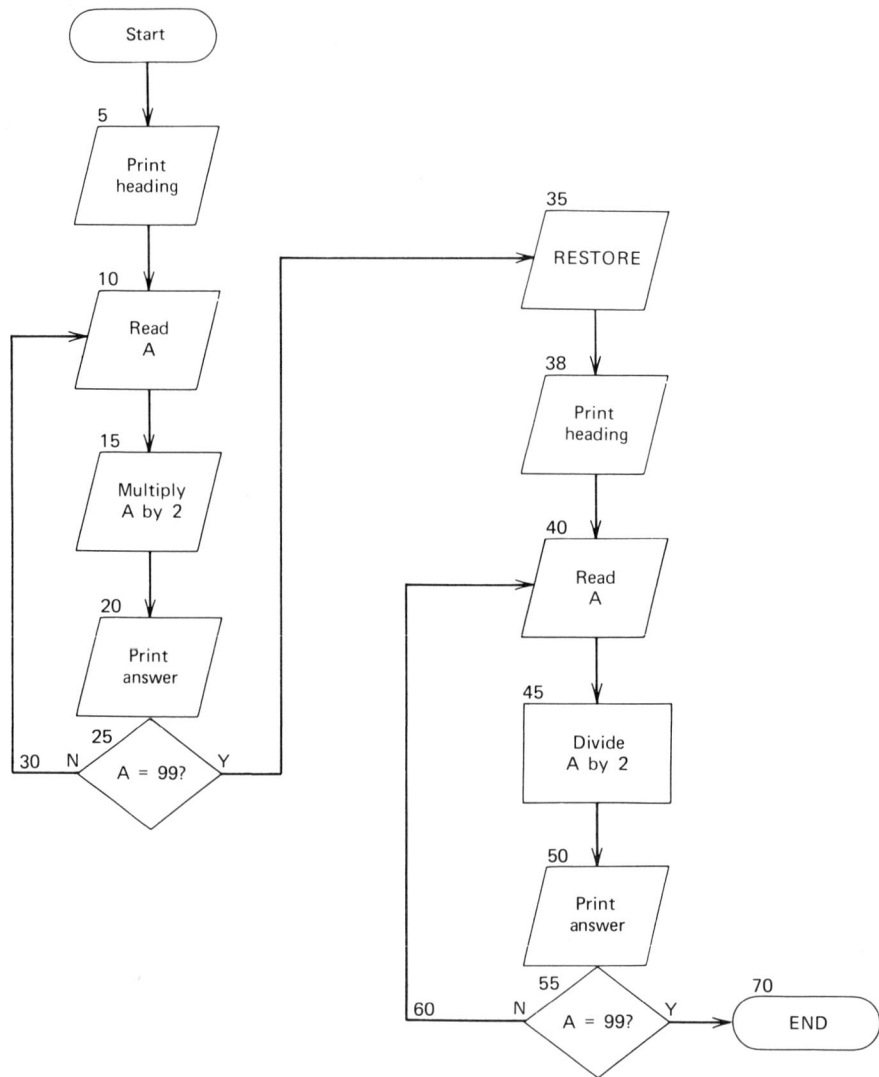

Fig. 8-1. *Program flowchart illustrating RESTORE.*

The coding and execution are shown in Fig. 8-2. The IF statement at line 25 tests for the last data item. When number 99 has been processed, the program branches to the RESTORE at statement 35. RESTORE "resets" the DATA in line number 65 and makes it possible for the computer to start reading that same DATA again. The IF state-

```
3     REM FIG. 8-2.
5 PRINT " A", "A*2"
8 PRINT
10 READ A
15 B = A * 2
20 PRINT A, B
23    REM TESTS FOR END OF DATA TO
24    REM AVOID OUT OF DATA MESSAGE.
25 IF A = 99 THEN 35
30 GO TO 10
33    REM RESETS DATA SO IT CAN BE READ AGAIN.
35 RESTORE
37 PRINT
38 PRINT " A", "A/2"
39 PRINT
40 READ A
45 B = A / 2
50 PRINT A, B
53    REM TESTS FOR END OF DATA ON
54    REM SECOND PASS THRU IT.
55 IF A = 99 THEN 70
60 GO TO 40
65 DATA 12, 19, 44, 86, 32, 99
70 END

READY
RUN NH


    A               A*2

    12               24
    19               38
    44               88
    86              172
    32               64
    99              198

    A               A/2

    12                6
    19                9.5
    44               22
    86               43
    32               16
    99               49.5

                    .

TIME:   0.15 SECS.

READY
```

Fig. 8-2.   The use of RESTORE.

ment in line 55 tests for the last DATA item on the second pass through the DATA so that the program can properly reach END.

Nonnumeric Data

Previously, the only way shown to handle nonnumeric (alphabetic and special characters) data has been through the use of a nonnumeric literal (as in printing of headings).

In order to provide for nonnumeric data in variable-named data fields, it is merely necessary to assign these fields a valid data name ending in a dollar sign ($). As we have seen, if you assign the variable name "A" to a data field, the computer will allow you to put only numeric data into field A. If you assign the name "A$," the computer will allow you to put any combination of valid characters into that field, including numeric characters.

A nonnumeric field (often called a character string) can be entered by assignment, by INPUT, and by DATA statements; it can be PRINTed); and it can be tested by the IF statement. But a nonnumeric field cannot have arithmetic performed on it.

Assume that we have a problem where we want to INPUT employee's names, hours worked, and pay rates. We want the computer to calculate and print each person's gross pay and to go on to the next person. A signal name of "ZZYZZ" represents the end of the input data, this unit not being a valid person.

The program in Fig. 8-3 will perform the functions described above. Significant statements in the program are:

10   INPUT N$ provides for alphabetic characters to be entered as the employee's name.

15   Tests an inputted name to see if it contains the characters "ZZYZZ". When a nonnumeric field is being tested, the specific characters being tested must be surrounded by quotes.

25   PRINT N$ allows the computer to print the alphabetic characters of each employee's name.

ON and GO TO

Assume a payroll problem where the raw data is: employee's names, hours worked, pay rate, and pay code. The pay code is to be used for bonus purposes. Total gross pay is to be regular pay (product of hours times rate) plus bonus.

```
3      REM FIG. 8-3.
5 PRINT "", "EMP NAME", "HOURS", "RATE", "GROSS"
7      REM PERMITS INPUT OF ALPHA LITERAL.
10 INPUT N$
12     REM TESTS INPUT FOR A SPECIFIC ALPHA LITERAL.
15 IF N$ = "ZZYZZ" THEN 35
18 INPUT H, R
20 G = H * R
23     REM USE OF "N$" PERMITS PRINTING
24     REM OF ALPHA LITERAL.
25 PRINT "", N$, H, R, G
30 GO TO 10
35 END

READY
RUN NH
```

	EMP NAME	HOURS	RATE	GROSS
?ED				
?8, 4				
	ED	8	4	32
?JOE				
?8.4, 3.20				
	JOE	8.4	3.2	26.88
?TOM				
?2.5, 4.58				
	TOM	2.5	4.58	11.45
?J0				
?8, 6.25				
	J0	8	6.25	50
?ZZYZZ				

```
TIME:  0.26 SECS.

READY
```

Variable Name Legend

N$	Employee name
H	Hours
R	Rate
G	Gross pay

Fig. 8-3. Handling a nonnumeric literal.

The pay code must be either a 1, 2, 3, or 4. The codes have the following meanings:

Pay Code	Bonus Amount
1	$ 50
2	75
3	100
4	200

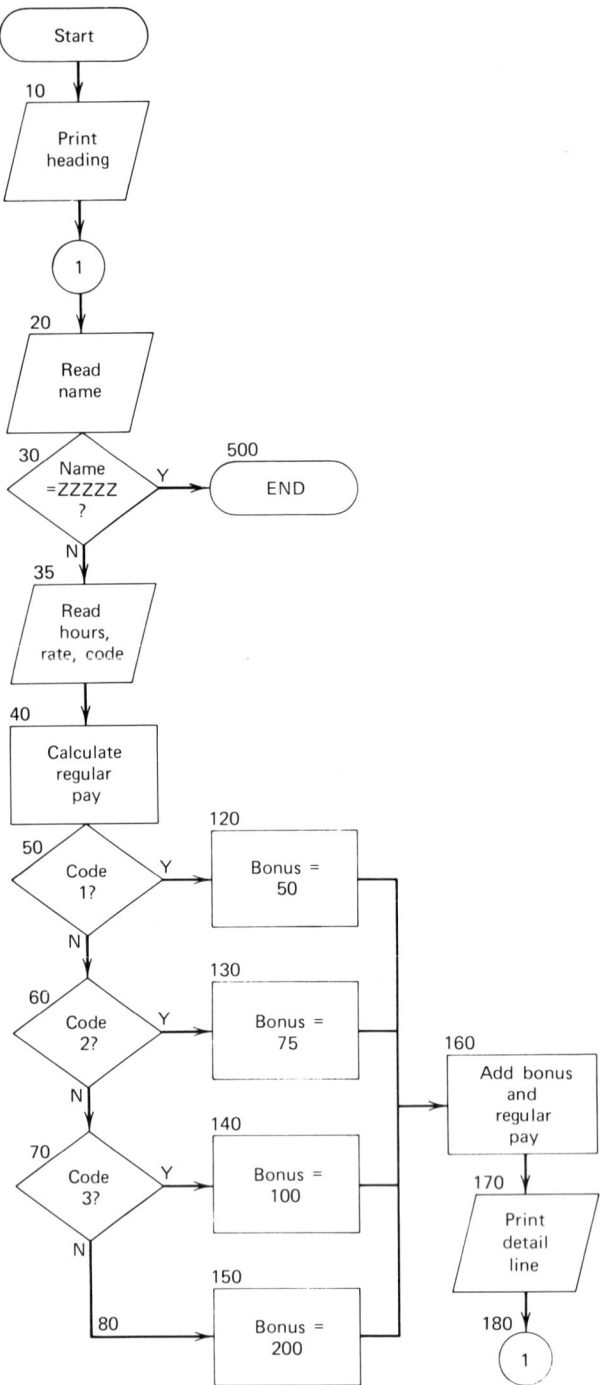

Fig. 8-4. Program flowchart with multiple decision points.

```
3     REM FIG. 8-5.
10  PRINT "NAME", "REG. PAY",
12  PRINT "BONUS", "TOT. GROSS"
20  READ N$
30  IF N$ = "ZZZZZ" THEN 500
35  READ H, R, C
40  R1 = INT (H * R * 100 + .5) / 100
45      REM TESTS FOR INPUT CODES.
50  IF C = 1 THEN 120
60  IF C = 2 THEN 130
70  IF C = 3 THEN 140
80  GO TO 150
120 B = 50
125 GO TO 160
130 B = 75
135 GO TO 160
140 B = 100
145 GO TO 160
150 B = 200
160 G = R1 + B
170 PRINT N$, R1, B, G
180 GO TO 20
200 DATA JOHN DOE, 24, 4,1
210 DATA JANE SMITH, 40, 5.25, 4
220 DATA BILL FRANK, 35, 3.50, 2
240 DATA PETE ROE, 34, 3.50, 3
270 DATA ZZZZZ
500 END

READY
RUN NH
```

	Variable Name Legend	
N$	Employee name
H	Hours
R	Rate
C	Bonus code
R1	Regular pay
B	Bonus
G	Gross pay

NAME	REG. PAY	BONUS	TOT. GROSS
JOHN DOE	96	50	146
JANE SMITH	210	200	410
BILL FRANK	122.5	75	197.5
PETE ROE	119	100	219

```
TIME:  0.14 SECS.

READY
```

Fig. 8-5. Use of multiple IF statements.

If you were to prepare the applicable program using the regular IF statement, the flowchart would resemble the one in Fig. 8-4, and the coding and execution would resemble that in Fig. 8-5. Observe that one IF statement was required to test for each of the first three pay codes. If a code was neither a 1, 2, nor 3, it was assumed to be a 4. This assumption could cause a serious problem, as described below.

These three IF statements can be replaced by one ON and GO TO statement. The replacement statement would be coded like this:

50 ON C GO TO 120, 130, 140. 150

The ON statement tests data field C to determine what numerical value it contains. If variable C contains a 1, the program branches to line number 120; if C contains a 2, the program branches to line number 130; if C contains a 3, the program branches to line number 140; and if C contains a 4, the program branches to line number 150.

Thus the program branches to the first line number following the word TO when the code is a 1, to the second line number when the code is 2, etc. Any number of codes could be tested with the ON statement if you are careful to provide a similar number of statements to branch to.

The revised program is listed and executed in Fig. 8-6. Notice that with line number 50 replacing line numbers 50–80 of the previous program, the results were the same.

```
3    REM FIG. 8-6.
10 PRINT "NAME", "REG. PAY",
12 PRINT "BONUS", "TOT. GROSS"
20 READ N$
30 IF N$ = "ZZZZZ" THEN 500
35 READ H, R, C
40 R1 = INT (H * R * 100 + .5) / 100
45    REM TESTS FOR INPUT CODES.
50 ON C GO TO 120, 130, 140, 150
120 B = 50
125 GO TO 160
130 B = 75
135 GO TO 160
140 B = 100
145 GO TO 160
150 B = 200
160 G = R1 + B
170 PRINT N$, R1, B, G
180 GO TO 20
200 DATA JOHN DOE, 24, 4,1
210 DATA JANE SMITH, 40, 5.25, 4
220 DATA BILL FRANK, 35, 3.50, 2
240 DATA PETE ROE, 34, 3.50, 3
270 DATA ZZZZZ
500 END

READY
RUN NH
```

Variable Name Legend	
N$	Employee name
H	Hours
R	Rate
C	Bonus code
R1	Regular pay
B	Bonus
G	Gross pay

NAME	REG. PAY	BONUS	TOT. GROSS
JOHN DOE	96	50	146
JANE SMITH	210	200	410
BILL FRANK	122.5	75	197.5
PETE ROE	119	100	219

```
TIME:   0.13 SECS.

READY
```

Fig. 8-6.   Use of ON- GO TO.

If the variable being tested should contain a decimal value, the computer simply truncates the decimal and tests the integer portion. The use of ON and GO TO does not work with zero nor with negative amounts.

Just a little experience with a computer quickly shows any programmer or user how easily errors can creep into the situation. For example, one new line of DATA, that for Emil Jones, has been added to the pro-

```
3     REM FIG. 8-7.
10  PRINT "NAME", "REG. PAY",
12  PRINT "BONUS", "TOT. GROSS"
20  READ N$
30  IF N$ = "ZZZZZ" THEN 500
35  READ H, R, C
40  R1 = INT (H * R * 100 + .5) / 100
45     REM TESTS FOR INPUT CODES.
50  ON C GO TO 120, 130, 140, 150
120 B = 50
125 GO TO 160
130 B = 75
135 GO TO 160
140 B = 100
145 GO TO 160
150 B = 200
160 G = R1 + B
170 PRINT N$, R1, B, G
180 GO TO 20
200 DATA JOHN DOE, 24, 4,1
210 DATA JANE SMITH, 40, 5.25, 4
220 DATA BILL FRANK, 35, 3.50, 2
230 DATA EMIL JONES, 38, 4.25, 5
240 DATA PETE ROE, 34, 3.50, 3
270 DATA ZZZZZ
500 END

READY
RUN NH
```

Variable Name Legend

N$	Employee name
H	Hours
R	Rate
C	Bonus code
R1	Regular pay
B	Bonus
G	Gross pay

NAME	REG. PAY	BONUS	TOT. GROSS
JOHN DOE	96	50	146
JANE SMITH	210	200	410
BILL FRANK	122.5	75	197.5

? ON EVALUATED OUT OF RANGE IN LINE 50

TIME: 0.18 SECS.

READY

Fig. 8-7. Program execution halted because of invalid data.

```
3      REM FIG. 8-8.
10 PRINT "NAME", "REG. PAY",
12 PRINT "BONUS", "TOT. GROSS"
20 READ N$
30 IF N$ = "ZZZZZ" THEN 500
35 READ H, R, C
40 R1 = INT (H * R * 100 + .5) / 100
41     REM TESTS FOR INPUT CODES.
42 IF C < 1 THEN 185
46 IF C > 4 THEN 185
50 ON C GO TO 120, 130, 140, 150
120 B = 50
125 GO TO 160
130 B = 75
135 GO TO 160
140 B = 100
145 GO TO 160
150 B = 200
160 G = R1 + B
170 PRINT N$, R1, B, G
180 GO TO 20
183    REM PRINTS ERROR MESSAGE FOR
184    REM ANYONE WITH INVALID CODE.
185 PRINT N$, R1, "ERROR", "ERROR"
187 GO TO 20
200 DATA JOHN DOE, 24, 4,1
210 DATA JANE SMITH, 40, 5.25, 4
220 DATA BILL FRANK, 35, 3.50, 2
230 DATA EMIL JONES, 38, 4.25, 5
240 DATA PETE ROE, 34, 3.50, 3
270 DATA ZZZZZ
500 END

READY
RUN NH
```

Variable Name Legend	
N$	Employee name
H	Hours
R	Rate
C	Bonus code
R1	Regular pay
B	Bonus
G	Gross pay

```
NAME            REG. PAY        BONUS           TOT. GROSS
JOHN DOE        96              50              146
JANE SMITH      210             200             410
BILL FRANK      122.5           75              197.5
EMIL JONES      161.5           ERROR           ERROR
PETE ROE        119             100             219


TIME:  0.16 SECS.

READY
```

Fig. 8-8. Testing for valid data.

gram that was shown in Fig. 8-6. The revised program listing and attempted execution are shown in Fig. 8-7.

Since the pay code for Emil Jones was a 5, which was beyond the range being tested by ON in line number 50, the computer printed an error message and stopped. Obviously, you can't always afford to have program executions stopped because of data errors. On the other hand, it is impractical to guarantee that there are no errors in the data.

The situation in Fig. 8-7 has been corrected by the revised program shown in Fig. 8-8. Line numbers 42 and 46 test the pay code to see if it is smaller than one or greater than four. If it is, the program branches to line number 185, where an appropriate error message is printed. The program then continues on to process the next person. Data for an ERROR condition would need to be corrected before processing could go on to the next phase.

EXERCISES

1. In a general sense, how does a computer make decisions?

2. What will happen in a computer program if a decision step that should be there is not present? Does the computer spot the omission? Why?

3. Describe some of the different situations that may be tested to determine when a program should branch to the END step.

4. If a programming language provides the ability to test for an equal condition and also for a greater than condition, does that language need the ability to test for a less than condition? Why?

5. Show two completely different ways to code:
    ```
    100 IF A < = 50 THEN 200
    150 GO TO 300
    ```

6. What is wrong with the following?
    ```
    300 IF C = D THEN 600
    400 IF C > D THEN 600
    500 IF D > C THEN 600
    ```

7. Review the following selected statements (from a complete program). Replace some existing statements with optional versions so that the total number of lines will be reduced.
    ```
    1  INPUT  A
    2  INPUT  B
    3  INPUT  C
       . . . . .
       . . . . .
       . . . . .
    85  D = A + B
    86  E = C
    87  IF D = E THEN 100
    88  IF D > E THEN 1
    100  END
    ```

8. What is the purpose of RESTORE? What will happen if you use RESTORE in a program that has no DATA statement? (Try this at your Computer Center and see what happens.)

9. Once RESTORE is used, do you still need to do something to prevent the OUT OF DATA message with subsequent use of READ? Why is that the case?

10. What are the differences among A, A1, A$, and "A"?

11. Can a "nonnumeric" field contain only alphabetic characters? Is this good or bad?

12. Should it be possible to perform arithmetic on nonnumeric data? Why?

13. Describe the nature of ON and GO TO. Under what circumstances will this particular coding have a payoff in programming productivity?

14. Assume that a variable field whose name is L has just been calculated; L contains any whole number between one and 11. If L is one to five, branch to statement 600. If L is six, branch to statement 700. If L is seven to eleven, branch to statement 800. Prepare the necessary BASIC coding, first using IF statements and then using ON and GO TO.

15. Change both Figures 8-1 and 8-2 to reflect a situation where DATA element 99 is not a valid transaction, but only a signal for the end of the data.

16. Can RESTORE be used to "undo" an OUT OF DATA condition once the condition has been signaled by the computer? Why?

17. Rewrite Fig. 8-2 so that there is only one pass through the DATA, and the result of A/2 is printed next to A and A * 2.

18. In Fig. 8-3:
    (a) What was the purpose of N$?
    (b) Would the printed results be different if line number 25 were PRINT, N$, H, R, G? Why?
    (c) What does this program do about overtime?
    (d) At your Computer Center try the following: enter " ZZYZZ" (note the space before the first Z) as the intended signal for the end of the INPUT. What happened? Why?

19. What was the deficiency with Fig. 8-7? Determine what would happen at your Computer Center with similar coding.

20. In Fig. 8-7, wouldn't it be a simple matter to avoid the DATA error by entering only correct data instead of having to change the program? Briefly discuss this point.

21. A factorial is the product of all the positive whole numbers from one to and including a given number. Thus the factorial of three is 1 * 2 * 3 or 6; the factorial of four is 1 * 2 * 3 * 4 or 24.
    Write a program flowchart and prepare the coding for a program that will calculate the factorial of any given valid value. Include steps that will reject invalid values.

22. What would be the results of the following program when it was run?

```
10 READ A1$, A2$, A3$, A4$, A5$, A6$, A7$, A8$, A9$
15 READ B1$, B2$, B3$, B4$, B5$, B6$, B7$, B8$, B9$
20 READ C1$, C2$, C3$, C4$, C5$, C6$, C7$, C8$
25 PRINT C6$;B4$;A1$;C1$
30 DATA A,B,C,D,E,F,G,H,I,J,K,L,M,N,O,P,Q,R,S,T,U,V,W,X,Y,Z
40 END

READY
```

23. Carefully review the program results shown below. Pay particular attention to the significance of the pay codes. Prepare a program flowchart and the BASIC coding that would produce such results.

CLOCK #	PAY CODE	REG PAY	BONUS	TOT. PAY
10	9	100	0	100
12	1	125	10	135
17	4	118	40	158
21	9	180	0	180
27	7	150	70	220
39	4	85	40	125
72	7	95	70	165
		853	230	1083

TIME: 0.25 SECS.

READY

24. A program is to develop one-digit random numbers. But instead of printing the random number, the program is to print the word that represents the number (one instead of 1, two instead of 2, etc.). Write this program, which uses ON- GO TO appropriately.

25. Clearly show the output results of the following program. Note that DATA statements appear in unusual, but acceptable, places.

```
5 A$ = "THATS ALL"
10 READ A
20 READ B
25 A$ = "THATS IT"
30 C = A + B
40 PRINT A, B, C
45 DATA 10, 20, 30
50 D = D + C
60 IF B > 60 THEN 100
70 GO TO 20
75 A$ = "NO MORE"
80 DATA 55, 70
100 PRINT A$, D
105 DATA 40, 90
110 END
```

READY

9 CHAPTER
DECISION
PROCESSES II

In Chapter 8 we saw examples of the statements needed to make any kind of decision required in the BASIC language. BASIC has additional statements that will do some of the same things but they will either make the programmer's job easier or permit a higher level of productivity.

FOR and NEXT

If the decision to be made by using IF and THEN relates to repeating a series of steps a given number of times, a variation using FOR and NEXT may be used. The two programs in Fig. 9-1 give examples of these two methods. The purpose of each program is to take the square root of the numbers from 1 to 10 and then to stop.

The general approach in program A is to set up a counter, add to that counter by one at a time, and to test that counter to see if it is equal to 10. When the counter is equal to 10, the program is to END.

Observe the difference in coding in the example labeled B. Instead of specifically setting up a counter to be used to control the number of loops, adding to the counter, and then testing the counter, the two lines numbered 10 and 40 take care of all of the decision making.

In line 10, the word FOR essentially sets up a counter with the desired beginning and ending values. In line 40, the word NEXT tells the computer to go back to the statement that contains FOR and to proceed with the next value of A. The statements between 10 and 40 (in this case

```
3     REM FIG. 9-1 - A.                3     REM FIG. 9-1-B.
10  A = 1                               5     REM CAUSES A TO VARY
15    REM CALCULATES SQUARE             7     REM FROM 1 TO 10.
17    REM ROOT OF VARIABLE A.           10  FOR A = 1 TO 10
20  R = SQR (A)                         15    REM CALCULATES SQUARE
30  PRINT A, R                          17    REM ROOT OF VARIABLE A.
40  IF A = 10 THEN 70                   20  R = SQR (A)
50  A = A + 1                           30  PRINT A, R
60  GO TO 20                            35    REM GETS NEXT VALUE OF A.
70  END                                 40  NEXT A
                                        50  END
READY
RUN NH                                  READY
                                        RUN NH

  1           1
  2           1.41421                     1           1
  3           1.73205                     2           1.41421
  4           2                           3           1.73205
  5           2.23607                     4           2
  6           2.44949                     5           2.23607
  7           2.64575                     6           2.44949
  8           2.82843                     7           2.64575
  9           3                           8           2.82843
  10          3.16228                     9           3
                                          10          3.16228


TIME:  0.11 SECS.
                                        TIME:  0.10 SECS.
READY
                                        READY
```

Fig. 9-1. IF-THEN versus FOR-NEXT.

20 and 30) are executed ten times. Thus A starts as 1, proceeds to 2, 3, etc., and terminates at 10.

In the FOR statement itself, the computer will increment or STEP by a value of 1 unless you state otherwise. For instance, if we had wanted the machine to take the square roots of all numbers from 1 through 10, increasing by .25 at a time, instruction 10 would have been written:

$$10 \quad FOR \ A = 1 \ TO \ 10 \ STEP \ .25$$

Thus the computer would have calculated the square root of 1, 1.25, 1.50, etc., up to 10.

The STEP can also indicate a decrement. If this is done, it is simply a matter of clearly indicating that intention with a minus value. If you want the computer to use a beginning value for A of 20 and to proceed by 4 at a time down to 8, the statement would be written like this:

$$10 \quad FOR \ A = 20 \ TO \ 8 \ STEP - 4$$

110   INSTRUCTION IN THE BASIC LANGUAGE

```
3     REM FIG. 9-2.
5     REM INPUTS THE BEGINNING VALUE,
6     REM THE ENDING VALUE,
7     REM AND THE STEP.
10 INPUT B, C, D
20 FOR A = B TO C STEP D
30 R = SQR(A)
40 PRINT A, R
45 NEXT A
50 END

READY
RUN NH


?1, 10, 1
1                 1
2                 1.41421
3                 1.73205
4                 2
5                 2.23607
6                 2.44949
7                 2.64575
8                 2.82843
9                 3
10                3.16228



TIME:   0.14 SECS.

READY
RUN NH


?1, 9, 2
1                 1
3                 1.73205
5                 2.23607
7                 2.64575
9                 3



TIME:   0.10 SECS.

READY
RUN NH


?97, 27, -14
97                9.84886
83                9.11043
69                8.30662
55                7.4162
41                6.40312
27                5.19615



TIME:   0.13 SECS.

READY
```

Variable Name Legend

B	Beginning value
C	Ending value
D	STEP
A	Value of which a square root is taken
R	Square root (answer)

Fig. 9-2.   Use of FOR-NEXT and STEP.

Observe that the STEP statement must be used when decrementing, regardless of the value of the decrement. When incrementing, STEP was required only when the value was other than 1, since the computer assumes a 1 unless the STEP statement is included.

The beginning, ending, and STEP values in a FOR statement, as opposed to being constant values (see above), could also be variables. Fig. 9-2 shows each of those being entered by means of INPUT. Any of those variables could also be read from DATA or could be the result of a calculation.

Subscripts

We have seen in previous programs that we can assign variable data names of either one alphabetic character or one alphabetic character followed by one digit. Each of these two methods can also be followed by a dollar sign to permit handling of nonnumeric characters.

The BASIC language also permits an extension of these methods. That is, either of the above naming methods can include a subscript.

A "subscript" is merely a character enclosed in parentheses, immediately following the variable name. The use of subscripts enhances data manipulation and decision-making processes. A subscript represents a "shorthand" way of referring to the individual elements that make up a related group.

Assume that we want to add five different types of numbers. INPUT values are to be added to one of five counters, depending upon the code following each input value. There is to be a separate counter for each of the values represented by valid codes 1 through 4; counter 5 will be used to total the values of all other codes. Counter 6 will be used to accumulate the totals from the five other counters (to provide a final total).

First, we will see a program that does not use subscripts. Please see the flowchart in Fig. 9-3. Notice that the logic has a decision step that tests for each individual valid code (1–4); there is also a way to test for invalid codes. The applicable amounts are added to the appropriate counters. The resulting coding and execution with sample data is shown in Fig. 9-4.

Most of the coding in Fig. 9-4 can be eliminated by the use of subscripts. Instead of individually naming each of the counters with a letter C followed by a digit, let's collectively name the counters with the letter C and refer to any single counter we want by using a digit in parentheses (by definition, a subscript). The counters could be set up this way:

$$10 \quad C(1) = 0$$
$$20 \quad C(2) = 0$$

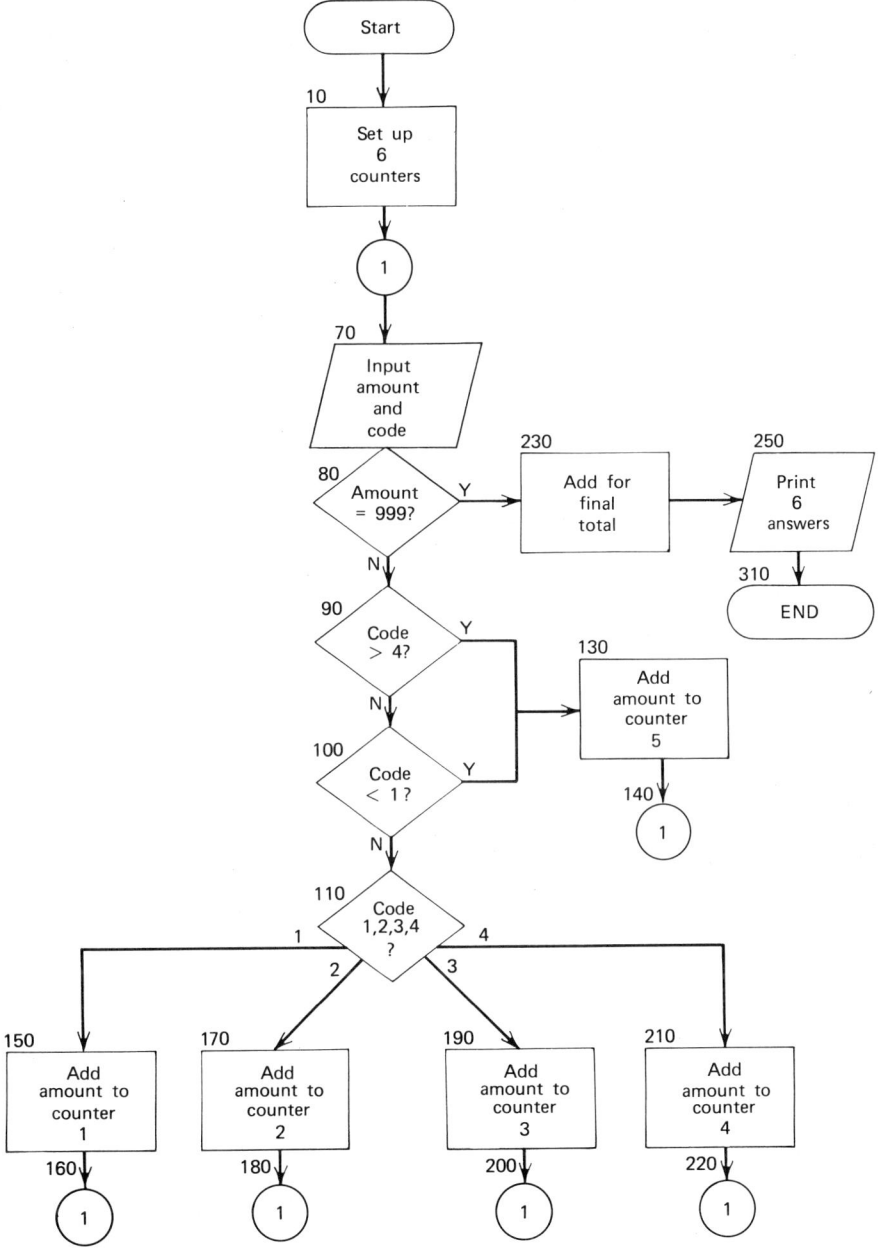

Fig. 9-3. *Program flowchart testing an INPUT code.*

```
5    REM FIG. 9-4.
10 C1 = 0
20 C2 = 0
30 C3 = 0
40 C4 = 0
50 C5 =0
60 C6 = 0
70 INPUT A, N
80 IF A = 999 THEN 230
85   REM TESTS FOR INVALID CODES.
90 IF N > 4 THEN 130
100 IF N < 1 THEN 130
110 ON N GO TO 150, 170, 190, 210
125    REM TOTALS VALUE OF INVALID CODES.
130 C5 = C5 + A
140 GO TO 70
150 C1 = C1 + A
160 GO TO 70
170 C2 = C2 + A
180 GO TO 70
190 C3 = C3 + A
200 GO TO 70
210 C4 = C4 + A
220 GO TO 70
225    REM TOTALS PRIOR 5 COUNTERS.
230 C6 = C5 + C4 + C3 + C2 + C1
240 PRINT
250 PRINT "C1=";  C1
260 PRINT "C2=";  C2
270 PRINT "C3=";  C3
280 PRINT "C4=";  C4
290 PRINT "C5=";  C5
300 PRINT "C6=";  C6
310 END

READY
RUN NH


 ?10, 2
 ?20, 3
 ?40, 5
 ?50, 1
 ?25, 4
 ?100, 2
 ?999, 9


C1= 50
C2= 110
C3= 20
C4= 25
C5= 40
C6= 245



TIME:  0.24 SECS.

READY
```

Variable Name Legend	
C1	Counter 1
C2	Counter 2
C3	Counter 3
C4	Counter 4
C5	Counter 5
C6	Counter 6
A	INPUT amount
N	INPUT code

Fig. 9-4. Use of ON-GO TO to test codes.

114 INSTRUCTION IN THE BASIC LANGUAGE

$$30 \quad C(3) = 0$$
$$40 \quad C(4) = 0$$
$$50 \quad C(5) = 0$$
$$60 \quad C(6) = 0$$

Or, the counters could be set up by using FOR and NEXT in this manner:

$$10 \quad \text{FOR } S = 1 \text{ TO } 6$$
$$20 \quad C(S) = 0$$
$$30 \quad \text{NEXT } S$$

```
5     REM FIG. 9-5.
10 FOR S = 1 TO 6
20 C(S) = 0
30 NEXT S
40 INPUT A, S
50 IF A = 999 THEN 80
53 IF S > 4 THEN 72
55 IF S < 1 THEN 72
60 C (S) = C (S) + A
70 GO TO 40
72 C(5) = C(5) + A
73 GO TO 40
80 C (6) = C(5) + C(4) + C(3) + C(2) + C(1)
85 PRINT
90 FOR S = 1 TO 6
110 PRINT "C"S; "="; C(S)
120 NEXT S
130 END
```

Variable Name Legend

C   Counter (composed of 6 individual counters)

S   Subscript (varies from 1 to 6)

A   INPUT amount

```
READY
RUN NH


 ?10, 2
 ?20, 3
 ?40, 5
 ?50, 1
 ?25, 4
 ?100, 2
 ?999, 9

C 1 = 50
C 2 = 110
C 3 = 20
C 4 = 25
C 5 = 40
C 6 = 245



TIME:  0.26 SECS.

READY
```

Fig. 9-5. Use of subscripts to test codes.

When S is 1, the computer will execute line 20 and set up the first counter (C(1)) with a value of zero. Then S is 2 and counter C(2) is established. It will continue to set up counters until it has provided for six of them.

Now let's take a look at how the complete program may appear in Fig. 9-5. Line numbers 10 through 30 replace 10 through 60 in Fig. 9-4. Line numbers 60 and 70 in Fig. 9-5 are doing all the work of statements 150 through 220 in Fig. 9-4.

Line number 60 in Fig. 9-5 essentially says: "Add the INPUT value of A into the counter whose number is S." When S is 1, A is added to counter 1; when S is 2, A is added to counter 2; etc. Note how line number 72 adds the values with invalid codes into counter 5.

The program is completed with the use of FOR and NEXT to print out the totals accumulated in each of the 6 counters.

DIM (Dimension)

When you subscript a data field, the computer will automatically provide 10 subscripted elements. But if a data field is to have more than 10 subscripted elements, you must specifically reserve the maximum number that you want.

Assume that you want to set 25 counters equal to zero at the beginning of a program. Observe what happens when you don't make a specific reservation:

```
10 FOR N = 1 TO 25
20 C(N) = 0
30 NEXT N
40 PRINT "OK"
50 END

READY
RUN NH



? DIMENSION ERROR IN LINE 20

TIME:  0.07 SECS.

READY
```

By using the DIM statement (an abbreviation for DIMENSION) in the following way, the computer will reserve the necessary space and respond as planned.

```
5 DIM C(25)
10 FOR N = 1 TO 25
20 C (N) = 0
30 NEXT N
40 PRINT "OK"
50 END

READY
RUN NH


OK


TIME:  0.04 SECS.

READY
```

Multiple fields can be set up like this:

$$DIM \ N(35), \ C\$(13)$$

This statement means that N has been set up with 35 subscripted elements (numeric), and C$ has been set up with 13 subscripted elements (able to hold nonnumeric characters).

The working storage area of the computer is similar to any other storage device; it has a limited capacity. Please determine what DIM restrictions apply to you.

Subroutines

A subroutine is a particular series of steps that will be executed at various, specific times in a program. I will first show a program that does not include a subroutine and then one that does.

If you put $1000 into a bank and three years later your account is worth $1331, what annual percentage of growth would that be? The answer can be calculated by the formula:

$$I = (E/B)^{1/N} - 1$$

The variable names in that formula have the following meanings.

I = Percent of growth.   E = Ending amount.
B = Beginning amount.   N = Number of years.

A

Positive Growth

Beg. Amt.	1000
End. Amt.	1331
Change	331
Yrs.	3
% Increase	10

B

Negative Growth

Beg. Amt.	100
End. Amt.	81
Change	−19
Yrs.	2
% Decline	−10

Fig. 9-6. Report format of GROWTH.

Let us assume that the format of the report we desire is the format shown in Fig. 9-6. Note that the only difference between the format of the Positive Growth in part A and that of the Negative Growth in part B is the word Increase or Decline in the last line of each printout.

An appropriate flowchart of a program is shown in Fig. 9-7. Notice that the first decision step tests to see whether growth has been positive or negative so that the computer can proceed to steps to print the appropriate headings and detail. The second decision step determines whether the user wants the program to branch back to the INPUT step for data to be entered for another situation.

Figure 9-8 shows the BASIC coding for that logic along with the execution using three sample situations. Note in line number 80 how the double asterisks (**) were used to raise E/B to the one divided by N (1/N) power. Line number 90 then took the decimal rate calculated in line 80 and converted it to a rounded percentage basis.

Line number 95 calculates the change (C) by subtracting the beginning amount (B) from the ending amount (E). Then line number 100 determines from the growth rate whether to proceed to the steps that handle the positive or the negative growth.

The first two examples executed in Fig. 9-8 can be proved to be correct based on the following calculations.

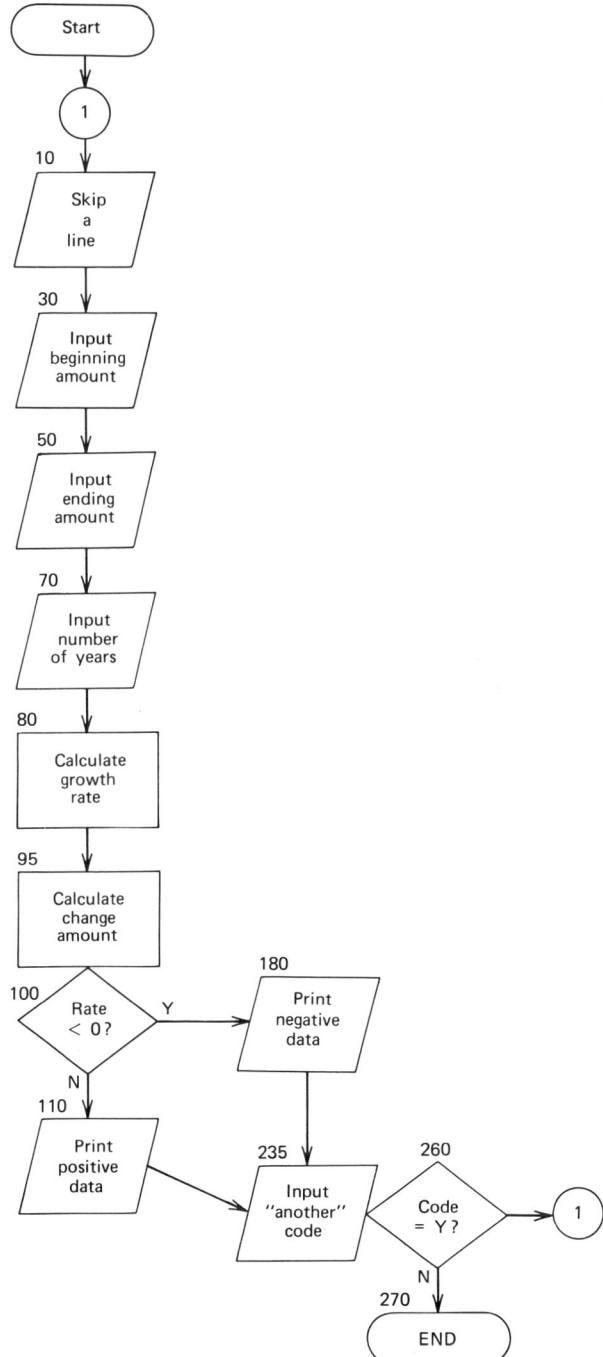

Fig. 9-7. *Program flowchart for GROWTH.*

	Positive Growth	Negative Growth
	10% Three Years	-10% Two Years
Beginning amount	1000	100
First year change	100	10
New amount	1100	90
Second year change	110	9
New amount	1210	81
Third year change	121	—
Ending amount	1331	81

```
5    REM FIG. 9-8.
10 PRINT
20 PRINT "ENTER BEG AMT';
30 INPUT B
40 PRINT "ENTER END AMT";
50 INPUT E
60 PRINT "ENTER # OF YEARS";
70 INPUT N
75 PRINT
80 I = ((E/B)**(1/N)) - 1
90 I = INT (I * 100() + .5) / 100
95 C = E-B
98   REM TESTS FOR + OR - GROWTH.
100 IF I < 0 THEN 180
105   REM HANDLES POSITIVE GROWTH.
110 PRINT "POSITIVE GROWTH"
120 PRINT "BEG AMT", B
130 PRINT "END AMT", E
140 PRINT "CHANGE", C
150 PRINT "YRS", N
160 PRINT "% INCREASE", I
170 GO TO 235
175   REM HANDLES NEGATIVE GROWTH.
180 PRINT "NEGATIVE GROWTH"
190 PRINT "BEG AMT", B
200 PRINT "END AMT", E
210 PRINT "CHANGE", C
220 PRINT "YRS", N
230 PRINT "% DECLINE", I
235 PRINT
240 PRINT "HAVE ANOTHER? ANS Y OR N";
250 INPUT Q$
260 IF Q$ = "Y" THEN 10
270 END
```

READY

Variable Name Legend

B	Beginning amount
E	Ending amount
N	Number of years
I	Growth rate
C	Amount of change
Q$	Code whether more data or not

Fig. 9-8. Listing and execution of GROWTH (completed on page 121).

```
ENTER BEG AMT ?1000
ENTER END AMT ?1331
ENTER # OF YEARS ?3

POSITIVE GROWTH
BEG AMT        1000
END AMT        1331
CHANGE         331
YRS            3
% INCREASE     10

HAVE ANOTHER? ANS Y OR N ?Y

ENTER BEG AMT ?100
ENTER END AMT ?81
ENTER # OF YEARS ?2

NEGATIVE GROWTH
BEG AMT        100
END AMT        81
CHANGE         -19
YRS            2
% DECLINE      -10

HAVE ANOTHER? ANS Y OR N ?Y

ENTER BEG AMT ?18.75
ENTER END AMT ?25.00
ENTER # OF YEARS ?10

POSITIVE GROWTH
BEG AMT        18.75
END AMT        25
CHANGE         6.25
YRS            10
% INCREASE     2.92

HAVE ANOTHER? ANS Y OR N ?N

TIME:   0.43 SECS.

READY
```

Fig. 9-8. cont.

If we refer again to the BASIC coding in Fig. 9-8, we observe that line numbers 120 through 150 are the same as those in line numbers 190 through 220. When this situation occurs in a program, it tends to suggest that some coding economies can be obtained.

One approach is to prepare another flowchart (Fig. 9-9). Note that the first "RATE < 0?" test is used to print one or the other of the two different headings. Then the steps merge to print the 4 common lines in

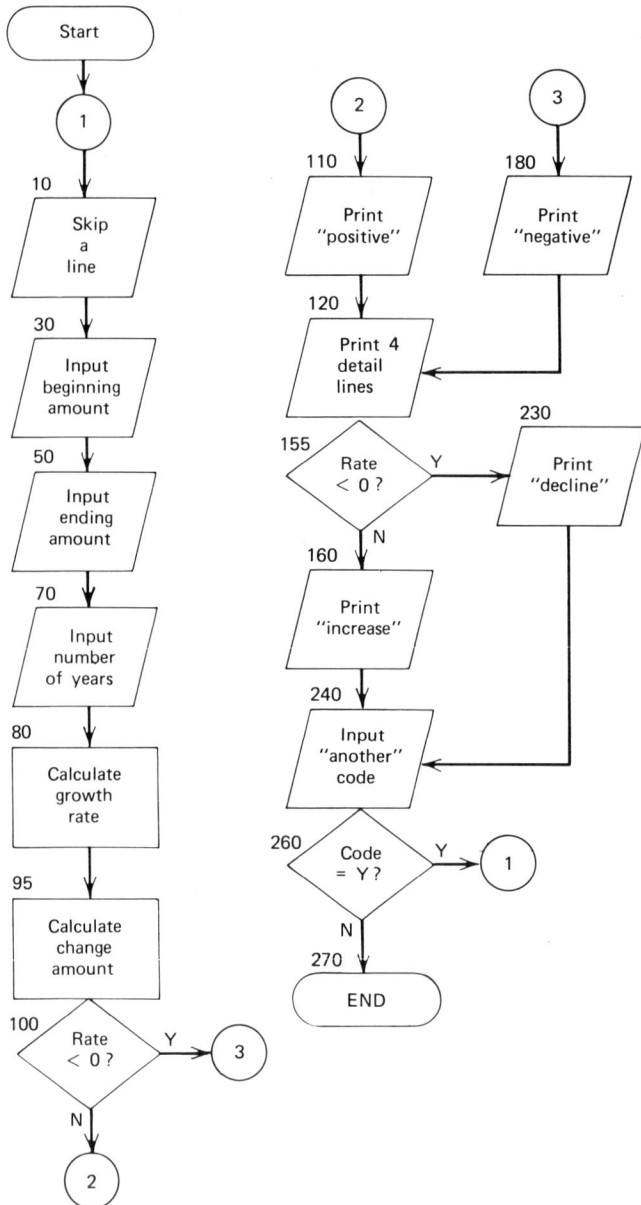

Fig. 9-9. *Program flowchart with a subroutine.*

the body of the report. The "minus" test is used again to cause the proper printing of the last line of the report.

Next, the steps merge again to test if there is another situation to calculate. The coding and execution for that solution appear in Fig. 9-10.

The coding method employed in both Figs. 9-8 and 9-10 was to use IF and THEN statements to branch around certain steps in order to do what you want when you want. In Fig. 9-10, line numbers 120 through 150 are referred to as a subroutine. Those lines represent a group of statements to be executed from one of several sources.

Another solution to the problem is to use a subroutine involving a specific statement called GOSUB. Conceptually, such a subroutine works according to the diagram in Fig. 9-11.

The subroutine, in effect, sits off by itself and is to be executed from point B. When the subroutine has been completed, control is to return to the step following the one that sent it there (C).

Eventually, the subroutine is to be executed from point E, and when the subroutine has been completed, control is to return to the step following the one that sent it there (F).

```
10 PRINT
20 PRINT "ENTER BEG AMT";
30 INPUT B
40 PRINT "ENTER END AMT";
50 INPUT E
60 PRINT "ENTER # OF YRS";
70 INPUT N
75 PRINT
80 I = ((E/B)**(1/N)) - 1
90 I = INT (I * 10000 + .5) / 100
95 C = E-B
100 IF I < 0 THEN 180
110 PRINT "POSITIVE GROWTH"
120 PRINT "BEG AMT", B
130 PRINT "END AMT", E
140 PRINT "CHANGE", C
150 PRINT "YRS", N
155 IF I < 0 THEN 230
160 PRINT "% INCREASE", I
170 GO TO 240
180 PRINT "NEGATIVE GROWTH"
190 GO TO 120
230 PRINT "% DECLINE", I
240 PRINT "HAVE ANOTHER? ANS Y OR N";
250 INPUT Q$
260 IF Q$ = "Y" THEN 10
270 END

READY
```

Variable Name Legend

B	Beginning amount
E	Ending amount
N	Number of years
I	Growth rate
C	Amount of change
Q$	Code whether more data or not

Fig. 9-10. Use of a subroutine (completed on page 124).

```
ENTER BEG AMT ?1000
ENTER END AMT ?1331
ENTER # OF YRS ?3

POSITIVE GROWTH
BEG AMT          1000
END AMT          1331
CHANGE           331
YRS              3
% INCREASE       10
HAVE ANOTHER? ANS Y OR N ?Y

ENTER BEG AMT ?100
ENTER END AMT ?81
ENTER # OF YRS ?2

NEGATIVE GROWTH
BEG AMT          100
END AMT          81
CHANGE           -19
YRS              2
% DECLINE        -10
HAVE ANOTHER? ANS Y OR N ?Y

ENTER BEG AMT ?18.75
ENTER END AMT ?25.00
ENTER # OF YRS ?10

POSITIVE GROWTH
BEG AMT          18.75
END AMT          25
CHANGE           6.25
YRS              10
% INCREASE       2.92
HAVE ANOTHER? ANS Y OR N ?N


TIME:   0.42 SECS.

READY
```

Fig. 9-10. cont.

GOSUB is the statement that must be used to cause branching to the subroutine. The word GOSUB must be followed by a line number that indicates where the subroutine is. The statement RETURN must be the last line in the subroutine. This causes the computer to return to the step following the one that sent it there.

The sample program has been redone using the GOSUB approach. The new flowchart is shown in Fig. 9-12 and the coding and execution in Fig. 9-13.

124   INSTRUCTION IN THE BASIC LANGUAGE

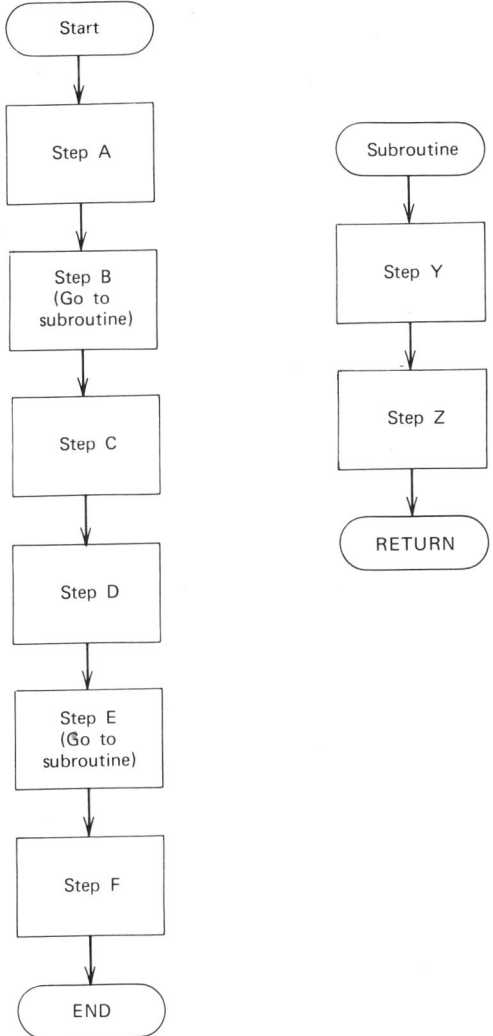

Fig. 9-11. *Concept of a subroutine.*

The coding steps down through line 100 are the same as those in the previous examples. In line number 100, control either goes to 180 to handle the negative situation or 110 to handle the positive situation.

If the rate is positive, the appropriate heading gets printed. Then line number 120 causes the computer to go to the subroutine located

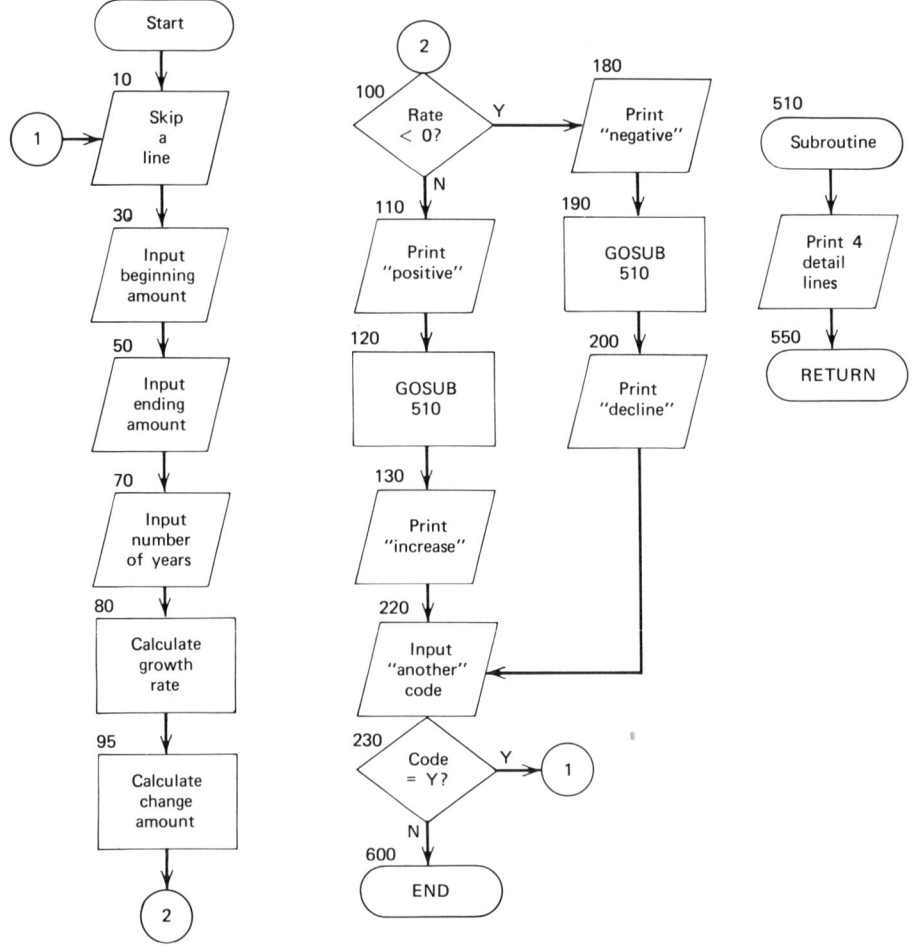

Fig. 9-12. Program flowchart using GOSUB and RETURN.

at 510. In the subroutine, the four lines of the body are printed, and RETURN causes the machine to branch back to line number 130.

When a negative value for I is encountered at line number 100, control branches to 180, where the negative heading is printed. Then the subroutine at 510 is accessed, and RETURN causes a return to line number 200.

It is obviously most important that the subroutine is executed only when it is supposed to be. That is, the subroutine should not be located in a place where the program would "fall into" it from a preceding step.

```
5     REM FIG. 9-13.
10 PRINT
20 PRINT "ENTER BEG. AMT";
30 INPUT B
40 PRINT "ENTER END AMT";
50 INPUT E
60 PRINT "ENTER # OF YEARS";
70 INPUT N
75 PRINT
80 I = ((E/B) **(1/N)) - 1
90 I = INT (I * 10000 + .5) / 100
95 C = E - B
100 IF I < 0 THEN 180
110 PRINT "POSITIVE GROWTH"
120 GOSUB 510
130 PRINT " % INCREASE", I
140 GO TO 210
180 PRINT "NEGATIVE GROWTH"
190 GOSUB 510
200 PRINT "% DECLINE", I
210 PRINT
215 PRINT "HAVE ANOTHER? ANS Y OR N";
220 INPUT Q$
230 IF Q$ = "Y" THEN 10
240 GO TO 600
500    REM THIS IS THE SUBROUTINE.
510 PRINT "BEG AMT",B
520 PRINT "END AMT ", E
530 PRINT "CHANGE",C
540 PRINT "YRS", N
550 RETURN
560    REM THIS COMPLETES THE SUBROUTINE.
600 END

READY
```

Variable Name Legend	
B	Beginning amount
E	Ending amount
N	Number oi ears
I	Growth rat
C	Amount of change
Q$	Code whether more data or not

Fig. 9-13. Program using GOSUB and RETURN (completed on page 128).

This has been prevented by having an unconditional branch immediately before the subroutine (see line number 240).

In another example, assume there is a need to write a program that will produce a report with the following specifications:

1. The results are to appear in a format so that the paper can be burst or cut into convenient page lengths.

2. The pages are to be numbered consecutively.

3. There is to be a dollar total on each page in addition to a final total at the end of the report. The final total must appear on a separate page (not on a page that contains detail items).

4. The number of detail lines per page is to be under control of the user.

```
ENTER BEG. AMT ?1000
ENTER END AMT ?1331
ENTER # OF YEARS ?3

POSITIVE GROWTH
BEG AMT          1000
END AMT          1331
CHANGE           331
YRS              3
  % INCREASE     10

HAVE ANOTHER? ANS Y OR N ?Y

ENTER BEG. AMT ?1200
ENTER END AMT ?1400
ENTER # OF YEARS ?4

POSITIVE GROWTH
BEG AMT          1200
END AMT          1400
CHANGE           200
YRS              4
  % INCREASE     3.93

HAVE ANOTHER? ANS Y OR N ?Y

ENTER BEG. AMT ?500
ENTER END AMT ?500
ENTER # OF YEARS ?5

POSITIVE GROWTH
BEG AMT          500
END AMT          500
CHANGE           0
YRS              5
  % INCREASE     0

HAVE ANOTHER? ANS Y OR N ?N


TIME:   0.47 SECS.

READY
```

Fig. 9-13.   cont.

The specific application here relates to a payroll. DATA statements contain clock number, hours worked, and pay rate. The product of hours times rate, a dollar value, is to be calculated and accumulated. Clock number 99 signals the end of the data (not an actual item).

The program flowchart in Fig. 9-14 provides for the above specifications. It provides for a page counter (N) to be set to zero. Then the user is to input the number of detail lines desired per page on the report.

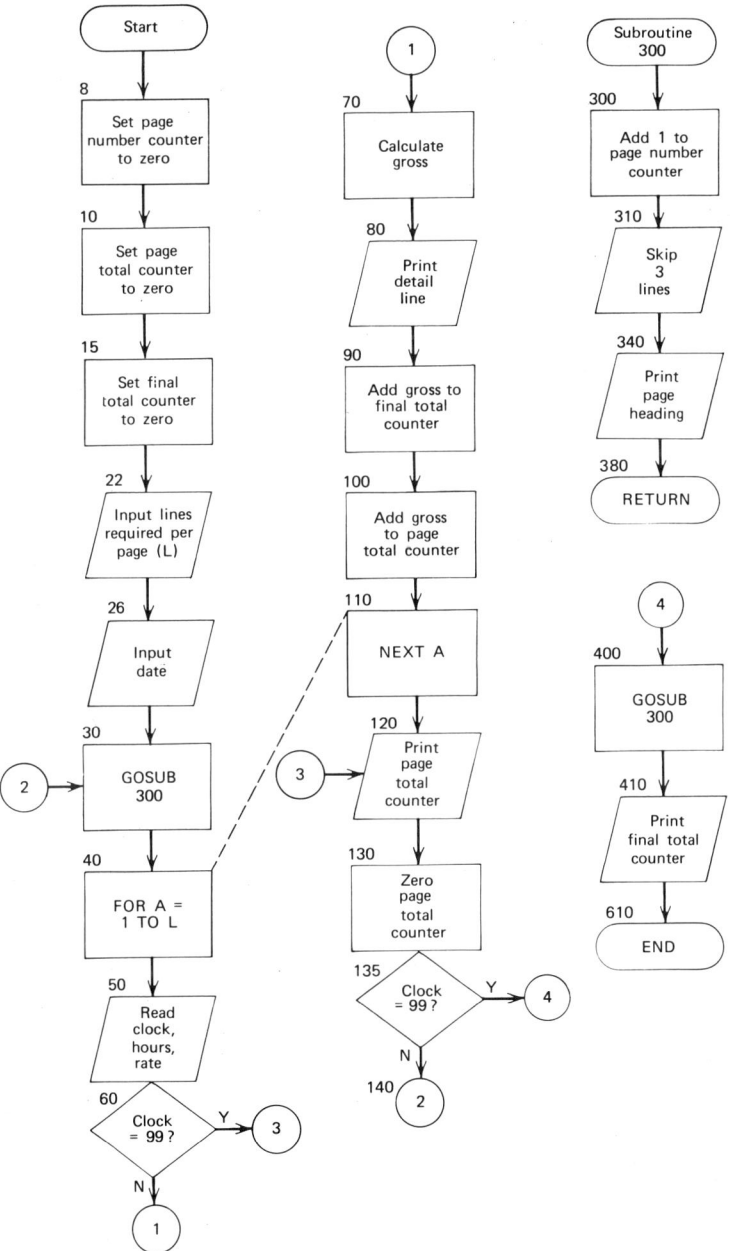

Fig. 9-14. Program flowchart using GOSUB and RETURN.

```
5    REM FIG. 9-15.
8 N = 0
10 P = 0
15 T = 0
18 PRINT "ENTER # OF DETAIL ";
20 PRINT "LINES REQUIRED PER PAGE";
22 INPUT L
24 PRINT "ENTER DATE";
26 INPUT D$
30 GOSUB 300
40 FOR A = 1 TO L
50 READ C, H, R
60 IF C = 99 THEN 115
70 G = INT (H * R * 100 + .5) / 100
80 PRINT C, H, R, G
90 T = T + G
100 P = P + G
110 NEXT A
115 PRINT
120 PRINT , , "PAGE TOTAL", P
130 P = 0
135 IF C = 99 THEN 400
140 GO TO 30
290    REM SUBROUTINE HANDLES PAGE HEADINGS.
300 N = N + 1
310 PRINT
320 PRINT
330 PRINT
340 PRINT TAB(50) "PAGE NO."; N
350 PRINT TAB(20) "JONES SUPPLY"
360 PRINT TAB(18) "WEEKLY PAY SCHEDULE"
365 PRINT TAB(22) D$
370 PRINT "CLOCK #", "HOURS", "RATE", "GROSS"
380 RETURN
400 GOSUB 300
405 PRINT
410 PRINT , , "FINAL TOTAL", T
500 DATA 12, 38, 4.00
510 DATA 18, 40, 5.25
520 DATA 27, 36, 4.24
530 DATA 31, 42, 7.20
540 DATA 38, 39.5, 4.20
550 DATA 39, 40, 5.20
560 DATA 47, 39, 5.10
570 DATA 49, 41, 5.10
580 DATA 53, 39, 4.10
590 DATA 57, 18, 2.90
600 DATA 61, 40, 4.50
605 DATA 99, 99, 99
610 END

READY
```

Variable Name Legend

N	Counter for page numbers
P	Counter for page totals
T	Counter for final total
L	Number of detail lines required per page
D$	Date
A	Counter in FOR-NEXT
C	Clock number
H	Hours
R	Rate
G	Gross pay

Fig. 9-15. Program listing with GOSUB and RETURN.

```
RUN NH


ENTER # OF DETAIL LINES REQUIRED PER PAGE ?5
ENTER DATE ?11/30/76



                                              PAGE NO. 1
                        JONES SUPPLY
                     WEEKLY PAY SCHEDULE
                        11/30/76
    CLOCK #         HOURS          RATE            GROSS
      12             38             4              152
      18             40            5.25            210
      27             36            4.24            152.64
      31             42            7.2             302.4
      38            39.5           4.2             165.9

                             PAGE TOTAL         982.94



                                              PAGE NO. 2
                        JONES SUPPLY
                     WEEKLY PAY SCHEDULE
                        11/30/76
    CLOCK #         HOURS          RATE            GROSS
      39             40            5.2             208
      47             39            5.1             198.9
      49             41            5.1             209.1
      53             39            4.1             159.9
      57             18            2.9             52.2

                             PAGE TOTAL         828.1



                                              PAGE NO. 3
                        JONES SUPPLY
                     WEEKLY PAY SCHEDULE
                        11/30/76
    CLOCK #         HOURS          RATE            GROSS
      61             40            4.5             180

                             PAGE TOTAL         180



                                              PAGE NO. 4
                        JONES SUPPLY
                     WEEKLY PAY SCHEDULE
                        11/30/76
    CLOCK #         HOURS          RATE            GROSS

                             FINAL TOTAL       1991.04


TIME:  0.67 SECS.
```

Fig. 9-16. Program execution of GOSUB and RETURN.

A branch to the subroutine causes page number one to be printed followed by appropriate headings. The mainstream of the program processes as many detail items per page as desired by the user in the INPUT step. When that number has been reached, the total for that page is printed; the counter that accumulates this total is zeroed; and the subroutine is accessed to prepare the beginning of the next page. When the end of the data is signaled, the subroutine is entered again so that the final total will be printed on a separate page.

Program coding is shown in Fig. 9-15, and execution is shown in Fig. 9-16. For execution purposes, only five detail lines per page were chosen because of limited space availability.

EXERCISES

1. Can anything be done with the decision steps in Chapter 9 that couldn't be done with the decision steps presented in Chapter 8? (Disregard the topics of programmer productivity and computer efficiency.) Explain.

2. How does the use of FOR and NEXT handle a decision-making process? What specific coding steps does it eliminate?

3. In your own words, describe how FOR and NEXT were being used in program B, Fig. 9-1.

4. How do you have to code a FOR instruction if you want the machine to proceed by increments other than one?

5. What is the purpose of a subscript? Does its use increase or decrease the amount of coding that has to be done?

6. What is the purpose of a DIM statement? Under what conditions must it be used?

7. How is a subroutine used? Is it possible that a subroutine may have to be entered to process every transaction?

8. How do you make sure that your program enters a subroutine only when it is supposed to?

9. Alter the coding in program B of Fig. 9-1 so that each square root is printed to thousandths, hundredths, and tenths, each answer being rounded according to common rules. Print the answers across the page with appropriate column headings.

10. In Fig. 9-4:
    (a) What was the purpose of counter 5?
    (b) What will happen to an INPUT item whose code is 7?; 0?; 3.5?
    (c) If ON and GO TO were not used, how many IF statements would be needed?

11. In Fig. 9-5:
    (a) What would happen if an INPUT item had code 7?
    (b) Can line number 80 be altered so that the accumulation of the first 5 counters into counter 6 can be accomplished by the use of FOR and NEXT? If yes, show how. If no, explain why.
    (c) Make the necessary changes so that the totals would be printed in six columns, properly headed, instead of in six rows.

12. In Fig. 9-8:
    (a) What would have been different if the semicolons had been removed from line numbers 20, 40, and 60?
    (b) Describe carefully what is being done in line number 90.
    (c) What change would have to be made to the program to make it print the percentage in tenths? To the nearest whole percent?
    (d) Under what data conditions do you expect the program would not work? Try several of them to see if you are right.
    (e) Will the program work if number of years contains a decimal value? Explain.
    (f) What would happen if your INPUT in line number 250 were M (for maybe)?

13. Alter the program in Fig. 9-13 so that it shows a detail "proof" of the annual growth similar to the examples shown on page 120.

14. Add the coding to the program in Fig. 9-15 so that the page total would be enclosed in asterisks:

15. Many corporations publish financial data showing the trend of sales, profits, and dividends over a period of 10 years. Often, any individual data item shows a growth percentage for the entire period. Write a program that would calculate three growth percentages for such data—one for the entire period, one for the first five years, and one for the second five years.

16. We have seen that BASIC does not print a comma between the thousandths and hundredths positions of a numerical value. Write

a program that would print a comma in that position, given any numerical value up to 9999. (You may get an unwanted space next to the comma.)

17. A program is to be written that will determine the starting salary of people about to enter a certain job position. The starting salary is to be based on "number of points" applicable to certain qualifications. The qualifications, input codes, and points allowable are:

	Qualifications	Code	Points
College graduate:			
	BS	B	4
	MS	M	7
	PhD	D	10
Work experience:			
	1–3 yrs.	1	4
	4–6 yrs.	2	7
	7 or more	3	10
Present salary:			
	<$10,000	L	4
	$10,000–$17,000	M	7
	>$17,000	H	10

Have the program accumulate each applicant's points by using one or more subroutines (with GOSUB and RETURN). Be sure to reject any invalid codes.

18. What would be the results of the following program when carriage return was pushed?

```
10 DIM D(10)
20 FOR A = 1 TO 10
30 READ D(A)
40 NEXT A
50 INPUT N
60 PRINT D(N), D(N+1), D(N*2), D(N**2), D(N/2)
70 DATA 1, 2, 3, 4, 5, 6, 7, 8, 9, 10
80 END

READY
RUN NH
```

?3

19. Given the following program and INPUT data, what results would occur when carriage return was pushed? What caused that problem? (Check the data carefully.)

```
10 FOR S = 1 TO 6
20 C(S) = 0
30 NEXT S
40 INPUT A, S
50 IF A = 999 THEN 80
60 C(S) = C(S) + A
70 GO TO 40
80 PRINT
90 FOR I = 1 TO 5
100 C(6) = C(6) + C(I)
110 NEXT I
120 FOR S = 1 TO 6
130 PRINT "C" S; "="; C(S)
140 NEXT S
150 END

READY
RUN NH


?5,4
?3,5
?8,2
?6,1
?5,6
?8,2
?9,5
?999,999
```

20. Show what output would occur from the following program when carriage return is pushed.

```
10 INPUT N1
20 FOR N = 1 TO N1
30 READ N2
40 N3 = N2 * N
50 PRINT N, N2, N3
60 IF N3 > N2 THEN 110
70 NEXT N
100 DATA -3, -1, 2, 4, 7, 9
110 END

READY
RUN NH


?5
```

21. The names of the twelve months are presently contained in DATA statements. Write all of the steps needed to print out the proper month name when the appropriate month number is entered by means of INPUT.

136 INSTRUCTION IN THE BASIC LANGUAGE

10 CHAPTER
ARRAYS

In computer programming, it is often desirable to set up data as an array in the computer. Certain desirable processing techniques can be accomplished once data has been so set up.

An array is defined as an orderly arrangement of data. In programming, an array is a group of related data items that can be referenced by one variable name. Individual items within the group are referenced by subscripts.

In Fig. 9-5, we first saw the use of an array. In that program we used the variable name C to refer to a group of six counters. C in that situation is known as a one-dimensional array, since it is only one element wide but six elements long. We might say that C has one column and six rows.

It is often necessary to keep track of data in a fashion that involves two dimensions. Such an arrangement may be said to contain both length and width; it is commonly known as a table, an array, or a matrix. Within this section, I will consistently refer to such arrangements of data as an array.

When you are about to work with an array, first determine how much data you want to provide for. You can then establish the dimensions of that data. Although BASIC automatically provides a 10 X 10 (10 columns and 10 rows) array without the need to use dimensions, it is a good habit to always dimension an array.

Assume we have three years of numeric data by calendar quarter for

137

each year, and that we want to present the data in a format that has three rows (for the years) and four columns (for the quarters). If we wish to refer to all of the data by the variable name D, we can do so and reserve all of the necessary space in the computer with the following instruction.

DIM D(3, 4)

That instruction dimensions a variable data field whose name is D. Within parentheses, the first digit (3) indicates how many rows there will be, and the second digit (4) indicates how many columns there will be. Thus the array contains space for 12 data items.

```
5     REM FIG. 10-1.
10 DIM D (3,4)
20 READ D(1,1)
30 READ D (1,2)
40 READ D (1,3)
50 READ D (1,4)
60 READ D(2,1)
70 READ D (2,2)
80 READ D (2,3)
90 READ D (2,4)
100 READ D (3,1)
110 READ D ( 3,2)
120 READ D ( 3,3)
130 READ D (3,4)
140 PRINT "YEAR", "Q1", "Q2", "Q3", "Q4"
150 PRINT
155 PRINT "1974",
160 PRINT D(1,1), D(1,2), D(1,3), D(1,4)
165 PRINT "1975",
170 PRINT D(2,1), D(2,2), D(2,3), D(2,4)
175 PRINT "1976",
180 PRINT D(3,1), D(3,2), D(3,3), D(3,4)
190 DATA 15, 18, 20, 28
210 DATA 17, 24, 22, 29
220 DATA 16, 23, 25, 28
230 END

READY
RUN NH
```

YEAR	Q1	Q2	Q3	Q4
1974	15	18	20	28
1975	17	24	22	29
1976	16	23	25	28

```
TIME:  0.17 SECS.

READY
```

Fig. 10-1. Simple handling of an array.

How are we going to enter the data into the array? We can use the assignment, the READ and DATA, or the INPUT method.

Figure 10-1 shows one way you may enter data into an array by the READ and DATA method. The only purpose of this program is to enter the data into the array and to print it out in tabular form.

Note in Fig. 10-1 that 12 READ steps were used, one for each individual value. The DATA statement at line 190 contained the values for the first year, line 210 the second year, and line 220 the third year.

The program obviously does what it was intended to do. But, as we have seen in several prior instances, anytime there are a number of quite similar statements (such as the READ statements in lines 20 through 130) there may be a coding shortcut.

One "shortcut" is shown in Fig. 10-2. The FOR and NEXT state-

```
5    REM FIG. 10-2.
10 DIM D (3,4)
20 FOR Q = 1 TO 4
30 READ D(1,Q)
40 NEXT Q
50 FOR Q = 1 TO 4
60 READ D(2,Q)
70 NEXT Q
80 FOR Q = 1 TO 4
90 READ D (3,Q)
100 NEXT Q
140 PRINT "YEAR", "Q1", "Q2", "Q3", "Q4"
150 PRINT
155 PRINT "1974",
160 PRINT D (1,1), D(1,2), D(1,3), D(1,4)
165 PRINT "1975",
170 PRINT D(2,1), D(2,2), D(2,3), D(2,4)
175 PRINT "1976",
180 PRINT D(3,1), D(3,2), D(3,3), D(3,4)
190 DATA 15, 18, 20, 28
200 DATA 17, 24, 22, 29
210 DATA 16, 23, 25, 28
220 END

READY
RUN NH
```

Variable Name Legend

D	Array (data)
Q	Quarter

YEAR	Q1	Q2	Q3	Q4
1974	15	18	20	28
1975	17	24	22	29
1976	16	23	25	28

```
TIME:  0.17 SECS.

READY
```

Fig. 10-2. Using FOR-NEXT to read into an array.

ments in line 20 through 40 read the data for the first year, those in lines 50 through 70 read the data for the second year, etc. It is to be noted that 9 "READ" statements in Fig. 10-2 replaced 12 READ statements in Fig. 10-1.

A closer examination of the FOR and NEXT statements in Fig. 10-2 shows that they follow a pattern. That pattern can be condensed by setting up one FOR and NEXT loop within another FOR and NEXT loop. This technique is referred to as "nesting" loops (see Fig. 10-3).

Line numbers 20 through 60 in Fig. 10-3 have replaced line numbers 20 through 100 in Fig. 10-2. In Fig. 10-3, line number 30 is one that we have seen in the previous program. But immediately before it, in line 20, is another FOR. The statement in 20 is referred to as an outer FOR and the one in 30 as an inner FOR.

The effect is to hold Y equal to one while Q varies from one to four (caused by NEXT Q in 50). Thus the READ step reads into D(1, 1),

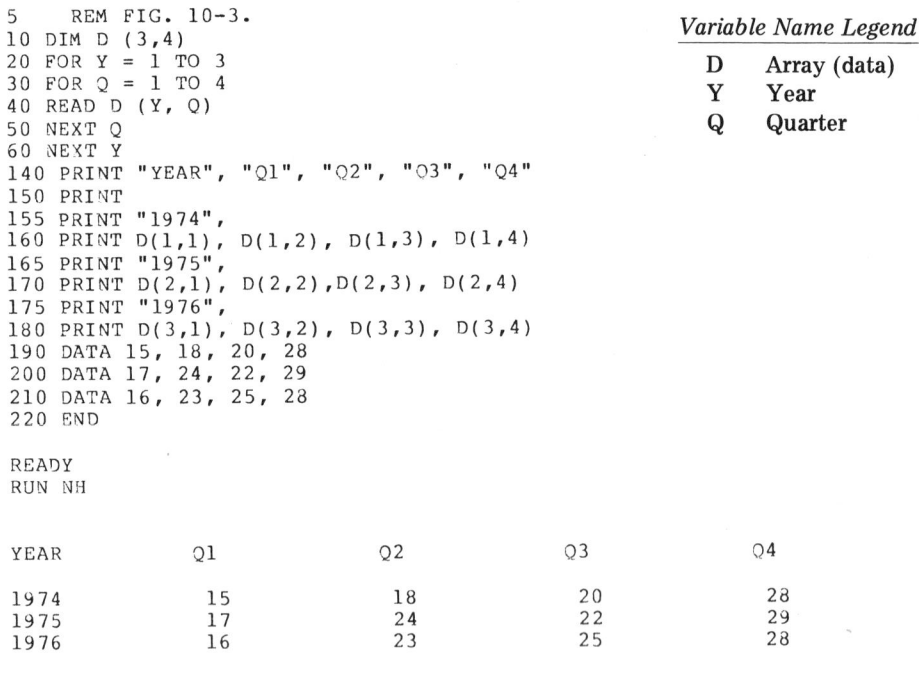

```
5     REM FIG. 10-3.
10  DIM D (3,4)
20  FOR Y = 1 TO 3
30  FOR Q = 1 TO 4
40  READ D (Y, Q)
50  NEXT Q
60  NEXT Y
140 PRINT "YEAR", "Q1", "Q2", "Q3", "Q4"
150 PRINT
155 PRINT "1974",
160 PRINT D(1,1), D(1,2), D(1,3), D(1,4)
165 PRINT "1975",
170 PRINT D(2,1), D(2,2),D(2,3), D(2,4)
175 PRINT "1976",
180 PRINT D(3,1), D(3,2), D(3,3), D(3,4)
190 DATA 15, 18, 20, 28
200 DATA 17, 24, 22, 29
210 DATA 16, 23, 25, 28
220 END

READY
RUN NH


YEAR          Q1            Q2            Q3            Q4

1974          15            18            20            28
1975          17            24            22            29
1976          16            23            25            28


TIME:   0.17 SECS.

READY
```

Variable Name Legend

D	Array (data)
Y	Year
Q	Quarter

Fig. 10-3. Using nested FOR-NEXT to read into an array.

140   INSTRUCTION IN THE BASIC LANGUAGE

D(1, 2), D(1, 3), and D(1, 4). At this point, the inner loop is said to be satisfied, and control passes back to the outer loop.

Y is now set equal to two, and Q is again varied from one to four. By the time Y has been advanced up through three, the outer loop will have been handled three times while the inner one will have been handled four times for every outer one. Hence, the READ step was accessed 12 times, and 12 data items will have been entered into the array.

Our attention will now be directed to using nested FOR and NEXT loops to print the contents of the array. The program in Fig. 10-4 does this, with a resulting print format equal to that of each of the prior three programs. Significant comments are:

1. Line number 160 establishes variable N as a year counter with a beginning value of 1974. N is to be printed only three times, so it is printed and incremented within the outer loop but outside of the

```
5     REM FIG. 10-4.
10 DIM D (3,4)
20 FOR Y = 1 TO 3
30 FOR Q = 1 TO 4
40 READ D (Y,Q)
50 NEXT Q
60 NEXT Y
140 PRINT "YEAR", "Q1", "Q2", "Q3", "Q4"
150 PRINT
160 N = 1974
170 FOR Y = 1 TO 3
180 PRINT N,
190 FOR Q = 1 TO 4
192 PRINT D (Y,Q),
194 NEXT Q
195 DATA 15, 18, 20, 28
196 N = N + 1
198 NEXT Y
200 DATA 17, 24, 22, 29
210 DATA 16, 23, 25, 28
220 END

READY
RUN NH
```

Variable Name Legend

D	Array (data)
Y	Year (FOR-NEXT use)
Q	Quarter
N	Year (printed value)

YEAR	Q1	Q2	Q3	Q4
1974	15	18	20	28
1975	17	24	22	29
1976	16	23	25	28

```
TIME:   0.15 SECS.

READY
```

Fig. 10-4. Using nested FOR-NEXT to handle an array.

inner loop. The comma following N in line 180 prevents vertical skipping of the printer so that the sales data can print on the same line.

2. The inner loop (lines 190–194) will be executed four times for each execution of the outer loop. Since there is a comma at the end of PRINT in line 192, all four numerical values of D print on the same line.

3. The program terminates when the outer loop has been executed three times.

You might find it desirable to compare the coding of Fig. 10-4 to the coding in Fig. 10-1 to review the build-up of nested FOR and NEXT statements.

Table Lookup

Occasionally, it is necessary to pull selected data from an array rather than to print out the whole array. Assume that a company has 12 different departments set up for payroll purposes. Within each department, there are six pay grades.

Instead of using clerical services to look up each employees pay rate, we will store the pay rates in an array in a computer program. (Although this technique could be called array lookup, it is popularly known as table lookup.) The program will locate the person's rate based on entering his or her department number and pay grade.

The program that meets our objective is illustrated in Fig. 10-5. The pay rates reside in DATA statements; at the beginning of execution, the pay rates are read into array R.

The statement at line 80 calls for the user to enter the clock number, department, grade, and hours of each employee. The purpose of line 90 is to calculate that worker's pay.

Assume the first input is for a person who works in Department 12 who is in pay grade 6. In line 90, D would then be 12 and G would be 6. The computer would go to the array and pick out the sixth pay rate (column six) of the twelfth department (row 12). The rate at that location is $5.78; the rate would be multiplied by hours to obtain pay.

The concept of table lookup is applied everywhere on almost a daily basis. We see it used in applications such as income tax tables, mileage tables on road maps, and telephone company rate schedules. Quite often, the lookup function is assigned to a computer rather than to a person.

```
5     REM FIG. 10-5.
10 DIM R (12, 6)
20 FOR D = 1 TO 12
30 FOR G = 1 TO 6
40 READ R(D,G)
50 NEXT G
60 NEXT D
70 PRINT TAB(18)"CLOCK #", "HRS", "RATE", "PAY"
80 INPUT C, D, G, H
90 P = R(D,G) * H
100 PRINT TAB(18)C, H, R(D,G), P
110 IF C = 999 THEN 250
120 GO TO 80
130 DATA 3.50, 3.58, 3.66, 3.74, 3.83, 3.94
140 DATA 3.20, 3.25, 3.30, 3.36, 3.43, 3.50
150 DATA 3.20, 3.25, 3.30, 3.36, 3.43, 3.50
160 DATA 3.33, 3.33, 3.33, 3.45, 3.45, 3.45
170 DATA 7.05, 7.10, 7.25, 7.45, 7.56, 7.75
180 DATA 6.60, 6.65, 6.70, 6.79, 6.89, 6.98
190 DATA 5.55, 5.55, 5.55, 5.75, 5.75, 5.75
200 DATA 7.00, 7.00, 7.45, 7.56, 7.80, 7.95
210 DATA 3.45, 3.46, 3.46, 3.67, 3.78, 3.90
220 DATA 4.00, 4.10, 4.20, 4.30, 4.40, 4.50
230 DATA 5.00, 5.00, 5.20, 5.20, 5.40, 5.40
240 DATA 5.34, 5.34, 5.56, 5.56, 5.78, 5.78
250 END

READY
RUN NH
```

Variable Name Legend	
R	Array
D	Department
G	Grade
C	Clock number
H	Hours
P	Pay

```
                    CLOCK #   HRS          RATE         PAY
?8, 12, 6, 40
                    8         40           5.78         231.2
?14, 1, 1, 40
                    14        40           3.5          140
?27, 8, 6, 23
                    27        23           7.95         182.85
?57, 8, 3, 35
                    57        35           7.45         260.75
?999, 12, 4, 8
                    999       8            5.56         44.48


TIME:  0.32 SECS.

READY
```

Fig. 10-5. Table lookup.

EXERCISES

1. Why would you ever want to employ an array in computer use?

2. What causes the need for two-dimensional arrays as opposed to that for one-dimensional arrays?

3. Under what circumstances must you dimension (DIM) a one-dimensional array? Determine what rules you need to follow in setting up two-dimensional arrays.

4. By what methods can data be placed into an array? What general method is used to print the contents of an array (to make sure all of it is printed)?

5. What is meant by "nesting" FOR and NEXT statements?

6. Describe what is incorrect about the following coding.
   ```
   100   FOR   A = 1 TO 5
   110   FOR   B = 1 TO 10
   120   NEXT A
   130   NEXT B
   ```

7. What is table lookup? Describe a common business application where it can be used?

8. How can you tell by merely glancing at Fig. 10-1 that some programming economies can be made?

9. In Fig. 10-4:
   (a) Make a list of the various statements that perform the same functions as their counterparts do in Fig. 10-1.
   For example, line number 10 in the former matches line number 10 in the latter.
   (b) Carefully describe the ideas behind line numbers 180 and 192.
   Why wasn't one PRINT statement used to print a complete data line? Could one statement do this efficiently?
   (c) Add the coding necessary to print totals by year.

10. Write a program that would calculate the mean (arithmetic average) of the 100 elements in a one-dimensional array.

Do a similar program where the data is in a 10 X 20 (two-dimensional) array.

11. What would be the output of the following program?

```
10 FOR A = 1 TO 2
20 FOR B = 1 TO 3
30 PRINT A + B
40 NEXT B
50 NEXT A
60 END

READY
```

12. The records in a series of DATA statements contain part number, part description, labor cost, material cost, and overhead cost. Write a program that would permit a user to obtain whichever cost desired for any part number.

13. The records in a series of DATA statements contain pay rates. A two-digit pay code will be used to search out the proper pay rate. The first digit of the pay code represents department number; the second digit of the pay code represents a pay grade. There are three departments and four pay grades. Write a program that would search out any pay rate, given the INPUT of a valid two-digit pay code. Use the table lookup approach.

14. A review of the program in Fig. 8-8 shows ERROR messages next to employees whose bonus code is invalid. Add the steps to this program that would print the names of such employees as a separate list when ZZZZZ is detected. (*Hint.* develop a method to save the names until they are needed.)

ARRAYS   145

11 CHAPTER
SORTING

All of the example programs and concepts in previous chapters have dealt with low volumes of data; furthermore, the data has been made available in a predetermined sequence. This chapter will introduce the topic of sorting, a process whereby the computer is programmed to take data and put it into whatever sequence is desired.

The data awaiting computer processing is often in random order or in a different order than what is required for current processing. In most cases, it is easier to cause the computer to sort the data than it is to manually sort the data outside the computer.

The detailed logic of a computer sorting process gets somewhat complicated. It is my opinion that sorting is one of those functions that the typical person can employ without needing to know how it works. Thus this chapter will only describe how to use a sorting program. Those interested in the details of sorting may refer to several of the publications mentioned in Appendix F.

A program that will sort numeric data into ascending sequence is shown in Fig. 11-1. The main categories of the program are:

LINE NUMBER	PURPOSE
10	Sets up 12 subscripted data areas in D, into which the DATA will be read. D may be referred to as a one-dimensional array, an orderly arrangement of data one column wide, but with 12 rows.

```
5    REM FIG. 11-1.
10 DIM D (12)
20 FOR I = 1 TO 12
30 READ D (I)
40 NEXT I
50 FOR I = 1 TO 11
60 FOR J = 1 TO 11
70 A = D (J)
80 B = D (J + 1)
90 IF A <= B THEN 120
100 D (J) = B
110 D (J + 1) = A
120 NEXT J
130 NEXT I
140 FOR I = 1 TO 12
150 PRINT D (I)
160 NEXT I
300 DATA 74, 12, 19, 5, 83, 18
305 DATA 4, 21, 36, 44, 62,50
310 END

READY
RUN NH


4
5
12
18
19
21
36
44
50
62
74
83



TIME:   0.14 SECS.

READY
```

Fig. 11-1.   A numeric sort.

20–40	Reads the DATA into array D.
50–130	Sorts the DATA into an ascending sequence, with the results remaining in D.
140–160	Prints the DATA in sequence.

The approach taken in Fig. 11-1 does have a major deficiency. It is limited because it can sort only 12 items, as evidenced by coding in such line numbers as 10, 20, and 140. You can verify this by inserting one additional item of DATA; the program as written does not have the capacity for more than 12 data items.

148   INSTRUCTION IN THE BASIC LANGUAGE

This particular deficiency in Fig. 11-1 has been corrected in the program in Fig. 11-2. In Fig. 11-2, a variable N is entered through an INPUT step at line number 15; the purpose of N is to inform the computer how many items there will be. Thus individual steps in the program (such as line numbers 20 and 140) do not have to be changed as the number of data elements to be sorted might vary.

Remember that the array must be dimensioned to a sufficient size. Fortunately, you do not need to take a lot of time to count exactly how many data items there are. Provided you make an estimate that is slightly

```
5     REM FIG. 11-2.
10 DIM D(100)
15 INPUT N
20 FOR I = 1 TO N
30 READ D (I)
40 NEXT I
50 FOR I = 1 TO N-1
60 FOR J = 1 TO N-1
70 A = D (J)
80 B = D (J + 1)
90 IF A <= B THEN 120
100 D (J) = B
110 D (J + 1) = A
120 NEXT J
130 NEXT I
140 FOR I = 1 TO N
150 PRINT D (I)
160 NEXT I
300 DATA 74, 12, 19, 5, 83, 18
305 DATA 4, 21, 36, 44, 62, 50
310 END

READY
RUN NH


?12
4
5
12
18
19
21
36
44
50
62
74
83


TIME:  0.17 SECS.

READY
```

Fig. 11-2. An improved version of a numeric sort.

high, the sort will work properly. (But be careful to avoid an "OUT OF DATA" condition when reading into the array.)

To perform a sort on a nonnumeric field, one basic change must be made. Wherever a variable name appears that involves this data, the "$" must be appended to it. Figure 11-3 shows an alphabetic sort; it uses the same general approach as the previous program does.

All of the programs shown previously do properly perform the func-

```
5     REM FIG.11-3.
10 DIM D$ (20)
20   INPUT N
25    REM READS DATA INTO ARRAY D$.
30 FOR I = 1 TO N
40 READ D$(I)
50 NEXT I
55    REM SORTS DATA WITHIN THE ARRAY.
60 FOR I = 1 TO N - 1
70 FOR J = 1 TO N - 1
80 A$ = D$(J)
90 B$ = D$ (J + 1)
100 IF A$ <= B$ THEN 130
110 D$(J) = B$
120 D$(J + 1) = A$
130 NEXT J
140 NEXT I
145   REM PRINTS THE SORTED DATA.
150 FOR I = 1 TO N
160 PRINT D$(I)
170 NEXT I
300 DATA POLAROID, GENERAL MOTORS, AT&T
305 DATA GENERAL FOODS, IBM, ZENITH
310 DATA CHRYSLER, EASTMAN, ANACONDA
320 END

READY
RUN NH


 ?9
ANACONDA
AT&T
CHRYSLER
EASTMAN
GENERAL FOODS
GENERAL MOTORS
IBM
POLAROID
ZENITH



TIME:  0.22 SECS.

READY
```

Fig. 11-3.   An alphabetic sort.

tion of sorting. However, each of them has provided for only one field of data (a number in the first two examples and a name in the third). A list of data is generally more meaningful if there are several fields available to describe each item.

Assume that we have sales data (see the left segment below); we want to have the computer sort it on the "code" and print it out as was done in the right segment:

Unsorted				Sorted		
Code	Name	Amount		Code	Name	Amount
67	Jones	22000		18	White	33333
44	Smith	18000		44	Smith	18000
62	Brown	15167		62	Brown	15167
18	White	33333		67	Jones	22000
92	Charles	24375		92	Charles	24375

Only the code variable will be sorted. The names and amounts will not be sorted; however, both the latter fields will be manipulated so that they can be properly printed once the codes are in sequence. The major segments of instructions in the resulting program in Fig. 11-4 are:

LINE NUMBERS	EXPLANATION
55–65	Reads each of the three fields from DATA into respective arrays.
70–80	Copies each of the codes from array D to array S.
90–170	Sorts the code variable within array D.
180–230	Prints the report.

The steps that actually print the results (line numbers 180–230) are explained in the following manner. When the sort has been completed, the codes, names, and amounts are still residing, respectively, in arrays S, C$, and V. At that time, the codes are also in array D, in ascending sequence. The problem is to cause the proper name and amount to print along with the code in code sequence.

The variable I is used to cause the computer to repeat an inner loop (190–220) as many times as there are codes. If the code in the first ele-

```
5     REM FIG. 11-4.
10 DIM D (20), S (20), C$(20), V(20)
20 INPUT N
30 PRINT
40 PRINT
50 PRINT "CODE", "NAME", "AMT."
52    REM READS CODE TO D, NAME TO C$, AND
53    REM AMOUNT TO V.
55 FOR I = 1 TO N
60 READ D(I), C$(I), V(I)
65 NEXT I
67    REM COPIES UNSORTED CODES IN D TO S.
70 FOR I = 1 TO N
75 S(I) = D (I)
80 NEXT I
85    REM SORTS CODE WITHIN D.
90 FOR I = 1 TO N - 1
100 FOR J = 1 TO N - 1
110 A = D(J)
120 B = D (J + 1)
130 IF A <= B THEN 160
140 D (J) = B
150 D (J + 1) = A
160 NEXT J
170 NEXT I
175    REM PRINTS NAMES & AMOUNTS TO
176    REM MATCH SORTED CODES.
180 FOR I = 1 TO N
190 FOR J = 1 TO N
200 IF D(I) = S(J) THEN 220
210 NEXT J
220 PRINT S(J), C$(J), V(J)
230 NEXT I
300 DATA 67,JONES,22000
310 DATA 44,SMITH,18000
320 DATA 62,BROWN,15167
330 DATA 18,WHITE,33333
340 DATA 92,CHARLES,24375
350 END

READY
RUN NH


   ?5


CODE           NAME           AMT.
  18           WHITE          33333
  44           SMITH          18000
  62           BROWN          15167
  67           JONES          22000
  92           CHARLES        24375


TIME:  0.22 SECS.

READY
```

Fig. 11-4. Sorting and printing.

152   INSTRUCTION IN THE BASIC LANGUAGE

ment of array D is equal to the code in the first element of array S, the program branches to line 220 to print a detail line. If the test results in an unequal compare, the code in the first element in array D is compared to the code in the second element of array S. When the name and amount can be printed for the code in the first element of array D, the computer goes on to the second.

All of the sorting programs in Chapter 11 have used a particular logical approach to the sorting process. An entirely different technique is illustrated in Appendix D.

EXERCISES

1. Why is it so necessary to use the computer to sort data? That is, why can't data be entered into the computer so that it is already in the proper sequence?

2. Is a DIM statement necessary to accomplish sorting? Why? Given the data used in Fig. 11-3, was a DIM statement necessary? Why?

3. What general procedure has to be followed in order to sort non-numeric data?

4. Describe the nature of the coding in Fig. 11-1 that causes that program to have a limited value.

5. In Fig. 11-1, change the less than symbol in line number 90 to the greater than symbol (let the equal sign remain). What were the results from running the program? What conclusion can you draw from having made that single change?

6. In Fig. 11-4:
   (a) Make the changes necessary to sort in ascending sequence on the amount field.
   (b) Why was it necessary to read three variables in line number 60?
   (c) When execution was completed, in how many storage locations could the code (67) for Jones be found? Explain.

7. Make the necessary additions to the coding in Fig. 9-5 so that the results would be printed with the largest counter value first (in descending order).

8. In baseball, a team's standing is based on its winning percentage, (games won divided by games played). Write a program whose INPUT is to be the team name, the games won, and the games lost. The program is to calculate each team's percentage and print the league standing in descending percentage order. Include steps to assure that total wins equal total losses within the entire league.

9.   Alter the coding in exercise eight above so that the computer aids the user by printing the team name, and the user has to enter only the number of wins and number of losses.

10.   In football, a tie game is treated as half a win and half a loss to calculate the winning percentage. Alter the coding in exercise eight above to properly handle the sport of football.

11.   In hockey, the standings are based on each team's number of "points." A win is two points, a tie is one point, and a loss is zero points. Write a program that would print out the standings in descending point order, given the input of team name and the number of wins, ties, and losses.

12.   A 20 X 4 (two-dimensional) array contains numerical values in random order.
      (a)   Find the range (the lowest and highest values) by using two completely different approaches. (Write two different programs.)
      (b)   Cause the computer to print the median value (in this case, the 41st value after having completed one of the programs in (a) above).

13.   Numerical data is contained in a two-dimensional array (a matrix). Read the data into a one-dimensional array and cause them to be sorted in ascending sequence.

14.   A current ratio is obtained by dividing current assets by current liabilities. Input data is composed of company name, current assets, and current liabilities. Prepare a program that would print out the detail data in descending order of current ratio.

12 CHAPTER
FILES

In all of the programs illustrated so far, the data we were working with arose from one of these four actions:

1. A simple assignment statement.

2. An INPUT statement.

3. A READ statement that read from a DATA statement contained within the program.

4. An arithmetic operation that obtained its raw data from one of the three previous sources.

Here we will see how data can be obtained from another source called a file. In the simplest context, a file is a collection of similar records. Everyone is familiar with how a desk drawer or a filing cabinet is used to store paper records. The major difference between a paper file and a computer file is that the latter is stored in a computer-sensible form such as magnetic tape or magnetic disk.

A program is a special type of file, since it is a collection of similar records (instructions). In this chapter, however, we are concerned with data when we discuss files.

There are several reasons why we may want to handle data as a file rather than as previously discussed:

1. Perhaps a program and the data to be processed by that program won't fit within the working storage area of the computer at the same time because there isn't enough room for both. Using a separate area (a file area) for the data itself leaves more space in working storage for the program.

2. Certain data for an application may be made available to a user, but the owner of that data may not want the user to have similar access to the related program. The program may be of a proprietary nature.

3. A user may want to enter data into a file by means of a program. This operation was not possible with previous instructions.

4. Creating or using a large volume of data may be much more efficient through the file approach rather than through any of the other methods.

Assume that we would like to set up a file containing employee's name, clock number, hours worked, and pay rate. You would begin by assigning a name to the file.

Then you would type the data for each person on a separate line, each with its own line number. You could use line numbers appropriate to the intended order of the records in the resulting file. (Or you could enter the data in random order and then sort the file.) Next, type SAVE to copy the data from working storage to the file. A sample program is shown in Fig. 12-1.

In that example, I assigned the name PAYFIL (A) to the file I want to create. Then the data was entered (B) and saved (C). The data was then scratched from working storage (D). An attempt to list it showed it was no longer in working storage (E).

Next the PAYFIL was accessed (F) and listed (G). It can now be verified that the data in the file is the data that was originally typed into the computer.

It is important to note that two different methods were used to separate data fields within a record. In the first two records, separation was caused by spacing; in the third and fourth records, separation was caused by placing a comma between data fields.

Deletions of whole line numbers and changes within existing line numbers can be made (as previously described) relating to instructions. Insertions of new lines can also be effected (remember to leave space between adjacent line numbers if you want to place insertions in correct sequence).

```
    NEW
A   NEW FILE NAME--PAYFIL

    READY
    10    26    JOHN    8.00    3.50
B   20    36    MARY    6.5     8.20
    30    47, RON, 4.0, 2.00
    40    98, BILL, 5.5, 3.86
C   SAVE

    READY
D   SCRATCH

    READY
E   LISTNH

    READY
    OLD
F   OLD FILE NAME--PAYFIL

    READY
G   LISTNH
    10    26    JOHN    8.00    3.50
    20    36    MARY    6.5     8.20
    30    47, RON, 4.0, 2.00
    40    98, BILL, 5.5, 3.86

    READY
```

Fig. 12-1. Creating a file.

Once a data file has been created, a program can be written that will do something with that data. Figure 12-2 shows a program that processes the data from the file created in Fig. 12-1.

There are only three statements in Fig. 12-2 that contain new coding. They are explained in this manner:

40   The word FILES is used to indicate that a file is involved. FILES must be followed by the name(s) of the data file that is to be used in the program (in this case, PAYFIL, as created in Fig. 12-1).

110   The IF END test is used to see if the end of the file has been reached (the computer automatically placed an appropriate signal at the end of the file when it was created). If it has, the program is to branch around the READ step. There must be a way to designate the file that you want to read, since you could have a program handling several of them. The designation "#1" refers to the first named file in the FILES statement (#2 would refer to the second, etc.).

```
20   REM FIG. 12-2.
40 FILES PAYFIL
50 PRINT "CLOCK", "NAME", "HOURS", "RATE", "PAY"
110 IF END # 1 THEN 170
120 READ # 1, C, N$, H, R
130 P = H * R
140 PRINT C, N$, H, R, P
150 T = T + P
160 GO TO 110
170 PRINT , , , , T
180 END

READY
RUN NH
```

Variable Name Legend

C	Clock number
N$	Name
H	Hours
R	Rate
P	Pay
T	Total pay

CLOCK	NAME	HOURS	RATE	PAY
26	JOHN	8	3.5	28
36	MARY	6.5	8.2	53.3
47	RON	4	2	8
98	BILL	5.5	3.86	21.23
				110.53

```
TIME:  0.16 SECS.

READY
```

Fig. 12-2.   Reading from and processing a file.

120   The word READ obtains the data from the file one record (one complete line) at a time. The designation "#1" refers to the file first named in the FILES statement. A variable name must be specified for each field to be read just as if you were reading from DATA statements. Note that the READ step does not read the line number of the records in the file (since no variable name was required for it).

The other statements in the program are straightforward.

Regarding the many versions of the BASIC language, there appear to be more differences among FILES instructions than in any other group of instructions. Thus you may need to spend considerable time learning how you need to proceed to process FILES.

A most frustrating problem concerns the separation of fields within a record (this was mentioned above). Using either spaces or commas to separate one field from another causes confusion when you have a valid field such as "NEW YORK" or "WALTHAM, MASS." The computer senses either the space or the comma and causes an error condition like this:

160   INSTRUCTION IN THE BASIC LANGUAGE

```
OLD FILE1                          OLD FILE2

READY                              READY
LISTNH                             LISTNH
10 NEW YORK 1250000                1000 WALTHAM, MASS., 02154

READY                              READY
OLD PROG1                          OLD PROG2

READY                              READY
LISTNH                             LISTNH
10 FILES FILE1                     10 FILES FILE2
20 IF END #1 THEN 50               20 IF END #1 THEN 50
30 READ #1, N$, P                  30 READ #1, N$, H
40 PRINT N$, P                     40 PRINT N$, H
50 END                            50 END

READY                              READY
RUN NH                             RUN NH


? BAD DATA IN LINE 30              ? BAD DATA IN LINE 30


TIME:  0.09 SECS.                  TIME:  0.09 SECS.

READY                              READY
```

In the left-hand example, NEW is read into N$, and then the computer tries to read YORK into P. But P can handle only numeric data, and the computer signals an error and stops. In the right-hand example, WALTHAM is read into N$, but MASS. cannot be read into H.

This dilemma is solved by placing quotation marks around nonnumeric fields in FILES (see below). You also must keep remembering not to use a comma to separate thousands from hundreds in numeric values.

```
OLD FILE1                          OLD FILE2

READY                              READY
LISTNH                             LISTNH
10 "NEW YORK", 1250000             1000 "WALTHAM, MASS.", 02154

READY                              READY
OLD PROG1                          OLD PROG2

READY                              READY
RUN NH                             RUN NH


NEW YORK       1250000             WALTHAM, MASS. 2154


TIME:  0.07 SECS.                  TIME:  0.07 SECS.

READY                              READY
```

FILES 161

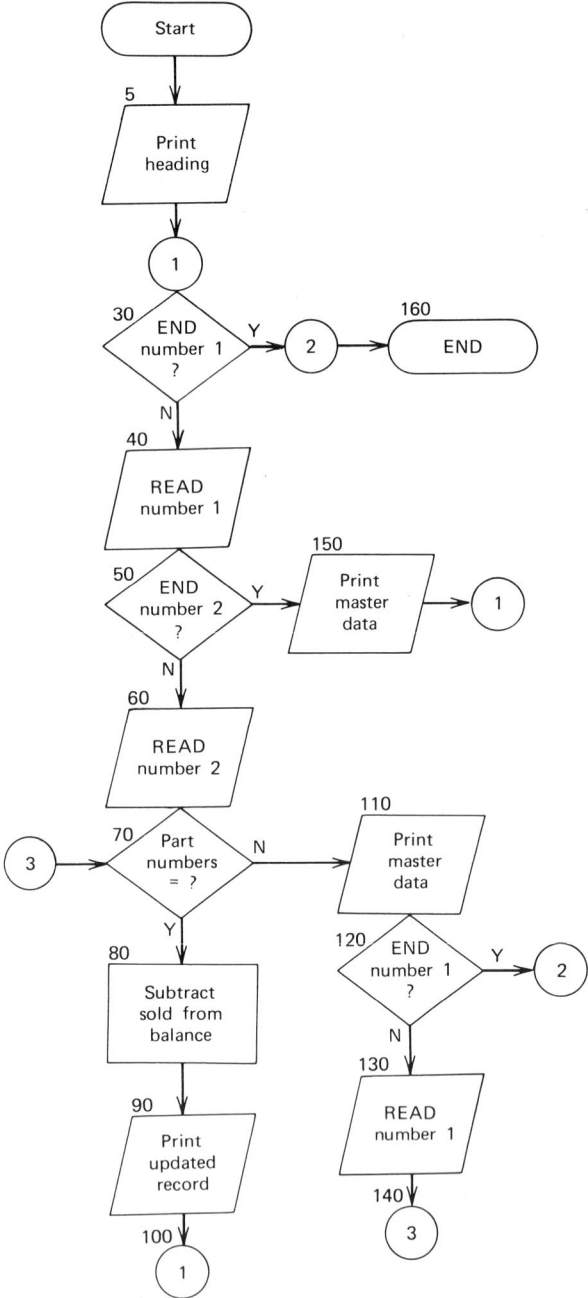

Fig. 12-3. *Program flowchart to read and process two files.*

Multiple Input Files

Possibly, you would want a program to obtain data from more than one file. Assume there is a MASTER file of inventory items. Each record in the file contains a part number, a description, and a current balance on hand.

At the same time, a DETAIL file contains a part number and the quantity sold. But the DETAIL file contains a record only for those items for which there has been a sale since the last time the MASTER was updated.

Figure 12-3 shows the logic of a program that selectively reads each record from each file. The purpose of the program is to print an up-to-date listing of new inventory balances. To keep the illustration simple, it is assumed that all items are in ascending sequence; there are no items in the DETAIL file for which there is no master; and no negative inventory balances result. Notice that even with all of these assumptions, the logic becomes quite involved. If you will spend a few minutes with it, along with some sample data, you will see why it contains the particular steps that it does.

The resulting coding appears in Fig. 12-4 along with the input data from both files and the resulting execution. Each of the statements that relates to a file was covered in the discussion of Fig. 12-2.

```
OLD OLDMAS

READY
LIST NH
10 17, BOLT, 15
20 18, NUT, 36
30 27, HAMMER, 7
40 31, SAW, 3
50 39, FILE, 20
60 44, BENCH, 2
70 47, SLEDGE, 3
80 53, RASP, 2

READY
OLD DETAIL

READY
LIST NH
10 17, 3
20 27, 2
30 39, 19
40 44, 1
50 53, 2

READY
```

Fig. 12-4. Reading from two files and processing (completed on page 164).

```
3      REM FIG. 12-4.
5  PRINT , , "PRIOR", , "NEW"
10 PRINT "PART #", "DESC.", "BALANCE", "SOLD", "BALANCE"
20 FILES OLDMAS, DETAIL
30 IF END # 1 THEN 160
40 READ # 1, P1, D$, B1
50 IF END # 2, THEN 150
60 READ # 2, P2, S
65    REM COMPARES PART NUMBERS.
70 IF P1<> P2 THEN 110
75    REM CALCULATES NEW BALANCE.
80 B2 = B1 - S
90 PRINT P1, D$, B1, S, B2
100 GO TO 30
110 PRINT P1, D$, B1, " 0", B1
120 IF END # 1 THEN 160
130 READ # 1, P1, D$, B1
140 GO TO 70
150 PRINT P1, D$, B1, " 0", B1
155 GO TO 30
160 END
```

Variable Name Legend

P1	Part No., master file
D$	Description
B1	Balance, master file
P2	Part No., detail file
S	Quantity sold
B2	New balance

```
READY
RUN NH
```

PART #	DESC.	PRIOR BALANCE	SOLD	NEW BALANCE
17	BOLT	15	3	12
18	NUT	36	0	36
27	HAMMER	7	2	5
31	SAW	3	0	3
39	FILE	20	19	1
44	BENCH	2	1	1
47	SLEDGE	3	0	3
53	RASP	2	2	0

```
TIME:  0.30 SECS.

READY
```

Fig. 12-4. cont.

Output Files

The previous examples involving FILES have dealt only with the topic of reading from FILES. But it may be desirable to output to a file, and this capability is provided. The program in Fig. 12-5 is a repeat of Fig. 12-4, except that Fig. 12-5 places the output into a third file in addition to printing the results on paper.

In Fig. 12-5, observe that line number 10 names the three files that are involved. OLDMAS and DETAIL are input files, and NEWMAS is to be the updated output file.

```
5     REM FIG. 12-5.
10 FILES OLDMAS, DETAIL, NEWMAS
20 PRINT "PART#", "DESC", "OLD", "SOLD", "NEW"
25 SCRATCH # 3
30 IF END # 1 THEN 160
40 READ # 1, P1, D$, B1
50 IF END # 2, THEN 150
60 READ # 2, P2, S
70 IF P1<> P2 THEN 110
80 B2 = B1 - S
90 PRINT P1, D$, B1, S, B2
93 L = L + 10
95 PRINT # 3, L, P1, D$, B2
100 GO TO 30
110 PRINT P1, D$, B1, " 0", B1
113 L = L + 10
115 PRINT # 3, L, P1, D$, B1
120 IF END # 1 THEN 160
130 READ # 1, P1, D$, B1
140 GO TO 70
150 PRINT P1, D$, B1, " 0", B1
153 L = L + 10
155 PRINT # 3, L, P1, D$, B1
157 GO TO 30
160 END

READY
```

Variable Name Legend	
P1	Part No., master file
D$	Description
B1	Balance, master file
P2	Part No., detail file
S	Quantity sold
B2	New balance
L	Line number counter

Fig. 12-5. Reading from two files and printing to a third file (completed on page 166).

Then there are only two new statements required. First, any file in BASIC is automatically only an input file at the beginning of program execution. Thus, at that time, it can only be read from. To be written to requires the SCRATCH instruction, as in line number 25. (Notice that SCRATCH here is an instruction, not a system command.)

Second, a special instruction is required to cause writing to an output file (see lines 95, 115, and 155). This is a PRINT statement, followed by the number that represents the output file according to the FILES statement (in this case #3). The purpose of the variable L in the program is to place a line number on each record of the output file.

Execution is completed below the listing of the program in Fig. 12-5. (The input data can be seen in Fig. 12-4.) To assure that output to the NEWMAS file was accurate and complete, the NEWMAS file is listed beneath execution of the program. Note that NEWMAS would become an input file the next time this program was to be executed.

We have now seen how a file can be created, how to read from it, and how to output to one (which is really an extension of how to create one). Coupling these steps with the sorting function covered in Chapter 11 gives you a broad ability to handle data in FILES.

PART#	DESC	OLD	SOLD	NEW
17	BOLT	15	3	12
18	NUT	36	0	36
27	HAMMER	7	2	5
31	SAW	3	0	3
39	FILE	20	19	1
44	BENCH	2	1	1
47	SLEDGE	3	0	3
53	RASP	2	2	0

TIME: 0.39 SECS.

READY
OLD NEWMAS

READY
LIST NH
```
10      17        BOLT        12
20      18        NUT         36
30      27        HAMMER      5
40      31        SAW         3
50      39        FILE        1
60      44        BENCH       1
70      47        SLEDGE      3
80      53        RASP        0
```

READY

Fig. 12-5. cont.

EXERCISES

1. Describe why files are such an important part of most computer applications. Name several files that most every organization would have.

2. Is the instruction FILES needed to establish a file or just to be able to read from the file? Explain.

3. How do you test for the end of a file? How does this test differ from the end-of-data tests in previous chapters?

4. When does SCRATCH require a line number? When doesn't it?

5. What do you have to do to place line numbers in output files?

6. A file is composed of payroll records, each of which contains a clock number, year-to-date earnings, and year-to-date social security tax withheld. Current input is to be clock number and this week's earnings for each employee. Write a program that would calculate the proper current social security tax for each employee. The tax rate is 5.85%; no more tax is to be withheld when new year-to-date earnings reach $16,500. Also, produce a new file of updated records.

7. A file (FILES) contains each employee's name and net pay amount (other fields are not relevant.) Since the company pays its employees in cash, it needs to determine exactly how much money it should get from its bank. The treasurer wants the output of a program to show:

$20 bills	XXX	Quarters	XXX
$10 bills	XXX	Dimes	XXX
$ 5 bills	XXX	Nickels	XXX
$ 1 bills	XXX	Pennies	XXX

    Total net pay $XXXXX.XX
    Write the appropriate program.

8. An accounts receivable file contains a name and an amount due from each customer. Go through the entire file, but print only the name and amount of any random customer from each group of four customers. At the end, show the total file amount, the total amount that was printed in detail, and the percentage relationship of the smaller to the larger amount.

Part 2
Business Applications Using the BASIC Language

13 CHAPTER
INTEREST
RATES I

Interest is defined as the cost of using money. Interest (the cost) is generally expressed as a decimal or as a percentage in relationship to the principal (the amount obtained). Unless otherwise specifically stated, an interest rate is quoted on an annual basis.

The purpose of this chapter is to present a number of different uses of interest rates.

Effective Interest Rate (EFFINT)

If we buy something and pay for it over time with interest charges included in our payments, how can we determine the true annual interest rate that we are paying? The matter is quite important because it is the major way of comparing the cost of one financial transaction to another.

Truth-In-Lending laws now require creditors to quote the effective rate. The following formula can be used to calculate it.

$$\text{Rate} = \frac{2 * \text{number of payments in one year} * \text{amount of interest}}{\text{amount of loan} * (\text{total number of payments} + 1)}$$

From the standpoint of coding that formula into a BASIC instruction, we could set it up like this:

$$R = 2 * P * ((N * M) - (C - D)) / ((C - D) * (N + 1))$$

The variable names have the following meanings.

R = Effective interest rate on an annual basis.
P = Number of payments in one year.
N = Total number of payments.
M = Amount of each payment.
C = Cash price of the item.
D = Down payment, if any.

If you will relate the use of the variable names immediately above to the formula as it appears in words, you can see how the computer will calculate certain values. For instance, the amount of interest is calculated by comparing total payments made with the amount "borrowed" (cash price minus down payment). In the denominator, the amount of the loan (borrowed) is similarly calculated.

The program listing for EFFINT is shown in Fig. 13-1, and the execution with a number of examples is shown in Fig. 13-2. Since the logic flowed from one statement to the next in a straightforward fashion, a program flowchart was not deemed necessary. Notice the methods that are used to guide the user in entering data and when to terminate execution.

```
5     REM FIG. 13-1.
10 PRINT
20 PRINT "PAYMENTS IN 1 YEAR";
30 INPUT P
40 PRINT "TOTAL # OF PAYMENTS";
50 INPUT N
60 PRINT "AMOUNT OF EACH PAYMENT";
70 INPUT M
80 PRINT "WHAT IS CASH PRICE";
90 INPUT C
100 PRINT "WHAT IS DOWN PAYMENT? IF NONE, ANS. 0";
110 INPUT D
115    REM CALCULATES AN EFF. INT. RATE.
120 R = 2 * P * (( N * M) - (C - D)) / (( C - D) * (N + 1))
130 R = INT (R * 1000 + .5) / 10
135 PRINT
140 PRINT "THE EFFECTIVE INTEREST RATE ON THIS LOAN IS "R;"%"
150 PRINT
160 PRINT "HAVE ANOTHER? ANS Y OR N";
170 INPUT B$
180 IF B$ = "N" THEN 200
190 GO TO 10
200 END

READY
```

Variable Name Legend

P	Payments in 1 year
N	Number of payments
M	Amount of each payment
C	Cash price
D	Down payment
R	Effective interest rate
B$	Code to continue or not

Fig. 13-1. Program listing of EFFINT.

```
RUN NH


PAYMENTS IN 1 YEAR ?12
TOTAL # OF PAYMENTS ?36
AMOUNT OF EACH PAYMENT ?87.50
WHAT IS CASH PRICE ?2750
WHAT IS DOWN PAYMENT? IF NONE, ANS. 0 ?0

THE EFFECTIVE INTEREST RATE ON THIS LOAN IS  9.4 %

HAVE ANOTHER? ANS Y OR N ?Y

PAYMENTS IN 1 YEAR ?6
TOTAL # OF PAYMENTS ?6
AMOUNT OF EACH PAYMENT ?100
WHAT IS CASH PRICE ?499.50
WHAT IS DOWN PAYMENT? IF NONE, ANS. 0 ?10

THE EFFECTIVE INTEREST RATE ON THIS LOAN IS  38.7 %

HAVE ANOTHER? ANS Y OR N ?Y

PAYMENTS IN 1 YEAR ?12
TOTAL # OF PAYMENTS ?18
AMOUNT OF EACH PAYMENT ?9.50
WHAT IS CASH PRICE ?200
WHAT IS DOWN PAYMENT? IF NONE, ANS. 0 ?50

THE EFFECTIVE INTEREST RATE ON THIS LOAN IS  17.7 %

HAVE ANOTHER? ANS Y OR N ?Y

PAYMENTS IN 1 YEAR ?1
TOTAL # OF PAYMENTS ?1
AMOUNT OF EACH PAYMENT ?110
WHAT IS CASH PRICE ?100
WHAT IS DOWN PAYMENT? IF NONE, ANS. 0 ?0

THE EFFECTIVE INTEREST RATE ON THIS LOAN IS  10 %

HAVE ANOTHER? ANS Y OR N ?N


TIME:  0.68 SECS.

READY
```

Fig. 13-2. Execution of EFFINT.

Compounding Interest Other than Annually (CMPINT)

Imagine the following advertisement by a local banking institution: "Put your money in one of our savings accounts. We compound interest quarterly instead of annually as all the other banks do. Make considerably more on your hard-earned savings."

Does compounding more often than once a year create a greater amount of interest? It does, since later periods are earning interest not only on the beginning principal but also on the interest that has been earned in prior periods. Depending on the amount of the principal, the additional interest amount may or may not be significant.

An example of the extra earnings due to compounding two and four times a year versus just once a year is shown below. The interest rate is 5%, and four decimal positions are carried in the calculations:

	Quarterly	Semiannually	Annually
Principal	$1000.	$1000.	$1000.
First period interest	12.50	25.	50.
New amount	1012.50	1025.	
Second period interest	12.6563	25.625	
New amount	1025.1563		
Third period interest	12.8145		
New Amount	1037.9708		
Fourth period interest	12.9746		
Amount at year end	$1050.95	$1050.63	$1050.

The difference between year-end amounts for compounding annually and semiannually is $.63. This is due to the fact that in the semi-annual method, $25 of interest earned during the first period also earned interest during the second half of the year. Thus, $25 at 5% for six months is $.625, or $.63.

The formula that calculates the resulting amount is:

$$A = P * (1 + R)^{N * T}$$

P is the beginning principal; R is the interest rate (on an annual basis); N is the number of compounding periods in a year, and T is the number of years. Thus in semiannual compounding, R must be divided by 2 to put the interest rate on a semiannual basis, and T must be multiplied by an N of 2; in quarterly compounding, R must be divided by 4, and T must be multiplied by an N of 4.

The program flowchart for CMPINT, which compounds daily, monthly, quarterly, and annually, is shown in Fig. 13-3. It provides for the user to enter the annual interest rate as a decimal or as a whole number.

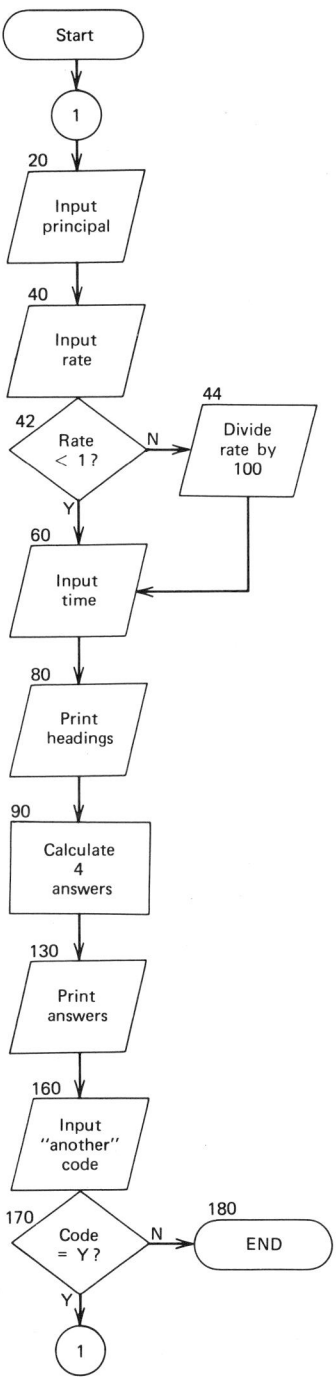

Fig. 13-3. Program flowchart—CMPINT.

```
5     REM FIG. 13-4.
8 PRINT
10 PRINT "ENTER PRIN";
20 INPUT P
30 PRINT "ENTER RATE";
40 INPUT R
42 IF R < 1 THEN 50
44 R = R/100
50 PRINT "ENTER TIME";
60 INPUT T
70 PRINT
80 PRINT TAB(1)"PRIN"; TAB(7)"%"; TAB(10)"YRS", "DAILY",
85 PRINT "MONTHLY", "QUARTERLY", "ANNUALLY"
88    REM COMPOUNDS DAILY.
90 D = P * (1 + R/360) ** (360 * T)
95 D = INT ( D * 100 + .5) / 100
98    REM COMPOUNDS MONTHLY.
100 M = P * ( 1 + R/12) ** ( 12 * T)
105 M = INT ( M * 100 + .5) / 100
108    REM COMPOUNDS QUARTERLY.
110 Q = P * ( 1 + R/4) ** ( 4 * T)
115 Q = INT ( Q * 100 + .5) / 100
118    REM COMPOUNDS ANNUALLY.
120 A = P * (1 + R) ** T
125 A = INT ( A * 100 + .5) / 100
130 PRINT TAB(1)P; TAB(7)R * 100; TAB(11)T; D, M, Q, A
140 PRINT
150 PRINT "HAVE ANOTHER? ANS Y OR N";
160 INPUT Z$
170 IF Z$ = "Y" THEN 8
180 END

READY
```

	Variable Name Legend
P	Principal
R	Rate
T	Time in years
D	Interest, compounded daily
M	Interest, compounded monthly
Q	Interest, compounded quarterly
A	Interest, compounded annually
Z$	Code to continue or not

Fig. 13-4. Program listing of CMPINT.

The appropriate BASIC coding is shown in Fig. 13-4. Whereas the interest rate must be in decimal form to calculate properly, it is converted to a whole number form for printing purposes. The program causes the computer to carry each calculation to the maximum number of decimal positions available. Then an INT instruction (such as those in line numbers 95 and 105) rounds each dollar answer to two decimals.

Observe the use of TAB instructions and semicolons in line 130 to force the printing of principal, %, and years into designated areas. Then spacing for DAILY, MONTHLY, QUARTERLY, and ANNUALLY was accomplished by just using commas. Program execution is shown in Fig. 13-5.

Present Value of $1 (PVALUE)

Assume you would like to have $5000 six years from now. If you could make an investment today that would earn 6% compounded annually, how much would you have to invest? You might try to determine

```
ENTER PRIN ?1000
ENTER RATE ?5
ENTER TIME ?1

  PRIN   %  YRS DAILY          MONTHLY          QUARTERLY          ANNUALLY
  1000   5   1  1051.27         1051.16          1050.95            1050

HAVE ANOTHER? ANS Y OR N ?Y

ENTER PRIN ?2500
ENTER RATE ?.08
ENTER TIME ?3

  PRIN   %  YRS DAILY          MONTHLY          QUARTERLY          ANNUALLY
  2500   8   3  3178.02         3175.59          3170.6             3149.28

HAVE ANOTHER? ANS Y OR N ?Y

ENTER PRIN ?100
ENTER RATE ?4
ENTER TIME ?.5

  PRIN   %  YRS DAILY          MONTHLY          QUARTERLY          ANNUALLY
  100    4   0.5  102.02        102.02           102.01             101.98

HAVE ANOTHER? ANS Y OR N ?N


TIME:   0.52 SECS.

READY
```

Fig. 13-5. Execution of CMPINT.

the required amount by the trial and error method, but that would be very time-consuming.

A formula that will enable you to simplify the process is $A = 1/((1 + I) ** N)$ where:

A = Amount needed now to have $1 at a future time.

I = Interest rate.

N = Number of years.

Observe carefully that A in the above formula provides the amount needed (usually called the present value) to produce just $1 at the specified future time. The program in this section will produce a table from which one can make a pencil and paper calculation to generate total present value dollars. In Chapter 14, the segment entitled Present or Future Value will expand the program to make the computer do all of the work.

Figure 13-6 shows the flowchart of the necessary logic. It is designed to handle whole percentage interest rates from 5 through 10% and years from 1 through 20.

INTEREST RATES I   177

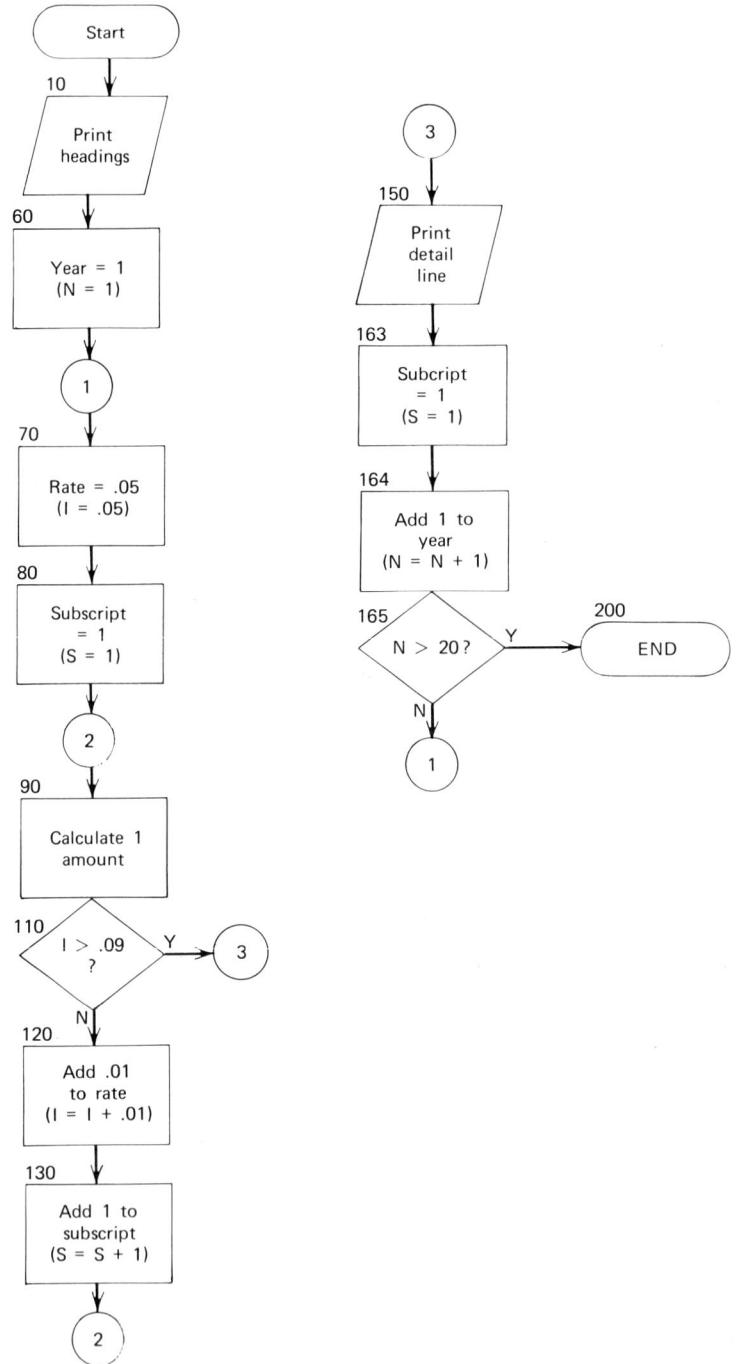

Fig. 13-6. Program flowchart—PVALUE.

Variable Name Legend

N   Year
I   Rate
S   Subscript for array A
A   Array (to contain answers)

```
5     REM FIG. 13-7.
7 DIM A(10)
10 PRINT
20 PRINT TAB(12)"PRESENT VALUE OF $1 LUMP SUM RETURN"
30 PRINT
40 PRINT TAB(1)"YEAR"; TAB(8)"5%"; TAB(18)"6%"; TAB(28)"7%";
50 PRINT TAB(38)"8%"; TAB(48)"9%"; TAB(58)"10%"
60 N = 1
70 I = .05
80 S = 1
85    REM CALCULATES A PRESENT VALUE
86    REM OF A FUTURE SUM.
90 A(S) = 1/ ((1 + I) ** N)
100 A(S) = INT (A(S) * 1000 + .5) / 1000
110 IF I > .09 THEN 150
120 I = I + .01
130 S = S + 1
140 GO TO 90
145    REM PRINTS 1 DETAIL LINE.
150 PRINT TAB(2)N; TAB(6)A(1); TAB(16)A(2); TAB(26)A(3);
160 PRINT TAB(36)A(4); TAB(46)A(5); TAB(56)A(6)
163 S = 1
164 N = N + 1
165 IF N > 20 THEN 200
170 GO TO 70
200 END

READY
```

Fig. 13-7. Program listing of PVALUE.

The program listing is shown in Fig. 13-7. Notice the use of TAB instructions so that a precise print format would be obtained. Execution of the program produced the present value table in Fig. 13-8.

You may verify any data value in the table through a process like this:

	5% One Year	8% Two Years	10% Three Years
Present value from Table	.952	.857	.751
First year earnings	.048	.069	.075
New value	1.000	.926	.826
Second year earnings		.074	.083
New value		1.000	.909
Third year earnings			.091
Future amount	1.000	1.000	1.000

PRESENT VALUE OF $1 LUMP SUM RETURN

YEAR	5%	6%	7%	8%	9%	10%
1	0.952	0.943	0.935	0.926	0.917	0.909
2	0.907	0.89	0.873	0.857	0.842	0.826
3	0.864	0.84	0.816	0.794	0.772	0.751
4	0.823	0.792	0.763	0.735	0.708	0.683
5	0.784	0.747	0.713	0.681	0.65	0.621
6	0.746	0.705	0.666	0.63	0.596	0.564
7	0.711	0.665	0.623	0.583	0.547	0.513
8	0.677	0.627	0.582	0.54	0.502	0.467
9	0.645	0.592	0.544	0.5	0.46	0.424
10	0.614	0.558	0.508	0.463	0.422	0.386
11	0.585	0.527	0.475	0.429	0.388	0.35
12	0.557	0.497	0.444	0.397	0.356	0.319
13	0.53	0.469	0.415	0.368	0.326	0.29
14	0.505	0.442	0.388	0.34	0.299	0.263
15	0.481	0.417	0.362	0.315	0.275	0.239
16	0.458	0.394	0.339	0.292	0.252	0.218
17	0.436	0.371	0.317	0.27	0.231	0.198
18	0.416	0.35	0.296	0.25	0.212	0.18
19	0.396	0.331	0.277	0.232	0.194	0.164
20	0.377	0.312	0.258	0.215	0.178	0.149

TIME: 0.66 SECS.

READY

Fig. 13-8. Execution of PVALUE.

Referring to the original question, what is the present value of money, which if invested at 6% for six years, would return $5000? See the table in Fig. 13-8. Follow across the line for year 6 to the 6% column. The present value necessary to produce $1 is $.705. If you have to invest $.705 to return $1 in six years at 6%, then you have to invest $.705 * $5000 or $3525 now to have $5000 in six years.

A serious limitation of the program in Fig. 13-7 is that it can handle only the specific interest rates and number of years, as evident in various instructions. It is conceptually better to design a program so that it is flexible enough to handle the particular data the user needs. To correct that limitation, the program above has been altered to the one shown in Fig. 13-9.

The new version allows the user to enter any beginning interest rate and number of years desired. Whereas the user can enter a rate of .05 as a whole number 5, the computer does require that the rate be in the former style. Therefore, line 210 converts the user input properly. The

```
10    REM FIG. 13-9.
20 DIM A(6)
30 PRINT "ENTER BEG. INT. RATE";
40 INPUT I
50 PRINT "ENTER STEP";
60 INPUT S
70 PRINT "ENTER BEG. YEAR";
80 INPUT Y
90 PRINT "ENTER END. YEAR";
100 INPUT N
110 PRINT
120 PRINT TAB(12)"PRESENT VALUE OF $1 LUMP SUM RETURN"
130 PRINT
140 PRINT TAB(1)"YEAR"; TAB(8)I"%"; TAB(18)I+S"%"; TAB(28)I+2*S"%";
150 PRINT TAB(38)I+3*S"%"; TAB(48)I+4*S"%"; TAB(58)I+5*S"%"
160    REM OUTER LOOP HANDLES YEARS (ROWS).
170 FOR L = Y TO N
180    REM INNER LOOP HANDLES VARYING INT. RATES (COLUMNS).
190 FOR K = 1 TO 6
200    REM CALCULATES A P. V. OF A FUTURE SUM.
210 A(K) = 1 / (( 1 + (I / 100 + (K-1) * S/100)) **L)
220 A(K) = INT (A(K) * 1000 + .5) / 1000
230 NEXT K
240    REM PRINTS 1 DETAIL LINE.
250 PRINT TAB(2)L; TAB(6)A(1); TAB(16)A(2); TAB(26)A(3);
260 PRINT TAB(36)A(4); TAB(46)A(5); TAB(56)A(6)
270 NEXT L
280 END
```

Variable Name Legend	
I	Beginning interest rate
S	STEP
Y	Beginning year
N	Ending year
L	Increment for years
K	Increment for interest rates
A	Array (to contain answers)

READY

Fig. 13-9. Program listing and execution of a more flexible version of PVALUE (completed on page 182).

program automatically provides for six detail output columns based on the STEP entered at line 60.

Present Value of an Annuity (ANUITY)

It should be made clear that the two previous programs (under PVALUE) dealt with a situation where there was a lump sum payment (an investment) and a lump sum return. But there are many situations where a lump sum investment is made, and the return flows back in the form of equal, annual payments (an annuity). The formula that will prepare the table of present values for the latter situation is:

$$A = (1 - (1 / (1 + I) ** N)) / I$$

where

A = Present value of an annual inflow of $1.
I = Interest rate.
N = Number of years.

The program listing is shown in Fig. 13-10. The coding is similar to the coding for the lump sum present value program in Fig. 13-9, the only

```
RUN NH


ENTER BEG. INT. RATE ?5
ENTER STEP ?1
ENTER BEG. YEAR ?1
ENTER END. YEAR ?4

              PRESENT VALUE OF $1 LUMP SUM RETURN

   YEAR    5 %       6 %       7 %       8 %       9 %      10 %
    1     0.952     0.943     0.935     0.926     0.917     0.909
    2     0.907     0.89      0.873     0.857     0.842     0.826
    3     0.864     0.84      0.816     0.794     0.772     0.751
    4     0.823     0.792     0.763     0.735     0.708     0.683



TIME:   0.35 SECS.

READY
RUN NH


ENTER BEG. INT. RATE ?8
ENTER STEP ?.2
ENTER BEG. YEAR ?5
ENTER END. YEAR ?8

              PRESENT VALUE OF $1 LUMP SUM RETURN

   YEAR    8 %      8.2 %     8.4 %     8.6 %     8.8 %      9 %
    5     0.681     0.674     0.668     0.662     0.656     0.65
    6     0.63      0.623     0.616     0.61      0.603     0.596
    7     0.583     0.576     0.569     0.561     0.554     0.547
    8     0.54      0.532     0.525     0.517     0.509     0.502



TIME:   0.32 SECS.

READY
RUN NH


ENTER BEG. INT. RATE ?12
ENTER STEP ?-2
ENTER BEG. YEAR ?1
ENTER END. YEAR ?3

              PRESENT VALUE OF $1 LUMP SUM RETURN

   YEAR   12 %      10 %       8 %       6 %       4 %       2 %
    1     0.893     0.909     0.926     0.943     0.962     0.98
    2     0.797     0.826     0.857     0.89      0.925     0.961
    3     0.712     0.751     0.794     0.84      0.889     0.942


TIME:   0.30 SECS.
```

Fig. 13-9. cont.

```
10    REM FIG. 13-10.
20  DIM A(6)
30  PRINT "ENTER BEG. INT. RATE";
40  INPUT I
50  PRINT "ENTER STEP";
60  INPUT S
70  PRINT "ENTER BEG. YEAR";
80  INPUT Y
90  PRINT "ENTER END. YEAR";
100 INPUT N
110 PRINT
120 PRINT TAB(12)"PRESENT VALUE OF $1 LUMP SUM RETURN"
130 PRINT
140 PRINT TAB(1)"YEAR"; TAB(8)I"%"; TAB(18)I+S"%"; TAB(28)I+2*S"%";
150 PRINT TAB(38)I+3*S"%"; TAB(48)I+4*S"%"; TAB(58)I+5*S"%"
160    REM OUTER LOOP HANDLES YEARS (ROWS).
170 FOR L = Y TO N
180    REM INNER LOOP HANDLES VARYING INT. RATES (COLUMNS).
190 FOR K = 1 TO 6
200    REM CALCULATES A P. V. OF A FUTURE SUM.
210 A(K) = (1-(1/(1+(I/100+(K-1)*S/100))**L))/(I/100+(K-1)*S/100)
220 A(K) = INT (A(K) * 1000 + .5) / 1000
230 NEXT K
240    REM PRINTS 1 DETAIL LINE.
250 PRINT TAB(2)L; TAB(6)A(1); TAB(16)A(2); TAB(26)A(3);
260 PRINT TAB(36)A(4); TAB(46)A(5); TAB(56)A(6)
270 NEXT L
280 END

READY
```

	Variable Name Legend
I	Beginning interest rate
S	STEP
Y	Beginning year
N	Ending year
L	Increment for years
K	Increment for interest rates
A	Array (to contain answers)

Fig. 13-10. Program listing of ANUITY.

difference being in the single step that contains the calculation (line 210). Notice again how an inner FOR-NEXT loop was used to calculate six values prior to printing a whole line of detail.

Two sample executions of the present value of an annuity of $1 are shown in Fig. 13-11. You can verify three different values from the table with a procedure as follows.

	5% One Year	6% Two Years	10% Three Years
Present value from Table	.952	1.833	2.487
First year earnings	.048	.110	.249
Resulting value	1.000	1.943	2.736
First year return	1.000	1.000	1.000
New value	-0-	.943	1.736
Second year earnings		.057	.174
Resulting value		1.000	1.910

	5% One Year	6% Two Years	10% Three Years
Second year return		1.000	1.000
New value		-0-	.910
Third year earnings			.090
Resulting value			1.000
Third year return			1.000
End value	-0-	-0-	-0-

If you could locate an investment that would earn 8% a year, how much would you have to invest now in order to get annual payments of $1000 for seven years? By referring to the row for year seven and the 8% column, we find a present value factor of 5.206. Since we have to invest $5.206 for seven years at 8% to get an annual return of $1, we would have to invest $5.206 times $1000 or $5206 to get back $1000 annually.

```
    RUN NH


    ENTER BEG. INT. RATE ?5
    ENTER STEP ?1
    ENTER BEG. YEAR ?1
    ENTER END. YEAR ?20

            PRESENT VALUE OF $1 LUMP SUM RETURN

    YEAR    5 %      6 %      7 %      8 %      9 %     10 %
     1    0.952    0.943    0.935    0.926    0.917    0.909
     2    1.859    1.833    1.808    1.783    1.759    1.736
     3    2.723    2.673    2.624    2.577    2.531    2.487
     4    3.546    3.465    3.387    3.312    3.24     3.17
     5    4.329    4.212    4.1      3.993    3.89     3.791
     6    5.076    4.917    4.767    4.623    4.486    4.355
     7    5.786    5.582    5.389    5.206    5.033    4.868
     8    6.463    6.21     5.971    5.747    5.535    5.335
     9    7.108    6.802    6.515    6.247    5.995    5.759
    10    7.722    7.36     7.024    6.71     6.418    6.145
    11    8.306    7.887    7.499    7.139    6.805    6.495
    12    8.863    8.384    7.943    7.536    7.161    6.814
    13    9.394    8.853    8.358    7.904    7.487    7.103
    14    9.899    9.295    8.745    8.244    7.786    7.367
    15   10.38     9.712    9.108    8.559    8.061    7.606
    16   10.838   10.106    9.447    8.851    8.313    7.824
    17   11.274   10.477    9.763    9.122    8.544    8.022
    18   11.69    10.828   10.059    9.372    8.756    8.201
    19   12.085   11.158   10.336    9.604    8.95     8.365
    20   12.462   11.47    10.594    9.818    9.129    8.514
```

Fig. 13.11. Execution of ANUITY.

```
TIME:   0.66 SECS.

READY
RUN NH


ENTER BEG. INT. RATE ?8
ENTER STEP ?3
ENTER BEG. YEAR ?5
ENTER END. YEAR ?9

           PRESENT VALUE OF $1 LUMP SUM RETURN

YEAR    8 %       11 %       14 %      17 %      20 %       23 %
  5   3.993     3.696      3.433     3.199     2.991      2.803
  6   4.623     4.231      3.889     3.589     3.326      3.092
  7   5.206     4.712      4.288     3.922     3.605      3.327
  8   5.747     5.146      4.639     4.207     3.837      3.518
  9   6.247     5.537      4.946     4.451     4.031      3.673


TIME:   0.35 SECS.

READY
```

Fig. 13.11.   Cont.

EXERCISES

1. What is the basic nature of compound interest as compared to that of simple interest?

2. Why don't all financial institutions just raise the interest rates that they pay on savings accounts instead of compounding more often than annually?

3. What practical use can be made of the program in Fig. 13-1?

4. Why isn't a program flowchart necessary for a program such as the one in Fig. 13-1? Regardless of any personal need you may have for a flowchart in such a situation, might some people benefit from a flowchart on even the most simple programs?

5. In Fig. 13-1:
   (a) Do you personally prefer the five different input items to be entered as they are on separate lines or would you like to enter all five items on one line?
   (b) Change the coding so that all five items are entered on one line.
   (c) Rewrite line number 130 so that exponentiation (raising to a power) is used as a part of the rounding process.
   (d) Delete line number 130. Alter line number 120 so that it provides for proper rounding.
   (e) Delete line number 130. Alter line number 140 so that it includes proper rounding of the interest rate in addition to printing.
   (f) What code must be entered to indicate that you have data for another calculation? Please test your answer to see if it is correct.

6. In Fig. 13-4:
   (a) In line number 120, why doesn't R need to be divided by some value as it was in lines 90, 100, and 110?
   (b) Prepare an instruction that would compound interest every six

months. Show the instruction that would compound interest
every 12 hours.

(c) How would the user enter a TIME (T) of 21 months?

(d) Observe in the sample runs in Fig. 13-5 that the values for YRS
and DAILY often are not well centered below the headings to
which they apply. Alter the program so that those data fields
are centered better than they are now.

7. In Fig. 13-6:

(a) What is the purpose of step 3—Rate = .05? How many times
is that step executed?

(b) What really ends the program—reaching a certain interest rate
or executing for a given number of years? Or a combination
of both?

(c) Why doesn't this flowchart INPUT "ANOTHER" code as does
Fig. 13-3?

8. In Fig. 13-7:

(a) Change line number 100 so that it rounds the values to four
decimal positions instead of three. Then run the program
again. Have those changes drastically altered the format of
the printed results? Why?

(b) Delete line number 100. Then run the program again. What
are the results like now? Why?

9. From a coding standpoint, what were the only differences between
Fig. 13-9 and Fig. 13-10?

10. Explain why the values in any section of the table of Fig. 13-11
were so much larger than the corresponding values in Fig. 13-9.

11. Based on the answer to exercise nine above, make the necessary
changes to Fig. 13-10 so that it would also handle the requirements
of Fig. 13-9. Set it up so that the user inputs a code indicating
whether the "lump sum" or the "annuity" table is required.

12. At a certain bank, a savings account file (FILES) contained customer records. In each record there was an account number, name
of the depositor, and account balance. The account balances were

to have interest calculated at a 5% annual rate in each one-month period. Checks in the proper amounts were to be mailed to depositors each month.

Instead of rounding to whole cents according to normal rounding rules, the program that was used truncated (chopped off) all decimal values beyond two decimals and accumulated a total for the benefit of the computer programmer. Write a program that would determine how much money the thief made, given any file of customer accounts.

14 CHAPTER
INTEREST
RATES II

Now that the concept of interest rates has been introduced, we are ready to see how some more complex problems can be solved. These solutions have practical applications to people whether on the job or for personal use.

Present or Future Value (PORFVL)

In those cases where you need to calculate present value data but computer facilities are not available, the tables prepared in Chapter 13 could be used in the manner described. When a time-sharing computer is available, you may take advantage of a program such as the one in this section. The program calculates:

1. The present value of a future lump sum payment.

2. The present value of future equal annual (annuity) payments.

3. The future value of a present lump sum, such as from putting $3000 in a bank now.

4. The future value of equal annual payments, such as from putting $1000 in a bank each year for a number of years.

In each of these four situations, the program multiplies the given number of dollars by the factor obtained from an appropriate formula—the user does not have to go to a table nor make any calculations.

A program flowchart is shown in Fig. 14-1. A significant feature is that the program will detect certain input errors and report them. For example, in step 90 the user must indicate whether the data applies to a lump sum (L) or to an annuity (A). If the input code is other than an L or an A, the computer will print a message INVALID CODE-TRY AGAIN. The program will not assume what code was intended; the user must respond with valid codes in order to get results.

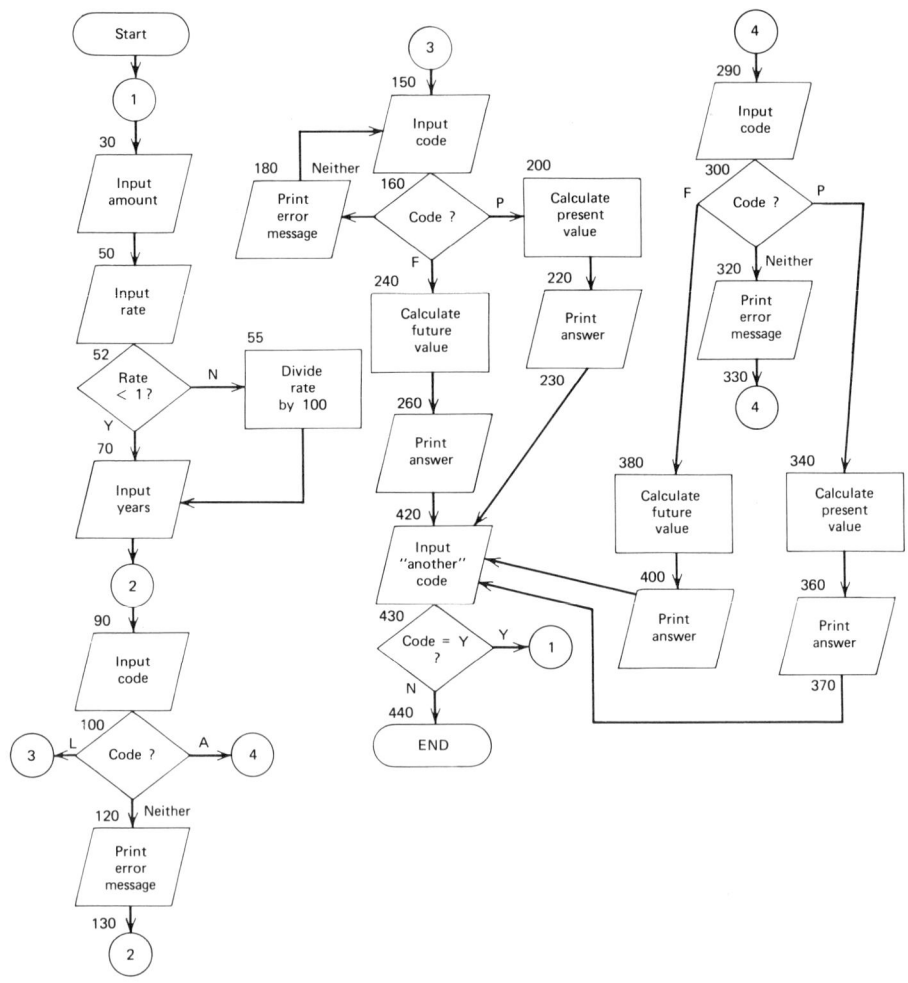

Fig. 14-1. Program flowchart—PORFVL.

There are two places in the logic where it is necessary to enter whether a present (P) or a future (F) value is desired (steps 150 and 290). An entry of other than a P or an F will cause the same error message.

The program listing appears as Fig. 14-2. The four formulas involved are:

1. Present value of a future lump sum (line 200)

$$B = D * (1 / ((1 + I) ** N))$$

2. Present value of an annuity (line 340)

$$B = D * (1 - (1 / (1 + I) ** N)) / I$$

3. Future value of a present lump sum (line 240)

$$B = D * ((1 + I) ** N)$$

4. Future value of an annuity (line 380)

$$B = (D * ((((1 + I) ** (N + 1)) - 1) / I)) - D$$

The uses of the variable data names are:

B   The final answer in dollars, rounded to the nearest whole dollar in the line following the calculation.

D   INPUT as either the present dollars in a future value situation or the future dollars in a present value situation.

I   The interest rate.

N   Number of years of life for the investment.

In Chapter 13 we saw a brief proof of each of the present value calculations. An example of each of the future value calculations is shown below.

	Lump Sum 10% Two Years	Annuity 10% Two Years
Original payment	100	100
First year earnings	10	10
Resulting value	110	110
Second year payment		100
New value		210
Second year earnings	11	21
Future value	121	231

```
5    REM FIG. 14-2.
10 PRINT
20 PRINT "ENTER AMT";
30 INPUT D
40 PRINT "ENTER INT RATE";
50 INPUT I
52 IF I < 1 THEN 60
55 I = I/100
60 PRINT "ENTER TIME IN YRS";
70 INPUT N
80 PRINT "LUMP SUM OR ANNUITY? -";
83 PRINT "ENTER L OR A";
90 INPUT Q$
100 IF Q$ = "L" THEN 140
110 IF Q$ = "A" THEN 280
120 PRINT "INVALID CODE -- TRY AGAIN"
130 GO TO 80
140 PRINT "DESIRE FUTURE OR PRESENT VALUE?";
143 PRINT "ENTER F OR P";
150 INPUT Q$
160 IF Q$ = "P" THEN 200
170 IF Q$ = "F" THEN 240
180 PRINT "INVALID -- TRY AGAIN"
190 GO TO 140
200 B = D * ( 1/(( 1 + I) ** N ))
210 B = INT ( B + .5)
215 PRINT
220 PRINT "P. V. OF $"; D; "IN"; N; "YRS AT"; I * 100; "% IS"; B
230 GO TO 405
240 B = D * (( 1 + I) ** N)
250 B = INT ( B + .5)
255 PRINT
260 PRINT "FUT. VAL. OF $"; D; "IN"; N; "YRS AT"; I * 100;"% IS"; B
270 GO TO 405
280 PRINT "DESIRE FUTURE OR PRES. VAL? ENTER F OR P";
290 INPUT Q$
300 IF Q$ = "P" THEN 340
310 IF Q$ = "F" THEN 380
320 PRINT "INVALID CODE - TRY AGAIN"
330 GO TO 280
340 B = D * (1-(1/(1 + I) ** N)) / I
350 B = INT ( B + .5)
355 PRINT
360 PRINT "P. V. OF $";D; "ANN. FOR"; N; "YRS AT"; I * 100;"% IS $";B
370 GO TO 405
380 B = (D * (((( 1 + I) ** ( N + 1)) - 1) / I)) - D
390 B = INT ( B + .5)
395 PRINT
400 PRINT "FUT. VAL. OF $"; D; "ANN. FOR"; N; "YRS AT";
402 PRINT I * 100;"% IS $"; B
405 PRINT
410 PRINT "HAVE ANOTHER? ANS Y OR N";
420 INPUT C$
430 IF C$ = "Y" THEN 10
440 END

READY
```

Variable Name Legend

D	Amount
I	Rate
N	Time in years
Q$	Code for:
	1. Lump sum or annuity
	2. Present or future value
C$	Code to continue or not
B	Answer in dollars

Fig. 14-2. Program listing of PORFVL.

```
ENTER AMT ?100
ENTER INT RATE ?.10
ENTER TIME IN YRS ?2
LUMP SUM OR ANNUITY? -ENTER L OR A ?L
DESIRE FUTURE OR PRESENT VALUE?ENTER F OR P ?F

FUT. VAL. OF $ 100 IN 2 YRS AT 10 % IS 121

HAVE ANOTHER? ANS Y OR N ?Y

ENTER AMT ?100
ENTER INT RATE ?.10
ENTER TIME IN YRS ?2
LUMP SUM OR ANNUITY? -ENTER L OR A ?A
DESIRE FUTURE OR PRES. VAL? ENTER F OR P ?F

FUT. VAL. OF $ 100 ANN. FOR 2 YRS AT 10 % IS $ 231

HAVE ANOTHER? ANS Y OR N ?Y

ENTER AMT ?100
ENTER INT RATE ?10
ENTER TIME IN YRS ?2
LUMP SUM OR ANNUITY? -ENTER L OR A ?L
DESIRE FUTURE OR PRESENT VALUE?ENTER F OR P ?P

P. V. OF $ 100 IN 2 YRS AT 10 % IS 83

HAVE ANOTHER? ANS Y OR N ?Y

ENTER AMT ?100
ENTER INT RATE ?10
ENTER TIME IN YRS ?2
LUMP SUM OR ANNUITY? -ENTER L OR A ?A
DESIRE FUTURE OR PRES. VAL? ENTER F OR P ?P

P. V. OF $ 100 ANN. FOR 2 YRS AT 10 % IS $ 174

HAVE ANOTHER? ANS Y OR N ?Y

ENTER AMT ?10000
ENTER INT RATE ?.12
ENTER TIME IN YRS ?7
LUMP SUM OR ANNUITY? -ENTER L OR A ?S
INVALID CODE -- TRY AGAIN
LUMP SUM OR ANNUITY? -ENTER L OR A ?A
DESIRE FUTURE OR PRES. VAL? ENTER F OR P ?E
INVALID CODE - TRY AGAIN
DESIRE FUTURE OR PRES. VAL? ENTER F OR P ?P

P. V. OF $ 10000 ANN. FOR 7 YRS AT 12 % IS $ 45638

HAVE ANOTHER? ANS Y OR N ?N

TIME:  1.11 SECS.
```

Fig. 14-3. Execution of PORFVL.

Figure 14-3 shows the program execution with a number of sample situations. Note that with this program, you can take present dollars and calculate their future value, or you can take future dollars and discount them back to their present value. Please keep in mind that this program reflects interest rates only and does not provide for inflation.

Terms of Payment (TERMS)

In business as in personal life, we typically have the opportunity to pay for an item when we buy it or to pay for it later. Sometimes we have the option of paying a discounted price immediately or paying the full list price at a later time. Another arrangement may be to pay list price at time of purchase or to pay somewhat more than list price later.

Occasionally, it is also possible to pay in advance for an item (before we receive it) and to get a price reduction for doing so. In any event, a vendor is typically happy to accept payment in advance even though there may be no discount attached to the prior payment.

With three such sets of possible, available terms and the potential to earn interest on money that we can hold and pay a bill later, how can one determine which method to use? What can be done to properly compare among the alternatives? If all of the alternatives are equated to present dollars at the time of purchase, then we will have a common denominator for decision-making purposes.

The program called TERMS will handle the three situations by equating each of them to present dollars in the following manner:

1. Advance payment (prior to receipt of purchased item)—the list price of the item less any price reduction for paying ahead of time. To that amount will be added the earnings that the buyer may have obtained if the money had been invested elsewhere for a while (a lost opportunity). The program will handle an advance payment of up to one year.

2. Discount at time of purchase—the list price less any discount for immediate payment. If there is no discount for immediate payment at the time of purchase, then this item is not applicable (N/A).

3. Net terms (payment later)—this is what you pay for the item minus that amount that could be earned by investing the value of the purchase elsewhere until actual payment must be made.

The logic of the program is shown in Fig. 14-4. There are three significant features that are evident. First, if the user does not provide

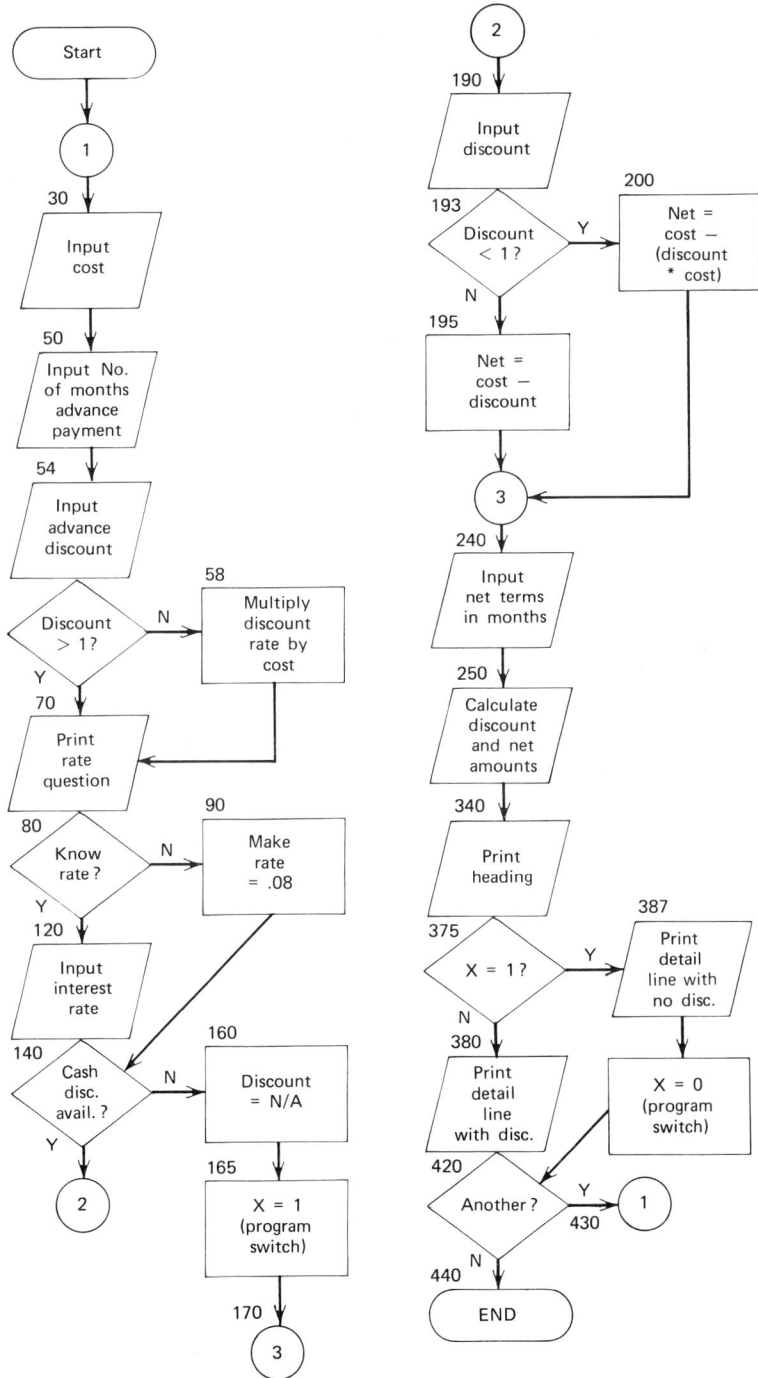

Fig. 14-4.   Program flowchart—TERMS.

```
5    REM FIG. 14-5.
10 PRINT
20 PRINT "WHAT IS COST OF ITEM";
30 INPUT C
40 PRINT "HOW MANY MONTHS IN ADVANCE";
50 INPUT M
52 PRINT "ADVANCE PAY DISC.";
54 INPUT Z
56 IF Z > 1 THEN 60
58 Z = C * Z
60 PRINT "DO YOU KNOW YOUR INT. RATE?";
70 INPUT Q$
80 IF Q$ = "Y  THEN 110
90 I = .08
100 GO TO 130
110 PRINT "ENTER YOUR INT. RATE";
120 INPUT I
130 PRINT "CASH DISC. TERMS AVAIL";
140 INPUT Z$
150 IF Z$ = "Y" THEN 180
160 D$ = "N/A"
165 X = 1
170 GO TO 220
180 PRINT "ENTER DISC.";
190 INPUT I1
193 IF I1 < 1 THEN 200
195 D = C - I1
197 GO TO 210
200 D = C * (1 - I1)
210 D = INT ( D * 100 + .5) / 100
220 PRINT "WHAT IS THE LATEST TIME AT WHICH A PAYMENT CAN BE MADE"
230 PRINT "WITHOUT ANY PENALTY? PLEASE ANSWER IN MONTHS OR A "
235 PRINT "DEC. PART OF A MONTH.";
240 INPUT M1
250 A = ( C - Z) * (1 / (1 +( I * M/12)))
260 A = INT ( A * 100 + .5) / 100
300 S = (1 + (I/12)) ** M1
310 R = (S * C) - C
315 R = INT (R * 100 + .5) / 100
320 N = C - R
340 PRINT
350 PRINT , "COST OF ITEM"
360 PRINT
370 PRINT "ADVANCE", "DISCOUNT",  "NET"
375 IF X = 1 THEN 387
380 PRINT A, D, N
385 GO TO 390
387 PRINT A, D$, N
388 X = 0
390 PRINT
400 PRINT "HAVE ANOTHER? ANS Y OR N";
410 INPUT Y$
420 IF Y$ = "N" THEN 440
430 GO TO 10
440 END

READY
```

C	Cost of item
M	No. of months advance payment
Z	Advance payment discount
Q$	Code for knowledge of interest rate
I	Rate
Z$	Code for cash discount terms
D$	Code for no cash discount terms
X	Program switch
I1	Cash discount
D	Net amount on discount terms
M1	Months grace on paying
A	Advance payment amount
S	Present value factor
R	Amount to be earned on investing cost amount for M1 months
N	Net amount from paying late
Y$	Code to continue or not

Fig. 14-5. Program listing of TERMS.

196 BUSINESS APPLICATIONS USING THE BASIC LANGUAGE

an interest rate appropriate to the value he or she places on money, the program uses a rate of 8% (see steps 80 and 90). Second, the user can enter the cash discount for immediate payment either as dollars or as a percentage of list price (see steps 190 and 193). In the latter case, the figure must be entered as a decimal (so the computer can distinguish between dollars and a percentage).

Third, we need a way to print N/A under the "discount" basis when there is no discount for immediate payment. In any situation where it has been determined that there is no discount, the digit one is placed in variable X in step 165 (known as a program switch). When it is later time to print a detail line, the variable X is tested (step 375). If X contains a

```
RUN NH


WHAT IS COST OF ITEM ?1524
HOW MANY MONTHS IN ADVANCE ?1
ADVANCE PAY DISC. ?25.00
DO YOU KNOW YOUR INT. RATE? ?Y
ENTER YOUR INT. RATE ?.12
CASH DISC. TERMS AVAIL ?Y
ENTER DISC. ?2
WHAT IS THE LATEST TIME AT WHICH A PAYMENT CAN BE MADE
WITHOUT ANY PENALTY? PLEASE ANSWER IN MONTHS OR A
DEC. PART OF A MONTH. ?2

              COST OF ITEM

ADVANCE         DISCOUNT       NET
  1484.16         1522           1493.37

HAVE ANOTHER? ANS Y OR N ?Y

WHAT IS COST OF ITEM ?100
HOW MANY MONTHS IN ADVANCE ?3
ADVANCE PAY DISC. ?1.05
DO YOU KNOW YOUR INT. RATE? ?N
CASH DISC. TERMS AVAIL ?N
WHAT IS THE LATEST TIME AT WHICH A PAYMENT CAN BE MADE
WITHOUT ANY PENALTY? PLEASE ANSWER IN MONTHS OR A
DEC. PART OF A MONTH. ?1

              COST OF ITEM

ADVANCE         DISCOUNT       NET
  97.01           N/A            99.33

HAVE ANOTHER? ANS Y OR N ?N


TIME:   0.70 SECS.

READY
```

Fig. 14-6. Execution of TERMS.

one, the program branches to a print step that prints the literal "N/A" under discount (step 387); then X must be set back to zero. If X does not contain a one, that means there is a discount, and a print statement is executed that can print a numerical value for it (step 380).

The program listing is shown in Fig. 14-5. The only new coding concept relates to the program switch (variable X) described above. The relevant coding is in line numbers 165, 375, and 388. Program execution is shown in Fig. 14-6.

Rate of Return When Annual Inflows Are Not Constant (RETURN)

If you should make an investment of $5000 and get back $2800 in each of two years, what rate of return would that be? The answer can be obtained once you have reduced the data to the common denominator calculated in Fig. 13-11. The nature of the data in Fig. 13-11 is as follows: the numbers in the body of that table indicate how much you would have to invest to get back $1 each year for the specified number of years at the specified interest rate. Referring to the question above, you have to invest $5000 to get back $2800 per year. Isn't it true then that you would have to invest $5000 ÷ $2800 or $1.786 to get back $1 each year on the same terms.

If we now look at the year two row of Fig. 13-11, we can follow across until we come to the factor nearest 1.786. Since 1.783 is the value closest to 1.786, we have determined the return on this investment to be slightly smaller than 8%.

The foregoing procedure works fine when the annual inflows are in equal (or constant) amounts. But a different approach is necessary when the inflows are not in constant amounts.

Suppose that an investment of $10,000 will have a life of only two years, the returns to be $5500 in the first year and $6000 in the second. The rate of return may be determined by trial and error, as follows (PVF stands for present value factor, as obtained from Fig. 13-9):

	8%		10%		12%	
	PVF	$	PVF	$	PVF	$
First year return $5500	.926	5093	.909	5000	.893	4912
Second year return $6000	.857	5142	.826	4956	.797	4782
		$10,235		$9956		$9694

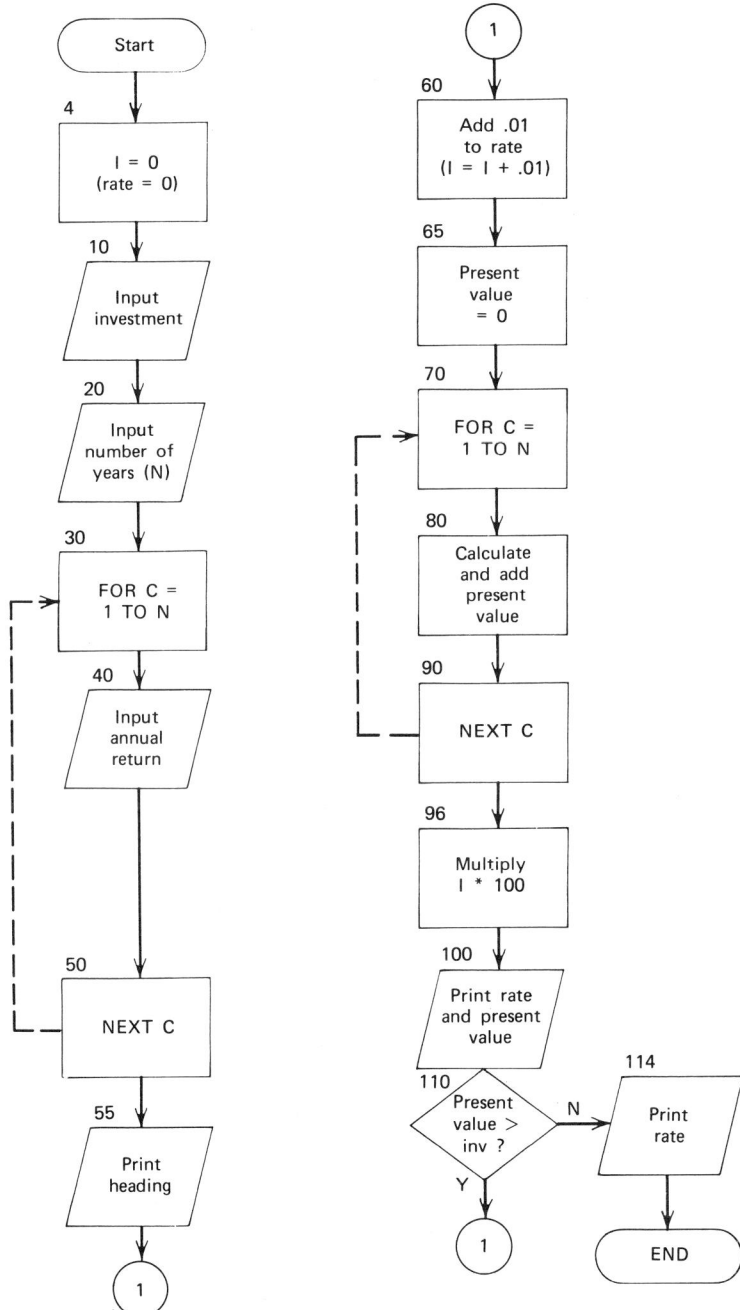

Fig. 14-7. Program flowchart—RETURN.

What I have done here is to use present value data from Fig. 13-9. I first assumed the rate of return to be 8%. Then I calculated the present value of $5500 one year from now plus that of $6000 two years from now. The total of $10,235 means that if we had invested $10,235 at 8%, we would get a return of $5500 in the first year and $6000 in the second.

But the problem states that we have to invest only $10,000 to get those returns. Therefore, the rate must be higher than 8%.

Both 10% and 12% were also tried, and we find that the present value in the 10% trial comes quite close to the amount of the investment (only a $44 difference).

To prevent the need for spending a lot of time making these trial-and-error calculations by hand, there is a computer program that will do this. The logic is shown in Fig. 14-7.

The nature of the logic is that the computer will first have the user input the amount of the investment. The computer then provides for a specific year at a time followed by a question mark; the user inputs the

Variable Name Legend

I	Interest rate (during calculations)
B	Array to hold annual $ returns
A	Investment amount
N	Number of years
C	Subscript for array B
P	Present value
R	Interest rate (for printing)

```
2     REM FIG. 14-8.
3 DIM B(20)
4 I = 0
5 PRINT "ENTER INV. AMT.";
10 INPUT A
15 PRINT "ENTER # OF YEARS";
20 INPUT N
24    REM LOOP PROVIDES FOR INPUT OF ANNUAL RETURNS.
30 FOR C = 1 TO N
35 PRINT C;
40 INPUT B(C)
50 NEXT C
53 PRINT
55 PRINT "%", "PRES VAL"
60 I = I + .01
65 P = 0
68    REM LOOP BUILDS UP A P. V. FOR ALL RETURNS AT A GIVEN RATE.
70 FOR C = 1 TO N
80 P = P + (B(C) / ( 1 + I) ** C)
90 NEXT C
93 P = INT ( P + .5)
96 R = I * 100
100 PRINT R, P
110 IF P > A THEN 60
112 PRINT
114 PRINT "RATE IS " R; "%"
120 END

READY
```

Fig. 14-8.   Program listing of RETURN.

```
RUN NH


ENTER INV. AMT. ?40000
ENTER # OF YEARS ?2
  1  ?22000
  2  ?30000

  %              PRES VAL
  1               51191
  2               50404
  3               49637
  4               48891
  5               48163
  6.              47455
  7.              46764
  8               46091
  9               45434
 10               44793
 11               44168
 12.              43559
 13.              42963
 14.              42382
 15.              41815
 16.              41260
 17.              40719
 18.              40190
 19.              39672

RATE IS  19. %



TIME:  0.34 SECS.

READY
RUN NH


ENTER INV. AMT. ?100000
ENTER # OF YEARS ?5
  1  ?24000
  2  ?24000
  3  ?24000
  4  ?24000
  5  ?24000

  %              PRES VAL
  1              116482
  2              113123
  3              109913
  4              106844
  5              103907
  6.             101097
  7.              98405

RATE IS  7. %



TIME:  0.30 SECS.
```

Fig. 14-9. Execution of RETURN.

cash return for that year. When all of the returns have been entered, the computer automatically goes to the calculation process.

The computer first determines the total present value of the returns at a rate of 1%. If that amount is greater than the investment, the program goes on and tries 2%. When the total present value is less than the original investment, the computer prints that rate of return and the program ends.

The program listing and execution are shown in Fig. 14-8 and 14-9, respectively. As the program is written, the array B is large enough to hold the return data for 20 years.

EXERCISES

1. Give an example of an investment whose returns would tend to be constant amounts in each period. Name one whose annual returns would fluctuate widely over its life.

2. In Fig. 14-2:
   (a) Does the computer care whether an interest rate is entered as a decimal or as a whole number? Why?
   (b) Is an interest rate (in an answer line) printed as a decimal or as a whole number? Which specific steps accomplish that?
   (c) What is the purpose of line numbers 120, 180, and 320? Does appropriate logic for those steps appear on the flow chart in Fig. 14-1?
   (d) Carefully explain the purpose of each segment of line number 220.
   (e) In line number 360, if "I * 100" had been eliminated, could line number 55 be removed? Why?
   (f) Carefully review line number 340. Why is that instruction different from line number 210 in Fig. 13-10? Give two reasons.

3. Regarding the program in Fig. 14-5:
   (a) How would the program be used in a practical sense?
   (b) What are some limitations of the program?
   (c) What would happen if the users response to line number 60 were anything other than Y? Is that problem serious enough to warrant making an appropriate change to the coding? Why?
   (d) Change the program so that it just prints the list price under DISCOUNT when there is no discount available as opposed to printing N/A as it does now.
   (e) Why are there presently two PRINT instructions that are so similar, namely lines 380 and 387?
   (f) What will be the results if the user enters a 3% discount as 3?

4. Describe the "trial and error" nature of the logic in Fig. 14-7.

5. As Fig. 14-7 now stands, what would be the output if the total of the yearly returns were less than the investment?

6.   (a) Make the needed changes to Fig. 14-7 so that an appropriate message would be printed if the total of the yearly returns were less than the investment.

      (b) Make the coding changes to Fig. 14-8 as suggested by your answer to (a) above.

7.   In Fig. 14-8:

      (a) Change the coding so that the computer would print only the final answer, not all the intermediate (trial and error) data.

      (b) What is the purpose of line number 65? Is that step executed more than once during the program? Why?

      (c) Make changes to the program so that the user has the opportunity to run another set of data without the need to type RUN again.

8.   Carefully study the data used in the second execution in Fig. 14-9. Prove the answer by referring back to the table generated in Fig. 13-11.

9.   A would-be traveler saw the following advertisement: "Traveler's checks normally cost $1.00 per $100 worth to buy. Buy yours in April and get them free of any service charge."

      Write a program that would determine how "free" the checks would be considering the purchaser could invest the money elsewhere and buy the checks instead on the day of the trip.

10.   Write a program that would print a table of "future values." Make the program flexible enough so that the user can obtain the choice of years, interest rates, and whether there will be a lump sum payment or annual payments.

15 CHAPTER BUDGETING

A budget is merely a quantitative plan by which you intend to operate in a future period. A budget may be expressed in units such as dollars, quantities of products, numbers of people, etc. Here, I will present some computer programs that could be used with certain facets of budget preparation.

A normal procedure in the preliminary stages of the budgeting process is to project certain data under a set of conditions and see what real life results would be created. If you aren't satisfied with the predicted results or if the underlying assumptions don't seem appropriate, you can try again. With a time-sharing computer environment, it is so easy to try again using different data or to alter the program.

Determining Gross Markup (MARKUP)

The accounting term for the difference between the acquisition cost of an item or service and its selling price is referred to as gross profit. Quite often, the gross profit is expressed as a percentage of either the cost or the selling price. This percentage is called markup.

The purpose of the program in this section is to calculate what the selling price has to be, given a particular cost and a desired markup. The markup can be based on either cost or selling price. Figure 15-1 shows an appropriate program flowchart.

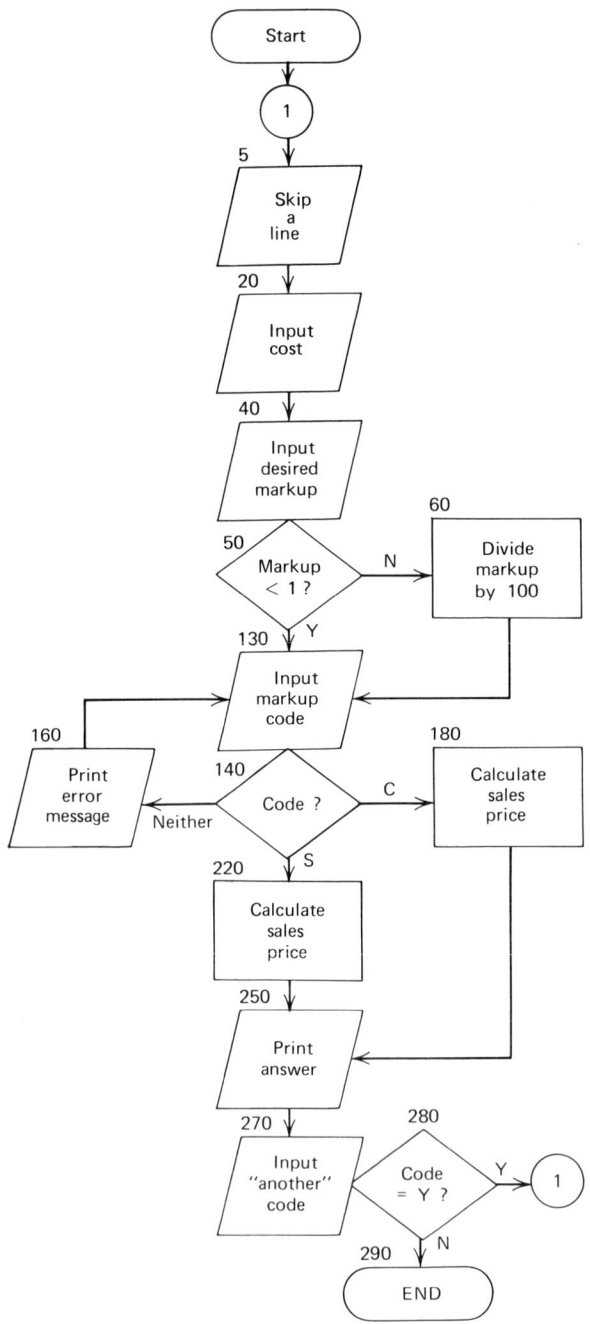

Fig. 15-1. Program flowchart—MARKUP.

Variable Name Legend

C	Cost
R	Markup desired
A$	Code for C (cost) or S (sales)
S	Sales price
B$	To hold literal "COST" or "SALES"
Q$	Code to continue or not

```
3     REM FIG. 15-2.
5 PRINT
10 PRINT "ENTER COST";
20 INPUT C
30 PRINT "ENTER MARKUP";
40 INPUT R
50 IF R < 1 THEN 120
60 R = R / 100
120 PRINT "DESIRE M/U ON COST(C) OR SELL. PRICE(S)";
130 INPUT A$
140 IF A$ = "C" THEN 180
150 IF A$ = "S" THEN 220
160 PRINT "INVALID CODE - TRY AGAIN"
170 GO TO 120
180 S = C + ( C * R)
190 S = INT ( S * 100 + .5) / 100
200 B$ = "COST"
210 GO TO 245
220 S = C / ( 1-R)
230 S = INT ( S * 100  + .5) / 100
240 B$ = "SALES"
245 PRINT
250 PRINT "WHEN COST IS $"C;"A MARKUP OF"R*100;"% ON";
255 PRINT B$; " GIVES SALES OF $"; S
258 PRINT
260 PRINT "HAVE ANOTHER";
270 INPUT Q$
280 IF Q$ = "Y" THEN 5
290 END

READY
```

Fig. 15-2. Program listing of MARKUP.

The logic calls for the user to enter three factors:

1. Acquisition cost.

2. Desired markup. This can either be a whole number percent or a decimal.

3. A code to indicate whether markup is to be on cost (C) or on selling price (S). Any other code will provide an error message.

The program listing and the execution with four examples are shown in Figs. 15-2 and 15-3. Sample data calculations are as follows:

BUDGETING   207

```
RUN NH


ENTER COST ?12.05
ENTER MARKUP ?34
DESIRE M/U ON COST(C) OR SELL. PRICE(S) ?C

WHEN COST IS $ 12.05 A MARKUP OF 34 % ONCOST GIVES SALES OF $ 16.15

HAVE ANOTHER ?Y

ENTER COST ?12.05
ENTER MARKUP ?34
DESIRE M/U ON COST(C) OR SELL. PRICE(S) ?S

WHEN COST IS $ 12.05 A MARKUP OF 34 % ONSALES GIVES SALES OF $
 18.26

HAVE ANOTHER ?Y

ENTER COST ?10.00
ENTER MARKUP ?.56
DESIRE M/U ON COST(C) OR SELL. PRICE(S) ?C

WHEN COST IS $ 10 A MARKUP OF 56. % ONCOST GIVES SALES OF $ 15.6

HAVE ANOTHER ?Y

ENTER COST ?10.00
ENTER MARKUP ?.56
DESIRE M/U ON COST(C) OR SELL. PRICE(S) ?S

WHEN COST IS $ 10 A MARKUP OF 56. % ONSALES GIVES SALES OF $ 22.73

HAVE ANOTHER ?N


TIME:  0.50 SECS.

READY
```

Fig. 15-3. Execution of MARKUP.

	Example 1		Example 2	
	Markup on Cost		Markup on Selling Price	
	$	%	$	%
Sales	16.15		18.26	100
Cost	12.05	100	12.05	66
Gross (markup)	4.10	34	6.21	34

In example 1, the selling price (S) is merely the cost (C) plus the cost times the desired markup (R). The formula as shown in line number 180 of Fig. 15-2 is S = C + (C * R).

In example 2, the cost must be divided by the relationship that cost has to selling price. If we know that markup has a .34 ratio to selling price, then cost must have a .66 (1 - .34) ratio to selling price. Dividing the known cost figure (C) of $12.05 by the cost ratio (1 - R) gives the required selling price (S). See line number 220 in Fig. 15-2.

Net Pay Requirements (NETPAY)

Certain people in professional positions have been known to enter salary negotiations by stating their required net pay instead of their expected gross pay. In proceeding on such a basis, it is necessary to work from net pay up to gross pay rather than in the usual direction of gross pay down to net pay.

The minimum required input data is desired net pay and certain knowledge about taxes and other deductions. In this sample program, taxes must be entered into the computer expressed as an effective rate of gross pay. The rate can be entered either as a decimal or as a whole number rate. Other deductions are to be entered in dollars.

The logic of the required calculation is similar to that necessary to calculate sales dollars when a certain markup on sales is required. Consider that a person's net take-home pay is really his or her gross profit.

Gross pay must be large enough to cover both taxes and deductions (cost) in addition to net pay. Thus the required amount of gross pay (G) is the total of the desired net pay (N) and other deductions (D) divided by the ratio that taxes have in relation to gross pay.

```
5     REM FIG. 15-4.
10 PRINT "ENTER REQ. NET PAY";
20 INPUT N
30 PRINT "EFFECTIVE TAX RATE";
40 INPUT T
45 IF T < 1 THEN 60
50 T = T / 100
60 PRINT "ENTER OTHER DEDUCTIONS";
70 INPUT D
80 G = INT ( (N + D) / (1.0 - T) + .5)
90 PRINT "REQUIRED GROSS PAY = $"; G
100 END

READY
```

Variable Name Legend

N	Required net pay
T	Tax rate
D	Deductions
G	Gross pay required

Fig. 15-4. Program listing of NETPAY.

```
RUN NH


ENTER REQ. NET PAY ?100
EFFECTIVE TAX RATE ?.12
ENTER OTHER DEDUCTIONS ?24
REQUIRED GROSS PAY = $ 141


TIME:   0.11 SECS.

READY
RUN NH


ENTER REQ. NET PAY ?2000
EFFECTIVE TAX RATE ?.34
ENTER OTHER DEDUCTIONS ?500
REQUIRED GROSS PAY = $ 3788


TIME:   0.14 SECS.

READY
RUN NH


ENTER REQ. NET PAY ?150
EFFECTIVE TAX RATE ?.15
ENTER OTHER DEDUCTIONS ?0
REQUIRED GROSS PAY = $ 176


TIME:   0.13 SECS.

READY
RUN NH


ENTER REQ. NET PAY ?360
EFFECTIVE TAX RATE ?27
ENTER OTHER DEDUCTIONS ?125
REQUIRED GROSS PAY = $ 664


TIME:   0.12 SECS.

READY
```

Fig. 15-5.   Execution of NETPAY.

The program listing is shown in Fig. 15-4. Four examples are run in Fig. 15-5. Through the use of the INT instruction, all answers have been truncated to whole dollars.

210   BUSINESS APPLICATIONS USING THE BASIC LANGUAGE

Variable Budgets (VARBUD)

If you were the supervisor of a manufacturing department, you would probably be furnished with a budget indicating how much you could spend for raw materials. Assume that you were expected to make 100 units of a finished product and that you were allowed to spend $500 for raw materials to do so.

Suppose orders for the finished product were heavier than originally planned, and management instead requested that you make 120 units of finished product. Shouldn't you be allowed to spend more on raw material if you made more units than had originally been the plan? On the other hand, if you make only 80 units of finished product, you should not be allowed as much money for raw materials.

Costs such as raw material, direct labor, and many of the payroll fringes should tend to fluctuate in almost direct proportion to output. These are typically called variable costs—in total, they vary with output.

Another category of costs is called fixed costs. These are costs that normally are pretty much the same, regardless of the level of activity over a given (short) period of time. Examples are depreciation of buildings and equipment, property taxes, and insurance.

Between variable costs and fixed costs is another category called semivariable or mixed costs. These costs have a portion that tends to be fixed and another portion that increases as the work effort increases. Examples are supervision and maintenance.

The program VARBUD (Fig. 15-6) provides for the user to enter variable, mixed, and fixed costs in order to develop a total budget. Variable costs are entered at 100% of normal capacity; the program calculates what those costs should be at 70, 80, and 90% of normal capacity.

Mixed costs are entered by inputting the fixed portion dollars and the variable portion at the rate at which it varies with direct labor. Again, the program calculates the budget amounts at the different levels. Fixed costs remain the same at all levels of capacity.

Program execution is shown in Fig. 15-7. Notice that the total budget at 70% is somewhat more than 70% of the 100% budget because there are some fixed elements that are the same at all four levels of production.

It is to be noted that this program is practical only as an illustration. Substantial changes would have to be made so that it could be used in any specific organization.

```
5     REM FIG. 15-6.
10 PRINT
20 PRINT "ENTER ALL COSTS AT 100%";
22 PRINT " OF NORMAL CAPACITY"
30 PRINT
40 PRINT "ENTER DIR. MAT.";
45 INPUT A
50 PRINT "ENTER DIR. LABOR";
55 INPUT B
60 PRINT "ENTER FRINGE BENEFITS AS % OF DIRECT LABOR";
70 INPUT C
74 IF C < 1 THEN 90
80 C = C / 100
90 PRINT "ENTER FIXED SUPER. EXP.";
95 INPUT D
100 PRINT "ENTER THE VARIABLE SUP. EXP. PER 1$ OF DIRECT LABOR";
110 INPUT E
120 PRINT "ENTER FIXED MAIN. EXP.";
125 INPUT F
130 PRINT "ENTER VARIABLE MAIN. EXP. PER $1 OF DIRECT LABOR";
140 INPUT G
150 PRINT "ENTER DEPRECIATION, INSURANCE, AND PROPERTY TAXES";
160 INPUT H, I, J
170 A1 = INT ( .7000 * A)
200 A2 = INT ( .8 * A)
210 A3 = INT ( .9 * A)
230 B1 = INT ( .7 * B)
250 B2 = INT ( .8 * B)
270 B3 = INT (.9 * B)
290 C1 = INT ( C * B1)
310 C2 = INT ( C * B2)
330 C3 = INT ( C * B3)
350 C4 = INT ( C * B)
370 K1 = INT ( D + ( E * B1))
390 K2 = INT ( D + ( E * B2))
410 K3 = INT ( D + ( E * B3))
430 K4 = INT ( D + ( E * B))
450 L1 = INT ( F + ( G * B1))
470 L2 = INT ( F + ( G * B2))
490 L3 = INT ( F + ( G * B3))
510 L4 = INT ( F + ( G * B))
530 M1 = A1 + B1 + C1 + K1 + L1 + H + I + J
540 M2 = A2 + B2 + C2 + K2 + L2 + H + I + J
550 M3 = A3 + B3 + C3 + K3 + L3 + H + I + J
560 M4= A + B + C4 + K4 + L4 + H + I + J
570 PRINT
580 PRINT "VARIABLE BUDGET( % OF NORMAL CAPACITY)"
590 PRINT
600 PRINT ,"70%", "80%", "90%", "100%"
610 PRINT "DIRECT MAT.",A1,A2,A3,A
620 PRINT "DIRECT LABOR", B1, B2, B3, B
630 PRINT "PAY FRINGES", C1, C2, C3, C4
640 PRINT "SUPERVISION", K1, K2, K3, K4
650 PRINT "MAINTENANCE", L1, L2, L3, L4
660 PRINT "DEPRECIATION", H, H, H, H
670 PRINT "INSURANCE", I, I, I, I
680 PRINT "PROP. TAXES", J, J, J, J
690 PRINT , "*****", "*****", "*****","*****"
700 PRINT "TOTAL BUDGET", M1, M2, M3, M4
710 END
```

READY

Fig. 15-6. Program listing of VARBUD (completed on page 213).

Variable Name Legend

A	Direct material $ @ 100%
B	Direct labor $ @ 100%
C	Fringe benefits %
D	Fixed supervisory expense $
E	Variable supervisory expense %
F	Fixed maintenance expense $
G	Variable maintenance expense %
H	Depreciation $
I	Insurance $
J	Property taxes $
A1	Direct material @ 70%
A2	Direct material @ 80%
A3	Direct material @ 90%
B1	Direct labor @ 70%
B2	Direct labor @ 80%
B3	Direct labor @ 90%
C1	Pay fringes @ 70%
C2	Pay fringes @ 80%
C3	Pay fringes @ 90%
C4	Pay fringes @ 100%
K1	Supervision @ 70%
K2	Supervision @ 80%
K3	Supervision @ 90%
K4	Supervision @ 100%
L1	Maintenance @ 70%
L2	Maintenance @ 80%
L3	Maintenance @ 90%
L4	Maintenance @ 100%
M1	Total costs @ 70%
M2	Total costs @ 80%
M3	Total costs @ 90%
M4	Total costs @ 100%

Fig. 15-6. cont.

```
ENTER ALL COSTS AT 100% OF NORMAL CAPACITY

ENTER DIR. MAT. ?1000
ENTER DIR. LABOR ?1000
ENTER FRINGE BENEFITS AS % OF DIRECT LABOR ?.10
ENTER FIXED SUPER. EXP. ?200
ENTER THE VARIABLE SUP. EXP. PER 1$ OF DIRECT LABOR ?.10
ENTER FIXED MAIN. EXP. ?100
ENTER VARIABLE MAIN. EXP. PER $1 OF DIRECT LABOR ?.10
ENTER DEPRECIATION, INSURANCE, AND PROPERTY TAXES ?300, 200, 100

VARIABLE BUDGET( % OF NORMAL CAPACITY)

               70%          80%          90%          100%
DIRECT MAT.    699          800          900          1000
DIRECT LABOR   699          800          900          1000
PAY FRINGES    69           80           90           100
SUPERVISION    269          280          290          300
MAINTENANCE    169          180          190          200
DEPRECIATION   300          300          300          300
INSURANCE      200          200          200          200
PROP. TAXES    100          100          100          100
               *****        *****        *****        *****
TOTAL BUDGET   2505         2740         2970         3200


TIME:   0.66 SECS.

READY
```

Fig. 15-7.   Execution of VARBUD.

Break-Even Analysis (BEANAL)

At some point in most budgeting processes, it is desirable to figure how many sales dollars will be required to just cover costs—to break even. The break-even point is the volume of sales that will equal total costs—there will be neither a profit nor a loss. Or, in other words, the net profit will be zero.

In an income statement format, an example would look like this:

Sales		100
Variable cost	60	
Fixed cost	<u>40</u>	
Total cost		<u>100</u>
Net		<u>-0-</u>

Stated verbally, the break-even point is:

$$\text{Sales} = \text{Variable costs} + \text{fixed costs}$$

In the preceding format, we really have an income statement shown in horizontal rather than in vertical form. Using appropriate variable names, the break-even formula can be shown as:

$S = (V * S) + F$, where S = sales; V equals the variable cost rate in relationship to sales; and F is total fixed costs. For computer purposes, the program will be:

$$S = F / (1.00 - V)$$

This formula states that the contribution to fixed cost (selling price minus the variable cost rate) is being divided into fixed cost. The quotient will be the amount of sales necessary to cover the total of variable and fixed costs. For example, if the variable cost rate to sales is 40% (.40), and if fixed costs are $600, then the sales required to break even is $600/ (1 - .40) or $1000.

Although it is often necessary to figure the break-even point, there is usually a greater need to figure the sales necessary to make a certain profit. The desired profit may be a fixed dollar amount or it may be quoted as a decimal in relationship to sales dollars.

The formulas we will use to calculate required sales dollars are:

1. $S = (N + F) / (1.00 - V)$ where:
    S = Required sales.
    N = Desired net profit dollars.
    F = Fixed costs.
    V = Variable cost rate to sales, as a decimal.

2. $S = F / (1.00 - V - N)$ where:
    S = Required sales.
    F = Fixed costs.
    V = Variable cost rate to sales, as a decimal.
    N = Desired profit rate to sales as a decimal.

A program flowchart of the logic is shown in Fig. 15-8. In addition to calculating the required sales on each of the two bases described above, it also calculates the net profit from the basic formula, Profit = Sales – Variable Cost – Fixed Cost when the Sales amount is provided in an INPUT step (170). The program listing is presented as Fig. 15-9.

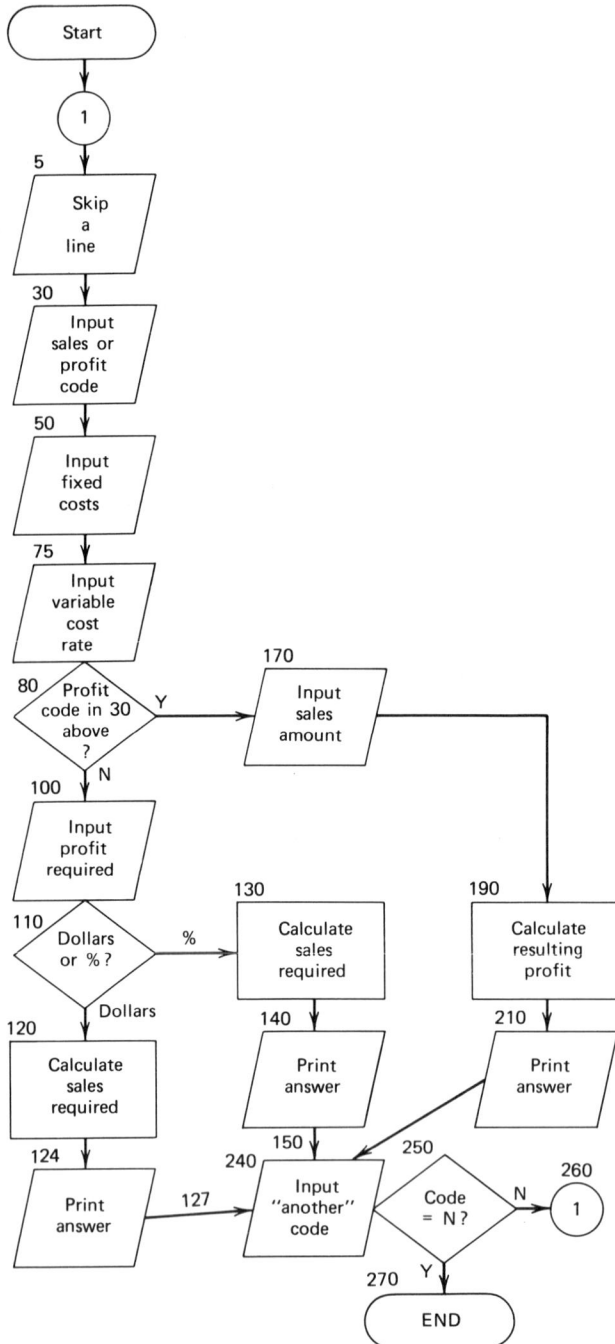

Fig. 15-8. Program flowchart—BEANAL.

A$	Code for sales or profit
F	Fixed costs
V	Variable cost rate
N	Desired net profit
S	Sales required
L	Estimated sales INPUT
E	Estimated profit
Z$	Code to continue or not

```
3    REM FIG. 15-9.
5 PRINT
10 PRINT "DESIRE SALES OR NET PROFIT?";
20 PRINT " ANS S(SALES) OR P";
30 INPUT A$
40 PRINT "FIXED COSTS";
50 INPUT F
60 PRINT "VARIABLE COST RATE? ENTER AS A DECIMAL"
65 PRINT "IN RELATION TO SALES";
75 INPUT V
80 IF A$ = "P" THEN 160
90 PRINT "DESIRED NET PROFIT? ENTER ";
95 PRINT " $ AMT OR DEC. PORTION OF SALES";
100 INPUT N
110 IF N < 1 THEN 130
120 S = INT (( N + F) / ( 1.00 - V))
122 PRINT
124 PRINT "FOR A NET PROFIT OF ";N;"THERE MUST BE";S;"IN SALES"
127 GO TO 215
130 S = INT (F/(1.00 - V - N))
135 PRINT
140 PRINT "FOR A NET PROFIT OF";N*100;"% THERE MUST BE"S;"IN SALES"
150 GO TO 215
160 PRINT "ESTIMATED SALES";
170 INPUT L
190 E = L - (L * V) - F
200 E = INT (E)
205 PRINT
210 PRINT "WITH SALES OF ";L;"YOUR PROFIT WILL BE"; E
215 PRINT
220 PRINT "HAVE ANOTHER? ANS Y OR N";
240 INPUT Z$
250 IF Z$ = "N" THEN 270
260 GO TO 5
270 END

READY
```

Fig. 15-9. Program listing of BEANAL.

Observe how N is used as a variable name for required profit. If the user inputs for N a number greater than one, the program treats N as dollars and uses the first formula above (see line number 120). If N is entered as less than one, the program treats N as a decimal in relationship to sales and goes to the second formula shown above (line number 130). If the program is to calculate a net profit, the coding in line 190 accomplishes that.

The program execution in Fig. 15-10 shows five different examples. Observe that in the fourth example, the variable cost rate and the desired

```
RUN NH
```

```
DESIRE SALES OR NET PROFIT? ANS S(SALES) OR P ?S
FIXED COSTS ?100000
VARIABLE COST RATE? ENTER AS A DECIMAL
IN RELATION TO SALES ?.34
DESIRED NET PROFIT? ENTER  $ AMT OR DEC. PORTION OF SALES ?100000

FOR A NET PROFIT OF  100000 THERE MUST BE 303030 IN SALES

HAVE ANOTHER? ANS Y OR N ?Y

DESIRE SALES OR NET PROFIT? ANS S(SALES) OR P ?P
FIXED COSTS ?100000
VARIABLE COST RATE? ENTER AS A DECIMAL
IN RELATION TO SALES ?.34
ESTIMATED SALES ?350000

WITH SALES OF  350000 YOUR PROFIT WILL BE 131000

HAVE ANOTHER? ANS Y OR N ?Y

DESIRE SALES OR NET PROFIT? ANS S(SALES) OR P ?S
FIXED COSTS ?50000
VARIABLE COST RATE? ENTER AS A DECIMAL
IN RELATION TO SALES ?.50
DESIRED NET PROFIT? ENTER  $ AMT OR DEC. PORTION OF SALES ?.23

FOR A NET PROFIT OF 23 % THERE MUST BE 185185 IN SALES

HAVE ANOTHER? ANS Y OR N ?Y

DESIRE SALES OR NET PROFIT? ANS S(SALES) OR P ?S
FIXED COSTS ?10000
VARIABLE COST RATE? ENTER AS A DECIMAL
IN RELATION TO SALES ?.50
DESIRED NET PROFIT? ENTER  $ AMT OR DEC. PORTION OF SALES ?.50

% DIVISION BY ZERO IN LINE 130

FOR A NET PROFIT OF 50 % THERE MUST BE 1.70141E+38 IN SALES

HAVE ANOTHER? ANS Y OR N ?Y

DESIRE SALES OR NET PROFIT? ANS S(SALES) OR P ?P
FIXED COSTS ?25000
VARIABLE COST RATE? ENTER AS A DECIMAL
IN RELATION TO SALES ?.50
ESTIMATED SALES ?300000

WITH SALES OF  300000 YOUR PROFIT WILL BE 125000

HAVE ANOTHER? ANS Y OR N ?N

TIME:  0.93 SECS.

READY
```

Fig. 15-10.   Execution of BEANAL.

profit rate were both entered as .50. This resulted in an attempt to use the second formula above when the divisor was zero. This attempt generated an error message and a meaningless answer.

Planning a Cost Increase (COSINC)

Assume a manufacturing company has a file that contains a particular record for each part they make. Each record contains a line number; a part number; a description; the number of hours spent on making the part in each of three manufacturing departments; and the present dollars of direct labor spent to produce it.

The company is experiencing the prospects of pay rate increases, and they want to know what the projected costs will be by item. They want a printed list of the projections, and they also want an updated file reflecting that situation. An immediate printout of the new file is also required.

A program flowchart is shown in Fig. 15-11. It begins with a step to input the new pay rates for the respective departments. The reason for obtaining records by means of INPUT instead of READ is described below.

Once the original file has been completely processed into a new file, it is time to input the new file in order to print its contents. Note the use of RESTORE to rewind file number 2 to its beginning point.

The first portion of Fig. 15-12 shows a list of the original file (MASCOS). Note that line number 400 (part number 33 for EX. MAN.) has quotes around its description to avoid the problem explained on pages 160 and 161.

The SCRATCH instruction is used in line 30 to make it possible to output to the PROCST file. The QUOTE in line 40 carries any quote symbols from the input file to the output file. Thus when the PROCST file is read later, no DATA ERROR problem will occur with nonnumeric fields.

Note the INPUT statement is used to obtain detail records in line 120 instead of the READ statement. INPUT, unlike READ, does read line numbers, and a variable name (L) is provided into which to read the line number. Thus that same line number is used when outputting to the PROCST file.

The RESTORE in line number 210 converts the output file PROCST to an input file and also "rewinds" it to its beginning point.

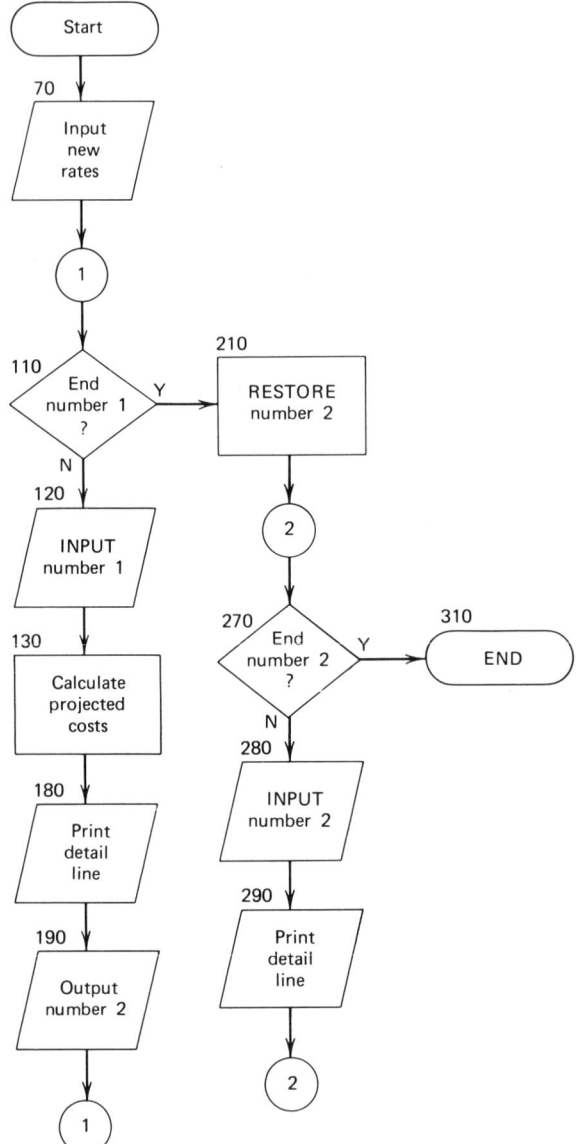

Fig. 15-11. Program flowchart—COSINC.

```
OLD MASCOS

READY
LISTNH
100 12 ENGINE 10, 14, 8, 134
200 18 TRANS. 5, 3, 0, 35
300 27  DIFF. 14, 0, 3, 65
400 33 "EX. MAN." 0, 1, 1, 8
500 41 RADIATOR 4, 3, 4, 43

READY
OLD COSINC

READY
LISTNH
10     REM FIG. 15-12.
20 FILES MASCOS, PROCST
30 SCRATCH # 2
40 QUOTE #2
50 PRINT "ENTER NEW LABOR RATES";
60 PRINT " FOR THE 3 DEPTS."
70 INPUT D1, D2, D3
80 PRINT
90 PRINT "PART NO.", "DESCR.", "PRES. COST",
100 PRINT "PROJ. INC.", "PROJ. TOT."
110 IF END # 1 THEN 210
120 INPUT #1, L, P, D$, H1, H2, H3, T
130 I1 = INT ( H1 * D1)
140 I2 = INT ( H2 * D2)
150 I3 = INT ( H3 * D3)
160 I4 = I1 + I2 + I3 -T
170 T1 = I1 + I2 + I3
180 PRINT P, D$, T, I4, T1
190 PRINT #2 L;P;D$;H1;H2;H3;T1
200 GO TO 110
210 RESTORE # .2
220 PRINT
230 PRINT TAB(20) "CONTENTS OF OUTPUT FILE"
240 PRINT
250 PRINT "LINE"; TAB(6)"PART"; TAB(11)"DESC"; TAB(19)"DEPT.1",
260 PRINT "DEPT.2", "DEPT. 3", "TOTAL"
270 IF END # 2 THEN 310
280 INPUT #2, L, P, D$, H1, H2, H3, T1
290 PRINT L; P; TAB(11)D$; TAB(21)H1, H2, H3, T1
300 GO TO 270
310 END

READY
```

Variable Name Legend

D1	} New labor rates for
D2	} 3 departments
D3	
L	Line number
P	Part number
D$	Description
H1	} Hours in each
H2	} department
H3	
T	Total cost, original
I1	
I2	} Projected increased costs
I3	
I4	Projected total increase
T1	Projected total cost

Fig. 15-12. Original data and program listing of COSINC.

Line numbers 270 through 300 then read the records from the file and print it in detail.

Program execution appears in Fig. 15-13. At the very bottom, the file PROCST is also listed. Note that the quotes have followed the description of line number 400.

```
RUN NH


ENTER NEW LABOR RATES FOR THE 3 DEPTS.
 ?6, 6, 5

PART NO.       DESCR.       PRES. COST    PROJ. INC.     PROJ. TOT.
   12          ENGINE          134           50             184
   18          TRANS.           35           13              48
   27          DIFF.            65           34              99
   33          EX. MAN.          8            3              11
   41          RADIATOR         43           19              62
                     CONTENTS OF OUTPUT FILE

LINE   PART DESC      DEPT.1    DEPT.2       DEPT. 3        TOTAL
 100   12   ENGINE      10        14           8             184
 200   18   TRANS.       5         3           0              48
 300   27   DIFF.       14         0           3              99
 400   33   EX. MAN.     0         1           1              11
 500   41   RADIATOR     4         3           4              62


TIME:  0.50 SECS.

READY
OLD PROCST

READY
LISTNH
100   12   ENGINE 10  14   8   184
200   18   TRANS. 5  3   0   48
300   27   DIFF. 14   0   3   99
400   33   "EX. MAN." 0  1   1   11
500   41   RADIATOR 4   3   4   62

READY
```

Fig. 15-13. Program execution—COSINC.

EXERCISES

1. What is the difference between a variable budget and a fixed budget?

2. Describe what break-even analysis means. How would a business use break-even analysis? How could we use the technique in our personal lives?

3. In Fig. 15-2:
   (a) On what basis does "INVALID CODE – TRY AGAIN" print?
   (b) Add the necessary steps to the program that will count the number of times an invalid code has been entered at line number 130. When the user has entered more than two invalid codes within one program execution, cause the computer to print an appropriate statement.
   (c) Make the changes to the program so that the printed results would be in either of these two formats:

	MARKUP ON SALES		MARKUP ON COST	
	$	%	$	%
Sales	100	100	150	—
Cost	50	50	100	100
	*****	*****	*****	*****
Markup	50	50	50	50

4. How complicated would the program NETPAY (Fig. 15-4) become if it had to provide for social security taxes on the basis of real life rates? Answer in a verbal sense unless you would like the challenge of preparing the specific coding.

5. In Fig. 15-6:
   (a) If it were required to calculate a budget at 110% of normal capacity, would it be a matter of just multiplying the cost at the normal capacity (the 100% column) by 110%? Why?
   (b) Add all of the steps necessary to provide for an additional category of expenses called OTHER (or MISCELLANEOUS). Provide for a fixed and a variable portion of that expense.

(c) Since depreciation, insurance, and property taxes are classified as fixed in this example, rewrite the program so they are totaled and printed as one line on the budget. Retain the present method of entering the raw data for those elements of cost.

(d) Change line number 580 so that the heading is centered over the budget.

(e) Cause a dollar sign to be printed in front of each amount on the total budget line.

6. Change the coding in Fig. 15-9 so that the printed results would appear in the following manner:

	$	%
Sales	1000	100
Variable costs	600	60
	*****	*****
Contribution	400	40
Fixed costs	200	20
	*****	*****
Net income	200	20

7. Write a program that would print a "break-even table." The rows should reflect fixed costs in increments of $1000; the columns should represent various variable cost rates; and the data in the body of the table (the answers) would show break-even sales dollars.

8. Write a program that would use the concept of MARKUP in this chapter. Provide for a table of output such as the one below.

MARKUP Based on Cost			
Required Selling Price			
COST	30%	40%	50%	60%
10	13	14	15	16
20	26	28	30	32
30	39	42	45	48

Also, provide for another segment of printed output that would show the required selling price with the MARKUP based on selling price.

9. The records in an inventory file (FILES) contain part number, description, quantity sold last year, quantity sold last month, and current balance on hand. A program is to be written that will print a reordering report by item.

If the annual rate of the quantity sold last month is equal to or greater than the quantity sold last year, order an amount equal to the quantity sold last month if the latter is greater than the current balance; otherwise, order none. If the annual rate of the quantity sold last month is less than the quantity sold last year, order an amount equal to 1/12 of the quantity sold last year if the latter is greater than the current balance; otherwise, order none.

Write the program so that it will print the status of all items or only those that need reordering (according to the user's wish).

Also, provide the user an option to output the status of all items to a new file. In addition, make it possible to obtain a random sample from the original file.

16 CHAPTER
FINANCE

In this chapter, we will see four programs directly related to the problems involved in finance—the raising of money. While many financial matters deal with the need to enter and manipulate large volumes of data, the topics chosen here require the use of relatively little data. The programs are quite appropriate for time-sharing solution.

Financial Ratios (FINRAT)

Ratio analysis is a financial tool that is used by the management of a business, its creditors, and its present or potential investors. The purpose of the analysis is to determine the interrelationships that exist among various financial accounts within the business. The accounts might represent historical data, or they could be estimated account balances based on proposed actions.

The ratios are typically prepared for several accounting periods in a row to check for trends. Also, the ratios are typically compared to those of other firms in the same or similar industries.

The program shown here calculates 17 of the common ratios. Rather than to go into the significance of each of the ratios here, the bibliography in Appendix F refers to accounting and financial sources for such information.

The program FINRAT does require the user to input 24 separate values. Since this program has not been designed to clearly lead the way

	INPUT Names		Calculated Values
A$	Date	A1	Working capital
B	Sales	B1	Current ratio
C	Cost of goods sold	C1	Acid test ratio
D	Net income	D1	Accounts receivable turnover
E	Cash	E1	Days sales in accounts receivable
F	Accounts receivable (current year end)	F1	Inventory turnover
		G1	Days sales in inventory
G	Accounts receivable (prior year end)	H1	Gross profit rate
		I1	Net profit to assets
H	Inventory (current year end)	J1	Net profit to net worth
I	Inventory (prior year end)	K1	Net worth to liabilities
J	Other current assets	L1	Fixed assets to long-term debt
K	Land, buildings, and equipment	M1	Net worth to fixed assets
L	Accumulated depreciation	N1	% of fixed assets depreciated
M	Other assets	O1	Book value per share
N	Total assets (prior year end)	P1	Earnings per share
O	Current liabilities	Q1	Price/earnings ratio
P	Long Term debt		
Q	Other liabilities		
R	Preferred stock		
S	Common stock		
T	Retained earnings		
U	Stockholders equity (prior year end)		
V	Market value common stock		
W	Shares of common outstanding		
X	Preferred stock dividends		

Fig. 16-1. Variable data names for FINRAT.

on providing for INPUT other than to print the ?, all of the variable data names and their meanings are separately shown in Fig. 16-1. (A much longer version of the program could provide this information and various options to the user.)

The program listing is reproduced in Fig. 16-2. The output variable names can easily be seen in PRINT line numbers 330 through 540. There are no new BASIC steps. The approach is quite straightforward; input the raw data, calculate all the ratios, and then print all the answers. Note that it doesn't make much difference if calculation is done in a wholesale fashion and then all output is performed later, as opposed to calculating one ratio; printing it; and then going on to calculate the next.

Program execution in Fig. 16-3 shows the financial ratios of a certain business calculated from data shown in their 1976 annual report. The

```
3    REM FIG. 16-2.
5     REM INPUT ALL DATA.
10 INPUT A$, B, C, D
20 INPUT E, F, G, H
30 INPUT I, J, K, L
40 INPUT M, N, O, P
50 INPUT Q, R, S, T
60 INPUT U, V, W, X
80    REM CALCULATE ALL ANSWERS.
100 A1 = E + F + H + J - O
110 B1 =INT ((( E + F + H + J) / O) * 100 + .5) / 100
120 C1 = INT ((( E + F) / O) * 100 + .5) / 100
130 D1 = INT ( B/ (( F + G) / 2) * 10 + .5) / 10
140 E1 = INT ( F/(B/300))
150 F1 = INT ( C/(( H + I) / 2) * 10 + .5) / 10
160 G1 = INT ( H / ( C / 300))
170 H1 = INT (( B - C) / B * 1000 + .5) / 10
180 I1 = INT(D/(((E + F + H + J + K - L + M + N) /2) * 1000 + .5) / 10
190 J1 = INT ( D / (( R + S + T + U) / 2) * 1000 + .5) / 10
200 K1 = INT (( R + S + T) / (O + P + Q) * 100 + .5) / 100
210 L1 = INT (( K-L) / P * 100 + .5) / 100
220 M1 = INT (( R + S + T) / (K -L) * 100 + .5) / 100
230 N1 = INT (L/K * 100 + .5)
240 O1 = INT (( S + T) / W * 100 + .5) / 100
250 P1 = INT (( D - X) / W * 100 + .5) / 100
260 Q1 = INT (( V / P1) * 10 + .5) / 10
280    REM PRINT ALL ANSWERS
300 PRINT
310 PRINT
320 PRINT TAB(60) A$
325 PRINT
330 PRINT TAB(1) "WORKING CAPITAL"; TAB(60)A1
340 PRINT TAB(1) "CURRENT RATIO"; TAB(60) B1
350 PRINT TAB(1)"ACID TEST"; TAB(60) C1
360 PRINT
370 PRINT TAB(1)"A/R TURN"; TAB(60) D1
380 PRINT TAB(1)"AVE DAYS SALES IN A/R @ YEAR-END"; TAB(60) E1
390 PRINT TAB(1)"INV. TURN."; TAB(60) F1.
400 PRINT
410 PRINT TAB(1)"# OF DAYS SALES IN INV. @ YEAR-END"; TAB(60)G1
420 PRINT TAB(1)"GROSS PROFIT RATE"; TAB(60) H1
430 PRINT TAB(1)"NET PROFIT TO AVERAGE ASSETS"; TAB(60) I1
440 PRINT
450 PRINT TAB(1)"NET PROFIT TO NET WORTH"; TAB(60) J1
460 PRINT TAB(1)"NET WORTH TO LIAB."; TAB(60) K1
470 PRINT TAB(1)"FIXED ASSETS TO L. T. D."; TAB (60) L1
480 PRINT
490 PRINT TAB(1)"NET WORTH TO FIXED ASSETS"; TAB(60) M1
500 PRINT TAB(1)"% FIXED ASSETS DEPRECIATED"; TAB(60) N1
510 PRINT TAB(1)"BOOK VALUE"; TAB(60) O1
520 PRINT
530 PRINT TAB(1) "EARNINGS PER SHARE"; TAB(60) P1
540 PRINT TAB(1)"P/E RATIO"; TAB(60) Q1
600 END

READY
```

Fig. 16-2. Program listing of FINRAT.

```
?12/31/76, 100000, 50000, 5000
?25000, 30000, 23000, 40000
?340000, 45000, 21000, 12000
?16000, 88000, 23000, 12000
?32000, 12200, 24000, 2000
?56000, 12.50, 1500, 2500
```

	12/31/76
WORKING CAPITAL	117000
CURRENT RATIO	6.09
ACID TEST	2.39
A/R TURN	3.8
AVE DAYS SALES IN A/R @ YEAR-END	90
INV. TURN.	0.3
# OF DAYS SALES IN INV. @ YEAR-END	240
GROSS PROFIT RATE	50
NET PROFIT TO AVERAGE ASSETS	4
NET PROFIT TO NET WORTH	10.6
NET WORTH TO LIAB.	0.57
FIXED ASSETS TO L. T. D.	0.75
NET WORTH TO FIXED ASSETS	4.24
% FIXED ASSETS DEPRECIATED	57
BOOK VALUE	17.33
EARNINGS PER SHARE	1.67
P/E RATIO	7.5

```
TIME:  0.76 SECS.

READY
```

Fig. 16-3. Execution of FINRAT.

ratio name has been clearly spelled out, the ratios themselves are printed starting in TAB position 60, and there is a blank line after each set of three ratios.

Paying Off a Mortgage (MTGE)

A mortgage is a particular type of long-term loan that is usually secured by title to real estate. The common mortgage arrangement is that the borrower will make equal monthly payments throughout the life of the loan. A portion of each payment will cover the interest applicable to the outstanding loan balance; the rest of the payment will be used to reduce the outstanding loan balance.

Based upon such factors as the original loan amount, the interest rate, and the life of the loan, the portion of the payment that goes to reduce the outstanding loan balance generally starts out rather small and slowly becomes larger as the interest amount applicable to the loan balance declines.

Both borrower and lender are naturally interested in the amount of the monthly payment that is required to pay off any given mortgage. In trying to develop the logic as to how to calculate that required amount, you might look at the situation from the standpoint of the lender. The lender is making a lump sum investment (the principal) and is getting that money and a return (the interest) back as an annuity in equal monthly receipts.

The general formula that will calculate the required payment is:

$$P1 = P * \frac{I}{1 - (1 / (1 + I)) * * L}$$

In the formula the variable names have the following uses.

> P1 = Required payment.
> P = Original loan amount (principal).
> I = Interest rate (annual basis).
> L = Life in years (number of annual periods).

Since in this case we are concerned about monthly payments, the formula in the program has been altered to use the interest rate on a monthly basis. Also, the mortgage life is multiplied by 12 to convert it to the number of months.

Both the borrower and the lender are also usually interested in their relative standings at any point during the life of the loan. To satisfy the need for such information, the program prints a complete schedule broken down by period. The program must break out those parts of the payment that apply to interest and to principal reduction, as well as calculate the remaining principal balance.

The logic of the program is shown in Fig. 16-4. The FOR and NEXT method is used instead of a counter and an IF statement to determine when the schedule has been completed.

The program listing appears as Fig. 16-5. Please carefully note the coding in line number 110. Since L, the life in years, could be whatever value the user chooses to enter, the factor following TO (in the FOR statement) is a variable rather than a constant amount and must be multiplied

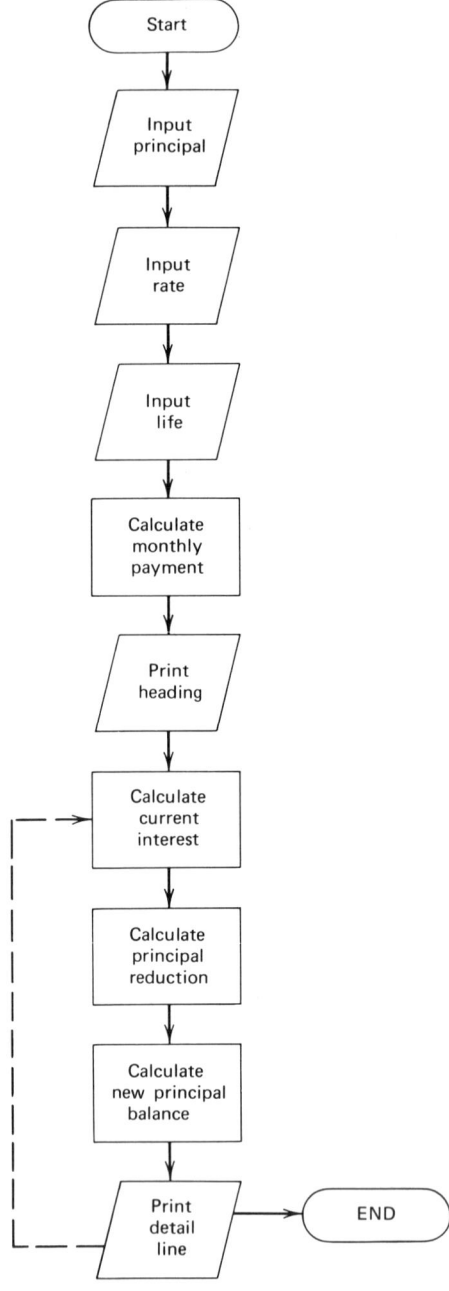

Fig. 16-4. Program flowchart—MTGE.

P	Principal balance		NEXT loop by month
I	Rate	P2	Interest (current)
L	Life		
P1	Monthly payment	P3	Principal reduction (current)
M	Value for FOR-		

```
5     REM FIG. 16-5.
10 PRINT "ENTER MTGE. PRIN.";
20 INPUT P
30 PRINT "ENTER INT. RATE";
40 INPUT I
50 PRINT "ENTER LIFE IN YEARS";
60 INPUT L
70 P1 = P * (I/12) / (1-(1/(1+(I/12)) ** (L * 12)))
80 P1 = INT (P1 * 100 + .5) / 100
85 PRINT
90 PRINT "PERIOD", "PAYMENT", "INTEREST", "PRIN RED.", "PRIN BAL."
100 PRINT " 0", , , , P
110 FOR M = 1 TO L * 12
120 P2 = P * I/12
130 P2 = INT (P2 * 100 + .5) / 100
140 P3 = P1 - P2
150 P = INT (( P - P3) * 100 + .5) / 100
160 PRINT M, P1, P2, P3 , P
170 NEXT M
180 END

READY
```

Fig. 16-5. Program listing of MTGE.

by 12 to convert it to months. This establishes the number of times the loop will be executed.

Three sample runs of the program appear in Fig. 16-6. Note that while a mortgage generally applies to a long term, the concept regarding payments and interest works just as well for short periods. When a fractional part of a year is entered, however, care must be taken so that the fractional part of a year represents a number of whole months, not any part of a month.

Establishing a Loan Rate (INRATE)

Interest rates on loans are generally set at a level to cover the pure cost of money plus a factor to cover the relative risk attached to the loan. The program in this section shows in a hypothetical manner how a financial institution might try to quantify the rate-setting aspect of a loan as much as it reasonably can.

Assume that the institution has already decided to grant the loan. The remaining part of the job is to establish the interest rate. You may find it an interesting task to work through the logic from the program list-

```
RUN NH

ENTER MTGE. PRIN. ?25000
ENTER INT. RATE ?.08
ENTER LIFE IN YEARS ?2
```

PERIOD	PAYMENT	INTEREST	PRIN RED.	PRIN BAL.
0				25000
1	1130.68	166.67	964.01	24036.
2	1130.68	160.24	970.44	23065.6
3	1130.68	153.77	976.91	22038.6
4	1130.68	147.26	983.42	21105.2
5	1130.68	140.7	989.98	20115.2
6	1130.68	134.1	996.58	19118.7
7	1130.68	127.46	1003.22	18115.4
8	1130.68	120.77	1009.91	17105.5
9	1130.68	114.04	1016.64	16088.9
10	1130.68	107.26	1023.42	15065.5
11	1130.68	100.44	1030.24	14035.2
12	1130.68	93.57	1037.11	12998.1
13	1130.68	86.65	1044.03	11954.1
14	1130.68	79.69	1050.99	10903.1
15	1130.68	72.69	1057.99	9845.11
16	1130.68	65.63	1065.05	8780.06
17	1130.68	58.53	1072.15	7707.91
18	1130.68	51.39	1079.29	6628.62
19	1130.68	44.19	1086.49	5542.13
20	1130.68	36.95	1093.73	4448.4
21	1130.68	29.66	1101.02	3347.38
22	1130.68	22.32	1108.36	2239.02
23	1130.68	14.93	1115.75	1123.27
24	1130.68	7.49	1123.19	0.08

```
TIME:   0.63 SECS.

READY
```

Fig. 16-6. Execution of MTGE (completed on page 235).

ing in Fig. 16-7. In all, there are 11 factors that are considered in arriving at the rate.

Two executions of the program are shown in Fig. 16-8.

Alternative Methods of Raising Money (LEVER)

While there are many means by which money may be obtained for business purposes, we will restrict ourselves to just three methods in this section. Those three are through the sale of either common stock or preferred stock, and borrowing through bonds.

```
RUN NH


ENTER MTGE. PRIN. ?12000
ENTER INT. RATE ?.10
ENTER LIFE IN YEARS ?1

PERIOD          PAYMENT         INTEREST        PRIN RED.       PRIN BAL.
0                                                               12000
1               1054.99         100             954.99          11045.
2               1054.99         92.04           962.95          10082.1
3               1054.99         84.02           970.97          9111.09
4               1054.99         75.93           979.06          8132.03
5               1054.99         67.77           987.22          7144.81
6               1054.99         59.54           995.45          6149.36
7               1054.99         51.24           1003.75         5145.61
8               1054.99         42.88           1012.11         4133.5
9               1054.99         34.45           1020.54         3112.96
10              1054.99         25.94           1029.05         2083.91
11              1054.99         17.37           1037.62         1046.29
12              1054.99         8.72            1046.27         0.02


TIME:   0.40 SECS.

READY
RUN NH


ENTER MTGE. PRIN. ?500
ENTER INT. RATE ?.09
ENTER LIFE IN YEARS ?.25

PERIOD          PAYMENT         INTEREST        PRIN RED.       PRIN BAL.
0                                                               500
1               169.17          3.75            165.42          334.58
2               169.17          2.51            166.66          167.92
3               169.17          1.26            167.91          0.01


TIME:   0.23 SECS.

READY
```

Fig. 16-6. cont.

The purpose of this program is to concentrate on the aspect of finance that will maintain the earning power of the common stock. Stating it in another way, the program will be written so that it will reveal any dilution in the ownership of the common stockholders.

Briefly, a significant feature of each of the three methods is:

1. Common stock—unless the additional profit generated by the use of

```
3    REM FIG. 16-7.
5  PRINT
10 PRINT "AMT OF LOAN";
15 INPUT A
20 IF A = 0 THEN 900
25 IF A > 1000 THEN 40
30 A1 = 4
35 GO TO 45
40 A1 = 2
45 PRINT "APPLICANTS AGE ";
50 INPUT B
55 IF B <= 25 THEN 75
60 IF B < 40 THEN 85
65 IF B < = 60 THEN 95
70 IF B > 60 THEN 105
75 B1 = 3
80 GO TO 110
85 B1 = 2
90 GO TO 110
95 B1 = 1
100 GO TO 110
105 B1 = 4
110 PRINT "APPLICANTS SALARY";
115 INPUT C
120 IF C = 0 THEN 140
125 IF C < 10000 THEN 150
130 IF C < 20000 THEN 160
135 IF C >= 20000 THEN 170
140 C1 = 16
145 GOTO 175
150 C1 = 12
155 GO TO 175
160 C1 = 8
165 GO TO 175
170 C1 = 4
175 PRINT "# OF JOBS IN LAST 5 YEARS";
180 INPUT D
185 IF D = 1 THEN 210
190 IF D = 2 THEN 220
195 IF D <= 4 THEN 230
200 IF D > 4 THEN 240
210 D1 = 3
215 GO TO 245
220 D1 = 6
225 GO TO 245
230 D1 = 12
235 GO TO 245
240 D1 = 15
245 PRINT "JOB SECURITY? ANS EXC = 1, GOOD = 2, POOR = 3 ";
250 INPUT E
255 IF E = 1 THEN 270
260 IF E = 2 THEN 280
265 IF E > 2 THEN 290
270 E1 = 3
275 GO TO 295
280 E1 = 6
285 GO TO 295
290 E1 = 12
295 PRINT "MARRIED OR SINGLE? ANS M OR S";
300 INPUT F$
```

Variable Name Legend

A	Amount of loan
A1	Points for loan amount
B	Age
B1	Points for age
C	Salary
C1	Points for salary
D	Number of jobs
D1	Points for number of jobs
E	Job security
E1	Points for job security
F$	Code for married or single
F1	Points for married or single
G1	Points for spouse's age
H1	Points for spouse's salary
G	Spouse's age
H	Spouse's salary
I	Credit rating
I1	Points for credit rating
J	Other debts
J1	Points for other debts
K	Prime interest rate
K1	Points for prime interest rate
L	Total points
Z$	Literal for "Interest Rate"

Fig. 16-7. *Program listing of INRATE* (continued on page 237).

```
305 IF F$ = "M" THEN 330
310 F1 = 7
315 G1 = 0
320 H1 = 0
325 GO TO 430
330 F1 = 1
335 PRINT "SPOUSES   AGE";
340 INPUT G
345 IF G <= 25 THEN 365
350 IF G < 40 THEN 375
355 IF G <= 60 THEN 385
360 IF G > 60 THEN 395
365 G1 = 3
370 GO TO 400
375 G1 = 2
380 GO TO 400
385 G1 = 1
390 GO TO 400
395 G1 = 4
400 PRINT "SPOUSES SALARY";
405 INPUT H
410 IF H > 15000 THEN 425
415 H1 = 4
420 GO TO 430
425 H1 = 2
430 PRINT "CREDIT   RATING - ANS EXC = 1, GOOD = 2";
433 PRINT "POOR = 3, NONE = 4";
435 INPUT I
440 IF I = 1 THEN 460
445 IF I = 2 THEN 470
450 IF I = 3 THEN 480
455 IF I = 4 THEN 470
457 GO TO 480
460 I1 = 4
465 GO TO 485
470 I1 = 8
475 GO TO 485
480 I1 = 16
485 PRINT "OTH. DEBTS - ANS NONE = 1, LOW OR AVE = 2, LARGE = 3";
490 INPUT J
495 IF J = 1 THEN 510
500 IF J = 2 THEN 525
505 IF J > 2 THEN 535
510 J1 = 3
520 GO TO 540
525 J1 = 6
530 GO TO 540
535 J1 = 12
540 PRINT "PRIME INT. RATE";
545 INPUT K
547 IF K < 1 THEN 550
548 K = K /100
550 IF K < .08 THEN 570
555 IF K < .085 THEN 580
560 IF K < .10 THEN 590
565 GO TO 600
570 K1 = 3
575 GO TO 605
580 K1 = 6
585 GO TO 605
590 K1 = 9
```

Fig. 16-7. cont. (completed on page 238).

```
595 GO TO 605
600 K1 = 12
603    REM TOTALS UP POINTS.
605 L = A1 + B1 + C1 + D1 + E1 + F1 + G1 + H1 + I1 + J1 + K1
610 Z$ = "INTEREST RATE"
612 PRINT
614    REM TESTS FOR POINT TOTAL.
615 IF L <= 33 THEN 700
620 IF L < 39 THEN 710
625 IF L < 45 THEN 720
630 IF L < 51 THEN 730
635 IF L < 57 THEN 740
640 IF L < 63 THEN 750
645 IF L < 69 THEN 760
650 IF L < 75 THEN 770
655 IF L < 81 THEN 780
670 IF L < 87 THEN 790
675 IF L < 93 THEN 800
680 IF L < 99 THEN 810
685 GO TO 820
690    REM PRINTS THE APPLICABLE RATE.
700 PRINT Z$, "9.3%"
705 GO TO 900
710 PRINT Z$, "9.5%"
715 GO TO 900
720 PRINT Z$, "9.8%"
725 GO TO 900
730 PRINT Z$, "10%"
735 GO TO 900
740 PRINT Z$, "10.3%"
745 GO TO 900
750 PRINT Z$, "10.7%"
755 GO TO 900
760 PRINT Z$, "11%"
765 GO TO 900
770 PRINT Z$, "11.5%"
775 GO TO 900
780 PRINT Z$, "12%"
785 GO TO 900
790 PRINT Z$, "12.5%"
795 GO TO 900
800 PRINT Z$, "13%"
805 GO TO 900
810 PRINT Z$, "13.5%"
815 GO TO 900
820 PRINT Z$, "14%"
900 END

READY
```

Fig. 16-7. cont.

the new funds is sufficient, the resulting earnings per common share will be less than they were before the financing.

2. Preferred stock—if there are any dividends to be paid, the preferred owners generally get paid before there are any earnings available to

```
RUN NH


AMT OF LOAN ?1000
APPLICANTS AGE   ?45
APPLICANTS SALARY ?10000
# OF JOBS IN LAST 5 YEARS ?1
JOB SECURITY? ANS EXC = 1, GOOD = 2, POOR = 3  ?1
MARRIED OR SINGLE? ANS M OR S ?M
SPOUSES   AGE ?32
SPOUSES SALARY ?5000
CREDIT  RATING - ANS EXC = 1, GOOD = 2POOR = 3, NONE = 4 ?1
OTH. DEBTS - ANS NONE = 1, LOW OR AVE = 2, LARGE = 3 ?1
PRIME INT. RATE ?8

INTEREST RATE 9.8%



TIME:  0.61 SECS.

READY
RUN NH



AMT OF LOAN ?1200
APPLICANTS AGE   ?21
APPLICANTS SALARY ?3500
# OF JOBS IN LAST 5 YEARS ?4
JOB SECURITY? ANS EXC = 1, GOOD = 2, POOR = 3  ?3
MARRIED OR SINGLE? ANS M OR S ?S
CREDIT  RATING - ANS EXC = 1, GOOD = 2POOR = 3, NONE = 4 ?4
OTH. DEBTS - ANS NONE = 1, LOW OR AVE = 2, LARGE = 3 ?3
PRIME INT. RATE ?12

INTEREST RATE 12%




TIME:  0.62 SECS.

READY
```

Fig. 16-8. Execution of INRATE.

common stockholders. Also, any dividends paid on the preferred stock
are not deductible (as an expense) for income tax purposes.

3. Bonds—bond interest expense is deductible (as a cost) for income tax
purposes. If the venture being financed is successful, the earnings over
and above interest costs will have been well worth it to common stock
owners.

FINANCE 239

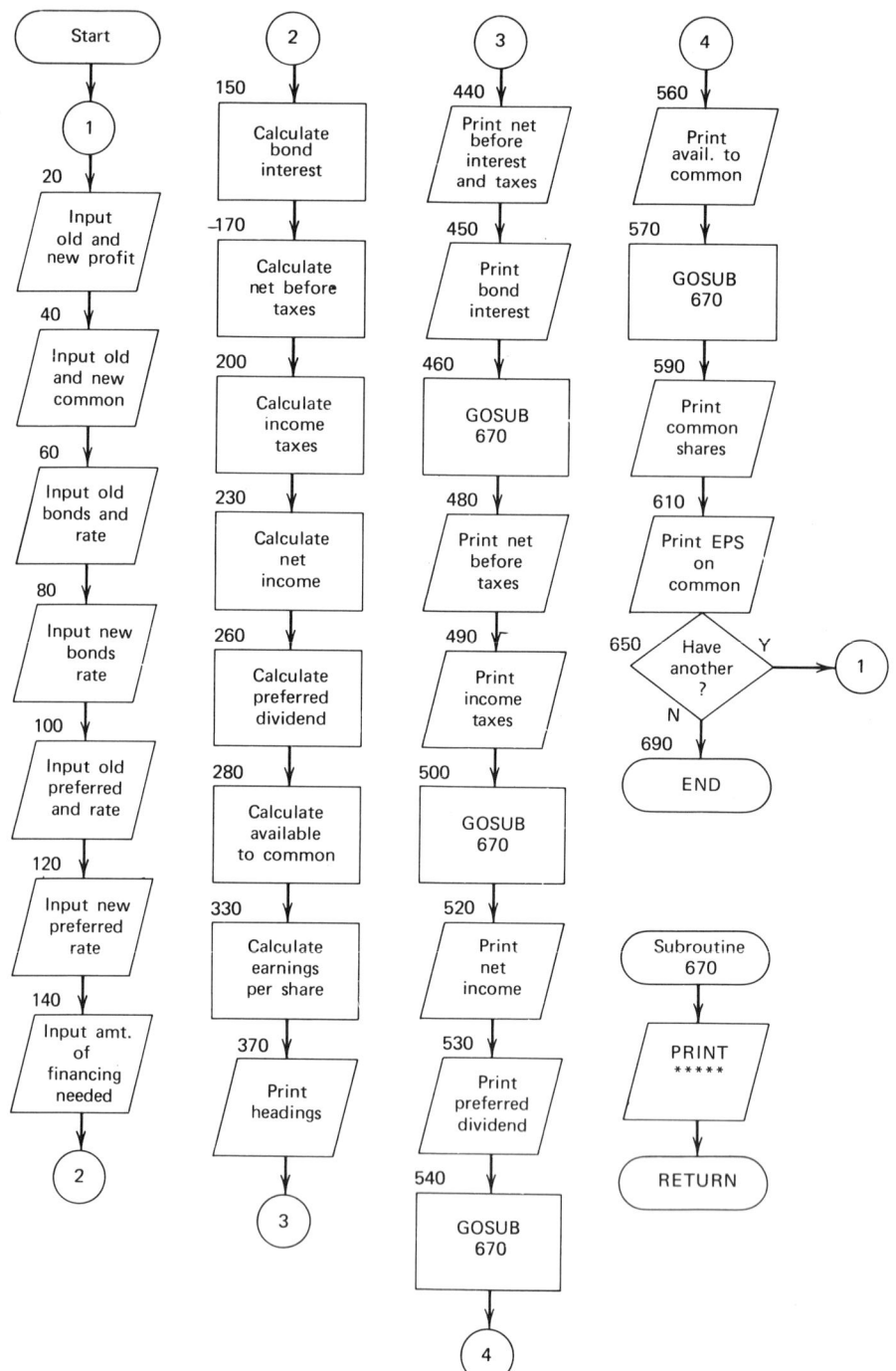

Fig. 16-9. Program flowchart—LEVER.

```
5     REM FIG16-10.
10 PRINT "ENTER OLD & NEW NET PROFIT BEFORE";
12 PRINT "TAXES & INTEREST";
20 INPUT A1, A2
30 PRINT "ENTER PRES. & ADDIT. # OF";
35 PRINT "COMMON SHARES";
40 INPUT B1, B2
50 PRINT "EMTER PRES. AMT. BONDS O/S";
55 PRINT "& INT. RATE";
60 INPUT C1, C2
70 PRINT "ENTER INT. RATE ON NEW BONDS";
80 INPUT D1
90 PRINT "ENTER PRES. AMT. PFD. O/S";
95 PRINT "& DIV. RATE";
100 INPUT E1, E2
110 PRINT "ENTER DIV. RATE ON NEW PFD.";
120 INPUT F1
130 PRINT "ENTER AMT. OF NEW FINANCING NEEDED";
140 INPUT G
150 H1 = INT (C1 * C2)
160 H2 = H1 + INT (D1 * G)
170 J1 = A1 - H1
180 J2 = A2 - H1
190 J3 = A2 - H2
200 K1 = INT (J1 * .50)
210 K2 = INT (J2 * .50)
220 K3 = INT (J3 * .50)
230 L1 = J1 - K1
240 L2 = J2 - K2
250 L3 = J3 - K3
260 M1 = INT (E1 * E2)
270 M2 = M1 + INT (F1 * G)
280 N1 = L1 - M1
290 N2 = L2 - M1
300 N3 = L2 - M2
310 N4 = L3 - M1
320 P1 = B1 + B2
330 Q1 = INT (N1 / B1 * 100 + .5) / 100
340 Q2 = INT (N2 / P1 * 100 + .5) / 100
350 Q3 = INT (N3 / B1 * 100 + .5) / 100
360 Q4 = INT ( N4 / B1 * 100 + .5) / 100
370 PRINT
380 PRINT "NPBT&I = NET PROFIT BEFORE TAXES & INTEREST"
390 PRINT "NPBT = NET PROFIT BEFORE TAXES"
400 PRINT
410 PRINT , "PRESENT", TAB(36) "PROJECTED POSITION"
420 PRINT , "POSITION", "COMMON", "PFD. STOCK", "BONDS"
430 PRINT
440 PRINT "NPBT&I", A1, A2, A2, A2
450 PRINT "INT. ON BONDS", H1, H1, H1, H2
460 GOSUB 670
470 PRINT
480 PRINT "NPBT", J1, J2, J2, J3
490 PRINT "TAXES(50%)", K1, K2, K2, K3
500 GOSUB 670
510 PRINT
520 PRINT "NET. INCOME", L1, L2, L2, L3
530 PRINT "PFD. DIV.", M1, M1, M2, M1
540 GOSUB 670
550 PRINT
```

Fig. 16-10. Program listing of LEVER (completed on page 242).

```
560 PRINT "AVAIL TO COMM", N1, N2, N3, N4
570 GOSUB 670
590 PRINT "COM SHARES", B1, P1, B1, B1
600 PRINT
610 PRINT "EPS ON COMMON", Q1, Q2, Q3, Q4
620 PRINT
630 PRINT "HAVE ANOTHER? ANS Y OR N";
640 INPUT R$
650 IF R$ = "Y" THEN 10
660 GO TO 690
670 PRINT , "*******", "*******", "*******", "*******"
680 RETURN
690 END

READY
```

Variable Name Legend

A1	Old net profit before interest and taxes	L3	New net with bonds
A2	New net profit before interest and taxes	M1	Old preferred dividend
		M2	New preferred dividend
B1	Old common shares	N1	Old available to common
B2	Additional common shares	N2	New available to common with common
C1	Old bonds		
C2	Rate on old bonds	N3	New available to common with preferred
D1	Rate on new bonds		
E1	Old preferred stock	N4	New available to common with bonds
E2	Dividend rate on old preferred stock		
		P1	New total common shares
F1	Dividend rate on new preferred stock	Q1	Old EPS
		Q2	New EPS with common
G	New financing needed	Q3	New EPS with preferred
H1	Interest on old bonds	Q4	New EPS with bonds
H2	Interest on new bonds	R$	Code to continue or not
J1	Old net before taxes		
J2	New net before taxes with common or preferred		
J3	New net before taxes with bonds		
K1	Old taxes		
K2	New taxes with common or preferred		
K3	New taxes with bonds		
L1	Old net income		
L2	New net with common or preferred		

Fig. 16-10. cont.

242 BUSINESS APPLICATIONS USING THE BASIC LANGUAGE

The program flowchart of the logic appears in Fig. 16-9. It begins with the user inputting the budgeted operating profit and the financial structure of the business as it now exists. Then the user enters the relevant factors regarding the financial terms surrounding new financing with common stock, preferred stock, and bonds.

Next, the logic proceeds through calculations whose goal is to prepare the bottom section of an income statement and, ultimately, to show earnings per share on the common stock.

The program listing is in Fig. 16-10 and the execution is in Fig. 16-11. While a number of trial runs with this program may tend to favor bonds as the best alternative, there are many other practical factors to be considered beyond those shown here.

```
RUN NH


ENTER OLD & NEW NET PROFIT BEFORETAXES & INTEREST ?100000, 200000
ENTER PRES. & ADDIT. # OFCOMMON SHARES ?25000, 15000
EMTER PRES. AMT. BONDS O/S& INT. RATE ?0, 0
ENTER INT. RATE ON NEW BONDS ?.12
ENTER PRES. AMT. PFD. O/S& DIV. RATE ?0, 0
ENTER DIV. RATE ON NEW PFD. ?.08
ENTER AMT. OF NEW FINANCING NEEDED ?250000

NPBT&I = NET PROFIT BEFORE TAXES & INTEREST
NPBT = NET PROFIT BEFORE TAXES
```

	PRESENT POSITION	PROJECTED POSITION COMMON	PFD. STOCK	BONDS
NPBT&I	100000	200000	200000	200000
INT. ON BONDS	0	0	0	30000
	*******	*******	*******	*******
NPBT	100000	200000	200000	170000
TAXES(50%)	50000	100000	100000	85000
	*******	*******	*******	*******
NET. INCOME	50000	100000	100000	85000
PFD. DIV.	0	0	20000	0
	*******	*******	*******	*******
AVAIL TO COMM	50000	100000	80000	85000
	*******	*******	*******	*******
COM SHARES	25000	40000	25000	25000
EPS ON COMMON	2	2.5	3.2	3.4

```
HAVE ANOTHER? ANS Y OR N ?N


TIME:  0.72 SECS.

READY
```

Fig. 16-11. Execution of LEVER.

EXERCISES

1. What is the basis on which monthly payments in equal amounts will pay off a mortgage?

2. What tends to make bonds a desirable financing instrument? What is undesirable about them?

3. If you attempted to execute the program in Fig. 16-2, you would find some difficulty in keeping everything straight, since 24 values have to be entered and the INPUT steps do not provide any guides for you. Make all the alterations necessary so that the computer will lead the way and tell you what value to enter next. Also, provide for only one or two input values per line. You might also provide for a way to verify a value after it has been entered (allow an error to be corrected on the spot without needing to start over).

4. In Fig. 16-5:
    (a) What specific coding causes nothing to print under PAYMENT, INTEREST, and PRIN RED. in period zero?
    (b) Change the coding so that the payment amount will appear in the PAYMENT column on the line for period zero only.
    (c) Add those coding steps needed to eliminate the few penny balance in the PRIN BAL. column for the last period. (*Hint.* Make the last payment for exactly the amount needed to retire the principal. Stop the FOR-NEXT loop one cycle earlier.)
    (d) It is obvious that the detail printout for a 20 or 30 year mortgage would be lengthy. Change the program so that, for any mortgage in excess of five years, the printout will show the status in totals only for each year rather than in detail by month.
    (e) Alter the program so that the interest rate can be entered either as a decimal or as a percent.
    (f) In line number 100, why was there one space in front of the zero in the literal? (Delete the space and see if the results differ.)

5. In Fig. 16-7:
    (a) Carefully study the coding in line numbers 485 through 535. Specifically, what would the program do if an OTH. DEBTS

code of 4 were entered? Should a situation such as this one be allowed to remain in a program?

(b) What will the program do if the PRIME INT. RATE would be entered as 12% (including the percent symbol)?

(c) The sample data for the second execution (shown in Fig. 16-8) shows a person who seems to have mostly poor qualities for a loan applicant, but the person still managed to get a loan. Pick some arbitrary but realistic maximum number of points above which the computer will print a RECONSIDER message.

(d) Under what different conditions does the program go to the END?

(e) Is it really possible for the program to specify a rate of 14%? That is, can an overall rating be so poor as to generate an L of 99 or more points?

(f) What is the purpose of line number 610? Show how the printing of "Z$" could be eliminated from all of the PRINT steps.

(g) Alter the coding so that ON and GO TO are used where appropriate.

6. In Fig. 16-10:

(a) What bearing, if any, do presently outstanding preferred stock and bonds have on the results from this program?

(b) Why are there only three lines of coding required to calculate income taxes (200, 210, and 220)?

(c) What would happen if variable A2 (New Net Profit Before Interest and Taxes) would be entered as a negative value? Should the program have a safeguard to prevent such input? Explain.

(d) Describe how the subroutine worked.

7. The program INRATE now provides a lower interest rate for a higher loan amount and a higher interest rate for a smaller loan amount. Change the "weighing" segment of the program so that there is a user option to provide a lower interest rate for small loans.

8. Use the concept of the program INRATE to determine how much maximum credit to allow a borrower based on salary, age, credit rating, outstanding debts, etc. Write such a program.

17 CHAPTER
DEPRECIATION AND TAXES

Both depreciation and income taxes are costs of doing business. The dollar amount of each cost can be accelerated or delayed based on certain acceptable methods of accounting. While neither topic will be presented in depth here, each is covered in a preliminary way to show alternative methods of handling.

Two Common Methods of Depreciation (SYDVSL)

Depreciation is the portion of the original cost of a long-lived asset that is charged to the expenses of operation in any given period of time. Since such an asset under normal conditions is not entirely used up in the year it is obtained, its total cost cannot be charged to the expenses of operation in that one period. Allocating that original cost over an asset's estimated life raises the problem of how much to charge each year, since total depreciation is not known until the asset is disposed of.

The two most common methods of depreciation are straight-line and sum-of-the-years-digits. The straight-line method charges the same amount per year, the amount being determined by dividing the depreciation base (original cost minus estimated scrap value) by the estimated life.

The sum-of-years-digits method is one of several "accelerated" methods. It permits the owner to charge proportionately more than the straight-line amount in the early years of the asset and less in the later

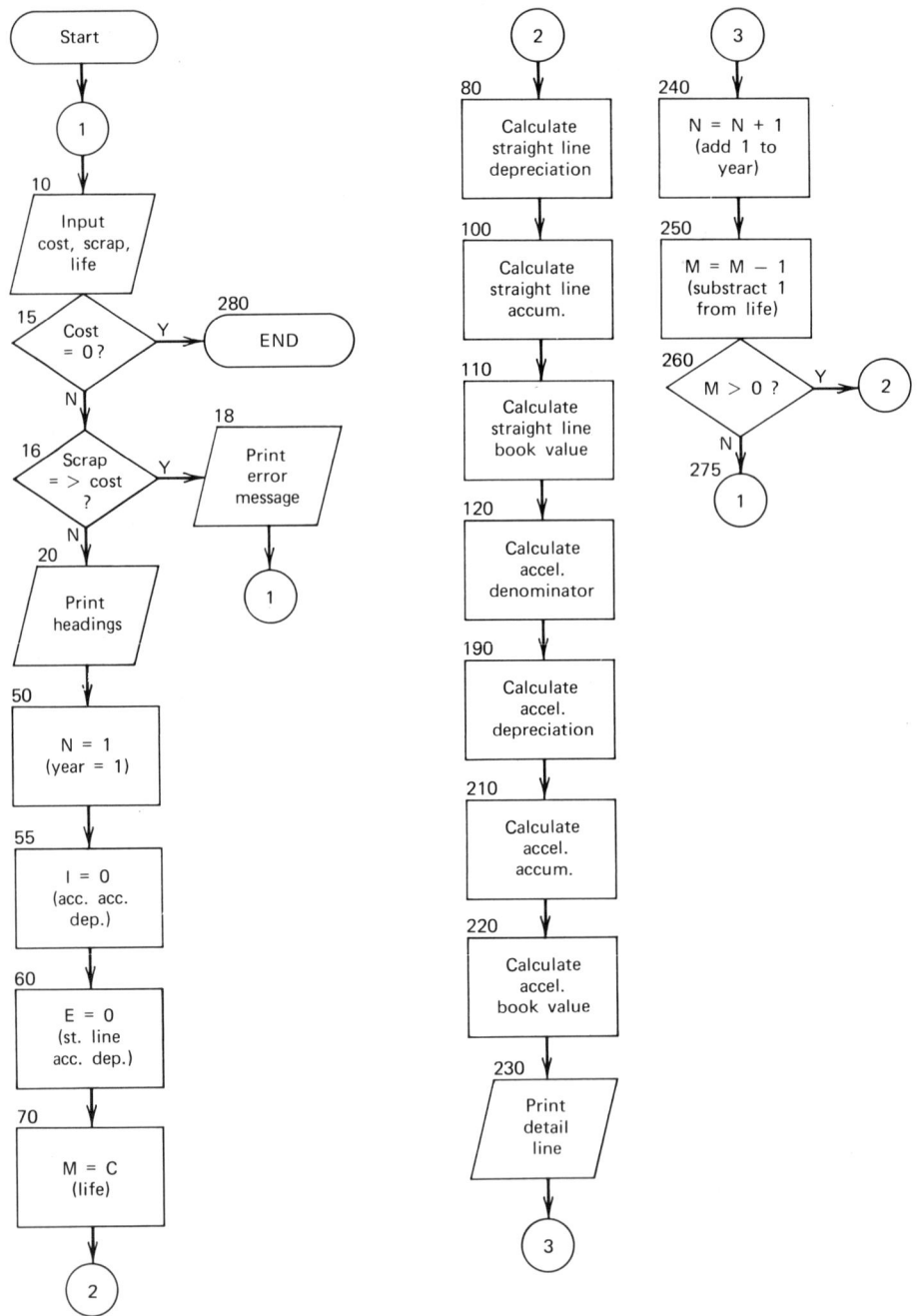

Fig. 17-1. Program flowchart—SYDVSL.

years. One justification for an accelerated method is that many assets become less efficient and require more maintenance as they get older. Thus total costs of using the asset tend to even out per year over the asset's life.

In the sum-of-the-years-digits method, it is necessary to determine a fraction that will be multiplied times the depreciation base. The denomi-

```
3     REM FIG. 17-2.
4 PRINT
5 PRINT "ENTER COST, SCRAP, & LIFE";
10 INPUT A, B, C
12 PRINT
15 IF A = 0 THEN 280
16 IF B > A THEN 18
17 GO TO 20
18 PRINT "SCRAP > COST"
19 GO TO 5
20 PRINT TAB(18) "STRAIGHT LINE"; TAB(45) "SUM OF YEARS DIGITS"
25 PRINT TAB(1)"YEAR"; TAB(9) "CURR DEP"; TAB(21) "ACC DEP";
26 PRINT TAB(30) "BOOK VAL."; TAB (41) "CURR DEP";
28 PRINT TAB(51)"ACC DEP"; TAB(60)"BOOK VAL."
30 PRINT "  0", TAB(31) A; TAB(61) A
50 N = 1
55 I = 0
60 E = 0
70 M = C
75    REM CALC. ST. LINE.
80 D = INT (( A - B) / C)
100 E = E + D
110 F = A - E
120 G = ( C ** 2 + C) / 2
185    REM CALC. SUM YEARS DIGITS.
190 H = INT ( M / G * ( A - B))
210 I = I + H
220 J = A - I
230 PRINT TAB(1);N;TAB(11);D;TAB(21);E;TAB(31);F;TAB(41);H;
235 PRINT TAB(51);I;TAB(61);J
240 N = N + 1
250 M = M - 1
260 IF M > 0 THEN 80
270 PRINT
275 GO TO 5
280 END

READY
```

	Variable Name Legend	E	Accumulated depreciation, straight-line
A	Cost	M	Life, to be decremented
B	Scrap	D	Straight-line depreciation
C	Life	F	Book value, straight-line
N	Increment for years	G	Denominator for accelerated
I	Accumulated depreciation, accelerated	H	Accelerated depreciation
		J	Book value, accelerated

Fig. 17-2. Program listing of SYDVSL.

nator of that fraction is calculated by adding the whole numbers from one through the number of years estimated life. For instance, the denominator would be six for an asset whose estimated life is three years (1 + 2 + 3), and it would be 15 for an asset whose life is five years (1 + 2 + 3 + 4 + 5). The denominator remains the same for all of the annual calculations for that asset.

The numerator of the fraction in the first year is the number that represents the estimated life. The numerator declines by one for each subsequent year until it is just one in the last year. Thus for an asset with a three-year life, one-half (3/6) is written off the first year, one-third (2/6) in the second, and one-sixth (1/6) in the third year. For an asset with a five-year life, one-third (5/15) is depreciated the first year, etc.

The program SYDVSL calculates the depreciation for any cost, scrap, and life, and it displays the results side by side for the two methods. Not only is the annual depreciation shown but also the depreciation as it accumulates and the resulting book value (original cost minus accumulated depreciation). Because of rounding, the book value at the end of the life

```
RUN NH


ENTER COST, SCRAP, & LIFE ?100000, 2500, 3

                    STRAIGHT LINE              SUM OF YEARS DIGITS
 YEAR    CURR DEP     ACC DEP    BOOK VAL.   CURR DEP   ACC DEP   BOOK VAL.
  0                               100000                          100000
  1       32500       32500        67500      48750     48750      51250
  2       32500       65000        35000      32500     81250      18750
  3       32500       97500         2500      16250     97500       2500

ENTER COST, SCRAP, & LIFE ?300000, 10000, 6

                    STRAIGHT LINE              SUM OF YEARS DIGITS
 YEAR    CURR DEP     ACC DEP    BOOK VAL.   CURR DEP   ACC DEP   BOOK VAL.
  0                               300000                          300000
  1       48333       48333       251667      82857     82857     217143
  2       48333       96666       203334      69047    151904     148096
  3       48333      144999       155001      55238    207142      92858
  4       48333      193332       106668      41428    248570      51430
  5       48333      241665        58335      27619    276189      23811
  6       48333      289998        10002      13809    289998      10002

ENTER COST, SCRAP, & LIFE ?0, 0, 0


TIME:  0.51 SECS.

READY
```

Fig. 17-3. Execution of SYDVSL.

of the asset may vary a few dollars from the scrap value, which is not part of the base.

The logic of the program is shown in Fig. 17-1. The program will end when a cost of zero is entered. Also, if a scrap value equal to or in excess of original cost is entered, the program notes this and goes back to the beginning.

The BASIC coding is in Fig. 17-2. Line 120 deserves a comment. The coding there calculates the denominator of the fraction needed for the sum-of-the-years-digits calculation. The formula $G = (C ** 2 + C) / 2$ will calculate the sum of all numbers consecutively from 1 through C (C being the life in years). Thus the user does not need to figure out what the denominator is.

Program execution with two samples is·shown in Fig. 17-3. In all cases the current depreciation for sum of the years digits starts out higher than but ends up lower than that for straight line. Thus the book value for the former is always lower than that of the latter except at the expiration of the life of the asset.

Effect of Depreciation on Income Tax (DEPTAX)

Since depreciation is an operating cost that is deductible for income tax purposes, a higher depreciation cost means there will be lower taxable income, lower taxes, and also lower net income. But this is not entirely a tax saving, since later in the life of the asset the accelerated depreciation is no longer available. Depreciation declines, taxable income increases, taxes increase, and net income increases. The direct impact of this situation may not be felt, however, as most companies are continually buying new assets.

The program DEPTAX shows the effect of straight-line versus sum-of-the-years-digits depreciation on income taxes and net income. Figure 17-4 reflects the logic. The same methods are used there to calculate annual depreciation as in SYDVSL in the previous section.

The major significant point of the logic in Fig. 17-4 is that federal income taxes are assessed at 22% of the first $25,000 of taxable income; any income above $25,000 is taxed at a rate of 48%.

Figure 17-5 shows the BASIC coding. Lines 120 and 130 calculate the applicable tax under the two depreciation methods when income exceeds $25,000. In either case, the tax is 48% of the income in excess of $25,000 plus $5500, which is 22% times $25,000. Line numbers 114 and 124 are used to figure the tax on incomes up to $25,000. If taxable in-

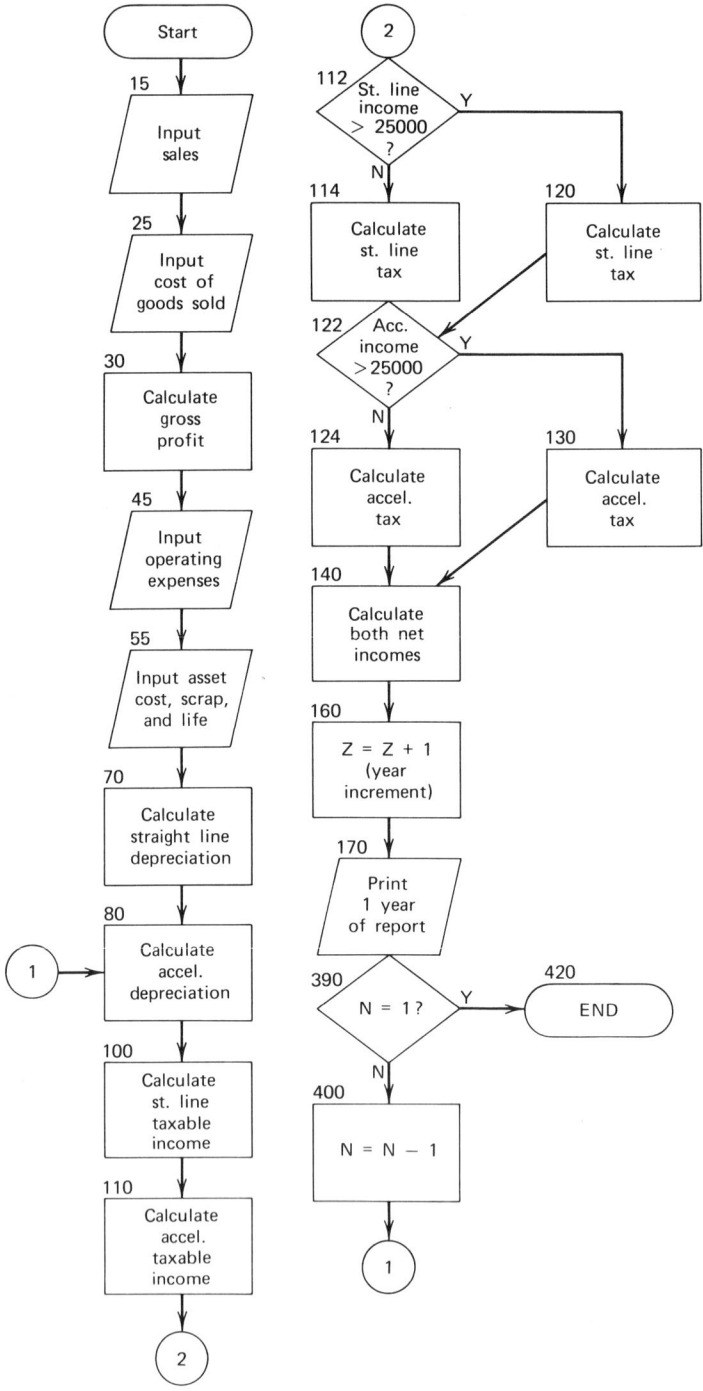

Fig. 17-4.   Program flowchart—DEPTAX.

```
5    REM FIG. 17-5.
10   PRINT "ENTER SALES";
15   INPUT A
20   PRINT "ENTER COST OF GOODS SOLD, EXC. DEPR.";
25   INPUT B
30   C = A - B
40   PRINT "ENTER OPER. EXP.";
45   INPUT D
50   PRINT "ENTER COST, SCRAP, & LIFE OF ASSET";
55   INPUT E, S, N
70   F = INT ((E - S) / N)
80   G = (N ** 2 + N) / 2
90   H = INT ( N/G * (E - S))
100  I = C - ( D + F)
110  J = C - ( D + H)
112  IF I > 24999 THEN 120
114  K = INT ( .22 * I)
116  GO TO 122
120  K = INT (( I - 25000) * .48 + 5500)
122  IF J > 24999 THEN 130
124  L = INT ( .22 * J)
126  GO TO 140
130  L = INT (( J - 25000) * .48 + 5500)
140  M = I - K
150  O = J - L
160  Z = Z + 1
170  PRINT
290  PRINT "YEAR"; Z
300  PRINT , "ST. LINE", "SOYD"
310  PRINT "NET SALES", A, A
320  PRINT "CGS", B, B
330  PRINT "GROSS PROFIT", C, C
340  PRINT "OPER EXP.", D, D
350  PRINT "DEPRECIATION", F, H
360  PRINT "INC. BEF. TAX", I, J
370  PRINT "INCOME TAX", K, L
380  PRINT "NET INCOME", M, O
390  IF N = 1 THEN 420
400  N = N - 1
410  GO TO 90
420  END

READY
```

Variable Name Legend	
A	Sales
B	Cost of goods sold
C	Gross profit
D	Operating expenses
E	Cost of asset
S	Scrap
N	Life of asset
F	Depreciation, straight-line
G	Denominator, accelerated
H	Depreciation, accelerated
I	Net before tax, straight-line
J	Net before tax, accelerated
K	Tax, straight-line
L	Tax, accelerated
M	Net, straight-line
O	Net, accelerated
Z	Year increment

Fig. 17-5. Program listing of DEPTAX.

come should be a negative number (a loss), the tax situation gets more complicated and this program is not designed to handle it.

Figure 17-6 contains a sample run. Observe that the program maintains all data constant each year down through the line OPER EXP.

For the life of the asset, total depreciation, total income tax, and total net income are the same for the two methods. But the accelerated method allows for some of the tax to be paid later instead of sooner. Depending on a company's financial objectives and certain operating policies, the accelerated depreciation method can be much preferred to the straight-line method.

```
ENTER SALES ?300000
ENTER COST OF GOODS SOLD, EXC. DEPR. ?175000
ENTER OPER. EXP. ?68000
ENTER COST, SCRAP, & LIFE OF ASSET ?75000, 3000, 4
```

YEAR 1

	ST. LINE	SOYD
NET SALES	300000	300000
CGS	175000	175000
GROSS PROFIT	125000	125000
OPER EXP.	68000	68000
DEPRECIATION	18000	28800
INC. BEF. TAX	39000	28200
INCOME TAX	12220	7036
NET INCOME	26780	21164

YEAR 2

	ST. LINE	SOYD
NET SALES	300000	300000
CGS	175000	175000
GROSS PROFIT	125000	125000
OPER EXP.	68000	68000
DEPRECIATION	18000	21600
INC. BEF. TAX	39000	35400
INCOME TAX	12220	10492
NET INCOME	26780	24908

YEAR 3

	ST. LINE	SOYD
NET SALES	300000	300000
CGS	175000	175000
GROSS PROFIT	125000	125000
OPER EXP.	68000	68000
DEPRECIATION	18000	14400
INC. BEF. TAX	39000	42600
INCOME TAX	12220	13948
NET INCOME	26780	28652

YEAR 4

	ST. LINE	SOYD
NET SALES	300000	300000
CGS	175000	175000
GROSS PROFIT	125000	125000
OPER EXP.	68000	68000
DEPRECIATION	18000	7200
INC. BEF. TAX	39000	49800
INCOME TAX	12220	17404
NET INCOME	26780	32396

```
TIME:  0.75 SECS.
```

READY

Fig. 17-6. Execution of DEPTAX.

Effect of Inventory Costing on Income Tax (INVTAX)

We saw in the previous section how a company may be able to defer some income taxes and net income by a choice of one depreciation method over another. A company has a similar opportunity in its choice of inventory-costing methods.

When a company sells a product, it charges the cost of that item as an expense for income tax and for net income purposes. (It either records the cost at the time of the sale or at a later time during that same accounting period.)

Regardless of whether the company sold the oldest item or the newest item from its stock on hand, it has the option to charge off the cost of either its oldest one or its newest one. If it charges off the cost of the oldest one, the company is said to be using the FIFO basis, the First one In being the First one Out. If the Last one In is the First one charged Out, they are using the LIFO basis.

Since the cost trend of most items is upward, a company can obviously make its cost in the current period higher by using the LIFO method. If that is the case, income before taxes will be lower, income taxes will be lower, and net income will be lower using LIFO.

In Fig. 17-7 is the listing of a program that reflects the effect of FIFO versus LIFO over a period of three years. Sales and all costs except those due to inventory costing valuation are held constant. The user inputs projected ending inventory figures under the two bases for each of the three years. Note that the cost of what was sold is obtained by adding purchases to beginning inventory and subtracting ending inventory.

In Fig. 17-8, there are two sample runs of the program with varying data. Note that inflation seems to have run rampant in the second example, based on the ending inventory figures under FIFO; the effects on income taxes and net income were substantial.

To Incorporate or Not (MINTAX)

When a person is about to start a business, one of the decisions that has to be made is whether to incorporate or to operate as a proprietorship. While there are several factors to consider before making that decision, the only one that we will examine here is the federal income tax aspect. Furthermore, the program MINTAX only concerns the income tax as a conceptual matter; this discussion is not intended to cover all the tax brackets, dividend exclusions, exemptions, etc.

The starting point for the program is the net income that the busi-

```
5    REM FIG. 17-7.
10   PRINT "ENTER SALES";
20   INPUT S
30   PRINT "ENTER PURCHASES";
40   INPUT P1, P2, P3
50   PRINT "ENTER BEG. INVENTORY";
60   INPUT B
70   PRINT "ENTER EXPENSES";
80   INPUT E
90   PRINT "ENTER FIFO INV. FOR 3 YEARS";
100  INPUT F1, F2, F3
110  PRINT "ENTER LIFO INV. FOR 3 YEARS";
120  INPUT L1, L2, L3
130  N1 = S - (B + P1 - F1) - E
140  N2 = S - (F1 + P2 - F2) - E
150  N3 = S - (F2 + P3 - F3) - E
160  N4 = S - (B + P1 - L1) - E
170  N5 = S - (L1 + P2 - L2) - E
180  N6 = S - (L2 + P3 - L3) - E
190  IF N1 > 25000 THEN 220
200  T1 = INT ( N1 * .22)
210  GO TO 230
220  T1 = INT ((( N1 - 25000) * .48) + 5500)
230  IF N2 > 25000 THEN 260
240  T2 = INT ( N2 * .22)
250  GO TO 270
260  T2 = INT ((( N2 - 25000 ) * .48) + 5500)
270  IF N3 > 25000 THEN 300
280  T3 = INT ( N3 * .22)
290  GO TO 310
300  T3 = INT ((( N3 - 25000) * .48) + 5500)
310  IF N4 > 25000 THEN 350
320  T4 = INT ( N4 * .22)
330  GO TO 360
350  T4 = INT (((N4 - 25000) * .48) + 5500)
360  IF N5 > 25000 THEN 390
370  T5 = INT ( N5 * .22)
380  GO TO 400
390  T5 = INT ( ((N5 - 25000) * .48) + 5500)
400  IF N6 > 25000 THEN 430
410  T6 = INT ( N6 * .22)
420  GO TO 440
430  T6 = INT ((( N6 - 25000) * .48) + 5500)
440  I1 = N1 - T1
450  I2 = N2 - T2
460  I3 = N3 - T3
470  I4 = N4 - T4
480  I5 = N5 - T5
490  I6 = N6 - T6
500  PRINT
510  PRINT, , "LIFO", "FIFO"
520  PRINT "YEAR 1"
530  PRINT "NET INCOME BEFORE TAXES", N4, N1
540  PRINT "INCOME TAX", , T4, T1
550  PRINT "NET INCOME AFTER TAXES", I4, I1
570  PRINT
580  PRINT "YEAR 2"
590  PRINT "NET INCOME BEFORE TAXES", N5, N2
600  PRINT "INCOME TAXES",, T5, T2
610  PRINT "NET INCOME AFTER TAX", I5, I2
```

Variable Name Legend

S	Sales
P1, P2, P3	Purchases
B	Beginning inventory
E	Expenses
F1	⎫
F2	FIFO inventory
F3	⎭
L1	⎫
L2	LIFO inventory
L3	⎭
N1	⎫
N2	Net before tax, FIFO
N3	⎭
N4	⎫
N5	Net before tax, LIFO
N6	⎭
T1	⎫
T2	Tax, FIFO
T3	⎭
T4	⎫
T5	Tax, LIFO
T6	⎭
I1	⎫
I2	Net, FIFO
I3	⎭
I4	⎫
I5	Net, LIFO
I6	⎭

Fig. 17-7. Program listing of INVTAX (completed on page 257).

```
620 PRINT
630 PRINT "YEAR 3"
640 PRINT "NET INCOME BEFORE TAX", N6, N3
650 PRINT "INCOME TAX",, T6, T3
670 PRINT "NET INCOME AFTER TAX", I6, I3
680 END

READY
```

Fig. 17-7. cont.

ness could earn before provision for the owner's salary or any income taxes that would have to be paid. If the business were incorporated, the owner would presumably take out a salary. The salary would thus reduce the corporation's taxable income, and income tax would be assessed on the remainder. Net income after tax would be taxable to the owner if it were paid out as a dividend. We will assume here that all net income is returned to the owner as a dividend.

If the business were not incorporated, all the net income of the business, including any amount taken out by the owner as a salary or as a draw, would be taxable to the proprietor at personal tax rates. Since corporate and personal income tax rates vary, the net effect to the owner can be substantial.

A program flowchart of the logic is seen in Fig. 17-9. The significant parts are:

1. If a salary would be entered that is greater than the net income of the corporation before taxes (step 30), the program prints an error message and goes back to the beginning. (We will not deal with losses.)

2. If the annual net income of the business being considered is less than $1000 (step 40), the program prints a message advising against the venture and the program ends.

3. The owner will be subject to personal income tax based on the total of his or her salary plus the dividends if incorporated, or on net profit from the business if not incorporated. Many possible steps are needed to calculate the personal income tax because the tax rate varies according to income "brackets." One set of steps is used for this purpose; it is coded as a subroutine and is entered from two places in the main program.

The BASIC coding is reproduced in Fig. 17-10. Program execution is shown in Fig. 17-11. Please recall the earlier statement that MINTAX

```
RUN NH

ENTER SALES ?500000
ENTER PURCHASES ?150000, 160000, 170000
ENTER BEG. INVENTORY ?45000
ENTER EXPENSES ?235000
ENTER FIFO INV. FOR 3 YEARS ?45000, 45000, 45000
ENTER LIFO INV. FOR 3 YEARS ?46000, 47000, 48000

                                  LIFO           FIFO
YEAR 1
NET INCOME BEFORE TAXES          116000         115000
INCOME TAX                        49180          48700
NET INCOME AFTER TAXES            66820          66300


YEAR 2
NET INCOME BEFORE TAXES          106000         105000
INCOME TAXES                      44380          43900
NET INCOME AFTER TAX              61620          61100


YEAR 3
NET INCOME BEFORE TAX             96000          95000
INCOME TAX                        39580          39100
NET INCOME AFTER TAX              56420          55900



TIME:  0.63 SECS.

READY
RUN NH


ENTER SALES ?500000,
ENTER PURCHASES ?150000, 180000, 200000
ENTER BEG. INVENTORY ?48000
ENTER EXPENSES ?240000
ENTER FIFO INV. FOR 3 YEARS ?54000, 66000, 78000
ENTER LIFO INV. FOR 3 YEARS ?49000, 48000, 49500

                                  LIFO           FIFO
YEAR 1
NET INCOME BEFORE TAXES          111000         116000
INCOME TAX                        46780          49180
NET INCOME AFTER TAXES            64220          66820


YEAR 2
NET INCOME BEFORE TAXES           79000          92000
INCOME TAXES                      31420          37660
NET INCOME AFTER TAX              47580          54340


YEAR 3
NET INCOME BEFORE TAX             61500          72000
INCOME TAX                        23020          28060
NET INCOME AFTER TAX              38480          43940



TIME:  0.65 SECS.

READY
```

Fig. 17-8. Execution of INVTAX.

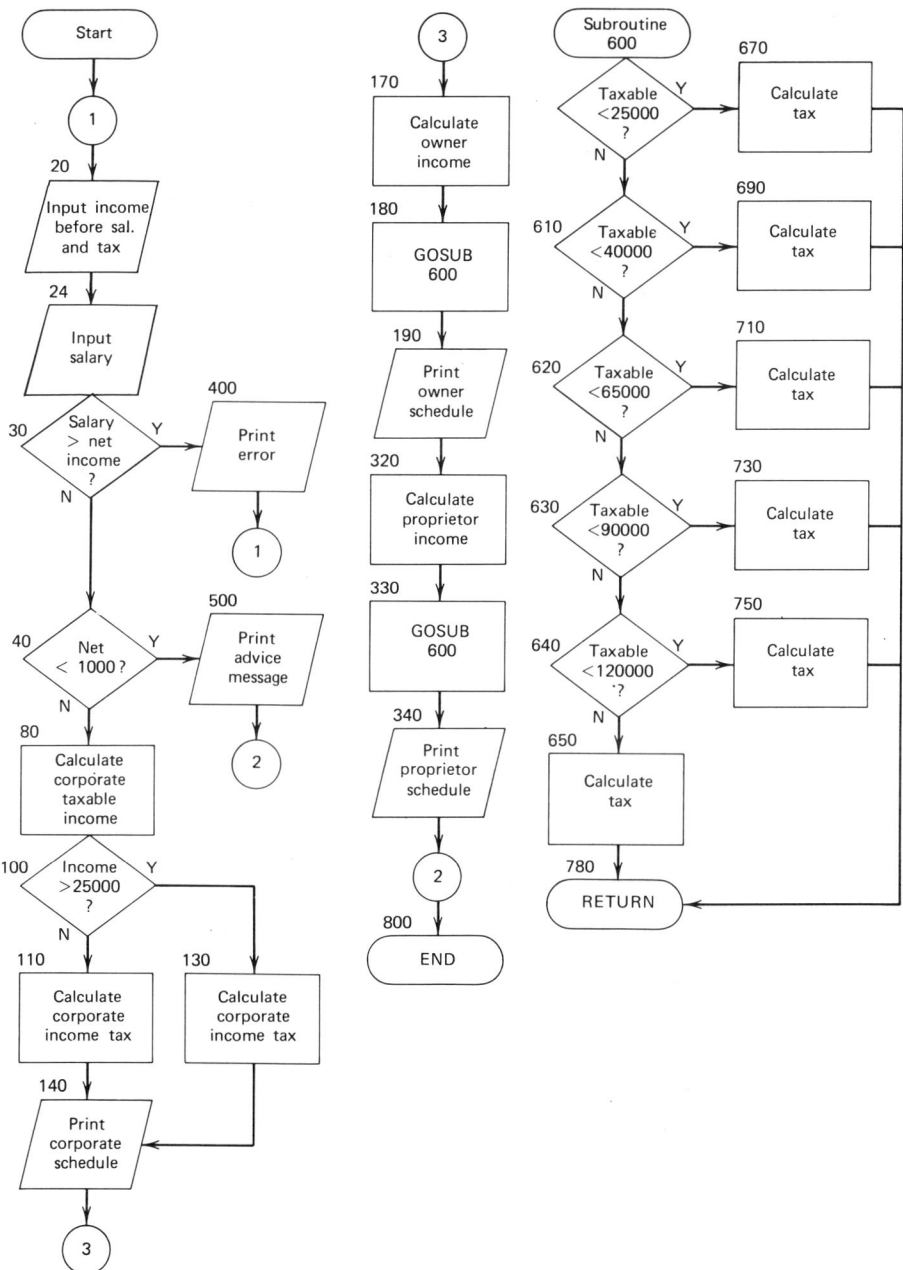

Fig. 17-9. Program flowchart—MINTAX.

```
5    REM FIG. 17-10.
10   PRINT "ENTER NET INCOME BEFORE SAL & TAXES";
20   INPUT A
22   PRINT "ENTER OWNER SAL";
24   INPUT B
30   IF B > A THEN 400
40   IF A < 1000 THEN 500
45   PRINT
50   PRINT , , "CORP."
60   PRINT "NET INC. BEFORE SAL & TAXES", A
70   PRINT "SALARY", , B
80   C = A - B
90   PRINT "NET INCOME BEFORE TAX", C
100  IF C > 25000 THEN 130
110  D = INT ( C * .22)
120  GO TO 140
130  D = INT ((C - 25000) * .48 + 5500)
140  PRINT "CORPORATE INCOME TAX", D
150  E = C - D
160  PRINT "CORP. NET INCOME", E
162  PRINT
164  PRINT , , "OWNER"
166  PRINT "SALARY, FROM ABOVE", B
168  PRINT "CORP NET INCOME, FROM ABOVE", E
170  F = B + E
174  PRINT "TOTAL INCOME", , F
180  GOSUB 600
190  PRINT "PERSONAL INCOME TAX", G
200  H = F - G
210  PRINT "EFFECTIVE NET INCOME", H; "**"
220  PRINT
280  PRINT , , , "PROP."
290  PRINT "PROP. PROFIT(SAME"
300  PRINT "   AS NET INCOME BEFORE"
310  PRINT "   SAL & TAXES ABOVE", , A
320  F = A
330  GOSUB 600
340  PRINT "PERSONAL INCOME TAX", , G
350  H = A - G
360  PRINT "EFFECTIVE NET INCOME", , H;"**"
370  GO TO 800
400  PRINT "SALARY > NET INCOME - TRY AGAIN"
410  GO TO 10
500  PRINT "NET INCOME TOO LOW TO ACCEPT RISK OF ENTERING BUSINESS"
510  GO TO 800
600  IF F < 25000 THEN 670
610  IF F < 40000 THEN 690
620  IF F < 65000 THEN 710
630  IF F < 90000 THEN 730
640  IF F < 120000 THEN 750
650  G = ( F - 120000) * .70 + 57580
660  GO TO 770
670  G = ( F - 10000) * .28 + 3260
680  GO TO 770
690  G = ( F - 25000) * .42 + 8660
700  GO TO 770
710  G = ( F - 40000) * .50 + 14060
720  GO TO 770
730  G = ( F - 65000) * .55 + 24420
740  GO TO 770
```

Variable Name Legend

A	Net before salary and tax
B	Owner salary
C	Net before tax
D	Corporate tax
E	Corporate net
F	Owner total income
G	Owner income tax
H	Effective net; corporate owner and proprietor

Fig. 17-10. Program listing of MINTAX (completed on page 261).

```
          750 G = ( F - 90000) * .62 + 45180
          770 G = INT (G)
          780 RETURN
          800 END

          READY
```

Fig. 17-10. cont.

```
RUN NH


ENTER NET INCOME BEFORE SAL & TAXES ?30000
ENTER OWNER SAL ?8000

                                    CORP.
NET INC. BEFORE SAL & TAXES   30000
SALARY                         8000
NET INCOME BEFORE TAX         22000
CORPORATE INCOME TAX           4840
CORP. NET INCOME              17160

                                    OWNER
SALARY, FROM ABOVE             8000
CORP NET INCOME, FROM ABOVE   17160
TOTAL INCOME                  25160
PERSONAL INCOME TAX            8727
EFFECTIVE NET INCOME          16433 **

                                                PROP.
PROP. PROFIT(SAME
   AS NET INCOME BEFORE
   SAL & TAXES ABOVE                            30000
PERSONAL INCOME TAX                             10760
EFFECTIVE NET INCOME                            19240 **



TIME:  0.50 SECS.

READY
RUN NH


ENTER NET INCOME BEFORE SAL & TAXES ?64000
ENTER OWNER SAL ?18500

                                    CORP.
NET INC. BEFORE SAL & TAXES   64000
SALARY                        18500
NET INCOME BEFORE TAX         45500
CORPORATE INCOME TAX          15340
CORP. NET INCOME              30160

                                    OWNER
SALARY, FROM ABOVE            18500
CORP NET INCOME, FROM ABOVE   30160
TOTAL INCOME                  48660
PERSONAL INCOME TAX           18390
EFFECTIVE NET INCOME          30270 **
```

Fig. 17-11. Execution of MINTAX (completed on page 262).

```
                                                    PROP.
PROP. PROFIT(SAME
      AS NET INCOME BEFORE
      SAL & TAXES ABOVE                             64000
PERSONAL INCOME TAX                                 26060
EFFECTIVE NET INCOME                                37940 **


TIME:  0.50 SECS.

READY
```

Fig. 17-11. cont.

does not include all relevant tax considerations. Therefore, it should not
be used on practical tax problems without considerable expansion.

EXERCISES

1. By what reasoning is depreciation considered a cost of doing business? Why isn't the cost of an asset just entirely written off in the year the asset is obtained?

2. How does one arrive at the "fraction" that is used to calculate depreciation in the sum-of-the-years-digits method? By what amount is that fraction then multiplied?

3. What inventory method, FIFO or LIFO, tends to create the higher net income during periods of severe inflation? Does the use of LIFO require that the last item bought be the first one sold (in a physical sense)?

4. In Fig. 17-2:
   (a) How often was line 80 executed in each of the sample runs? Would the program work properly if line 260 had used THEN 100? Explain.
   (b) Could line 120 have been written $G = C * (C + 1) / 2$? Explain. How many times does this instruction need to be executed for any given set of data?
   (c) Describe the results if a life of one year would be entered for any asset.
   (d) Make the coding changes that would furnish a book value exactly equal to the scrap value at the end of the estimated life.
   (e) Use a FOR-NEXT routine to handle the looping portion of the program.

5. Change the logic in Fig. 17-4 so that one subroutine is used to calculate taxes on income up to $25,000 and another subroutine is used to calculate taxes on income greater than $25,000.

6. In Fig. 17-5:
   (a) Make the coding changes appropriate to your logic in (5) above.
   (b) Add some coding that would prevent the income tax calculations if "INC. BEF. TAX" were negative.
   (c) Change the coding so that varying amounts (per year) for sales, cost of goods sold, and operating expenses could be entered.

7. In Fig. 17-7:
   (a) Change the coding so that subroutines would be used to calcu-
       late the taxes.
   (b) Provide for the entry of varying amounts (per year) for sales
       and expenses.
   (c) Cause the output to appear in the following format (with a
       similar segment for FIFO):

                                                        LIFO

YEAR 1
SALES   XXXXX
BEGINNING INVENTORY   XXX
PURCHASES   XXXX
TOTAL AVAILABLE   XXXX
ENDING INVENTORY   XXX
COST OF GOODS SOLD   XXXXX
GROSS PROFIT   XXXX
EXPENSES   XXX
NET INCOME BEFORE TAXES   XXX
INCOME TAX   XXX
NET INCOME AFTER TAX   XXX

8. In Fig. 17-9, could the subroutine be used efficiently to calculate
   the personal tax without the need to have so many decision steps
   within it? Why?

9. The program in Fig. 17-10 has been written so that all corporate
   net income is treated as wholly paid as a dividend to the owner
   under the OWNER section. Change the coding so that only the
   actual dividend paid would be treated as income instead of the
   total corporate net income (allow for the entry of a dividend figure). Then use that data plus the owner's salary to calculate an effective net income if the business were incorporated.

10. Prepare a flowchart and the coding for a program that would com-
    bine the features of Figs. 17-5 and 17-7. Set it up so that both
    FIFO and LIFO would be related to straight-line and sum-of-the-
    years-digits depreciation; that is, have four columns of output
    values.

11. Assume that individual income tax rates are expected to change soon. Change all the constants in the program in Fig. 17-10 to INPUT variables under user control so that the program will handle any new tax rates easily.

Summary of
BASIC Instructions
APPENDIX A

Instruction	Explained in Part One on Page:	Required in Part One in Exercise:	Illustrated in Part Two in Figure:	Required in Part Two in Exercise:
ABS	77	7-18		
DATA	37	4-11, 4-14		
DIM	116	9-21, 10-10	13-10, 14-8	15-8
END	9	2-15, 5-8	ALL	ALL
FILES	157	12-6, 12-7	15-12	13-12, 15-9
FOR(NEXT)	109	10-10, 10-14	13-10, 14-8	14-10, 15-7
GOSUB(RETURN)	123	9-17	16-10, 17-10	17-5
GO TO	13	2-15, 3-19	15-12	13-12, 16-8
IF (THEN)	14	2-15, 2-17	ALL	ALL
IF END #	159	12-6, 12-7	15-12	13-12, 15-9
INPUT	39	4-14	13-4, 17-10	14-10, 16-3
INPUT #			15-12	15-9
INT	73	7-6, 7-20	13-7, 17-10	13-12
LET	8	2-15, 2-18		
NEXT	109	10-10, 11-12	13-10, 14-8	14-10, 15-7
ON	96	8-14		16-8
PRINT	9	2-15, 3-18	ALL	ALL
PRINT #	165	12-6	15-12	15-9
QUOTE #			15-12	15-9
RANDOMIZE	83	7-19		15-9
READ	37	4-11, 4-14		
READ #	160	12-6		13-12, 15-9
REM	26	3-19	ALL	ALL
RESTORE	93	8-8		
RESTORE #			15-12	
RETURN	124	9-17	16-10, 17-10	17-5
RND	79	7-19, 8-24		15-9
SCRATCH #	165	12-6		15-9
SQR	76	7-17, 7-20		
STEP	110		13-10	14-10, 15-7
TAB	29	3-19	13-9, 17-2	14-10
THEN	14	2-15, 5-9	ALL	ALL

System Commands APPENDIX B

System commands are those words that tell the computer to do something to your program. They are not part of a program, and hence they do not use line numbers.

The purpose of this appendix is to show the commonly used system commands. Most of these commands will be helpful to you in your use of BASIC in a time-sharing environment. After carefully studying this material, please consult your own operating situation to determine any exceptions appropriate to you.

Rather than describing each command and then referring to a figure elsewhere, an appropriate narrative will appear on the left side of the page and an actual example immediately to the right. It is to be emphasized that, in each case, the operator typed the system command, which has been underlined.

LOGIN

A certain procedure is necessary to sign on to the computer. This includes entering a number and a password. (The password does not get printed.) In my case, I also need to show that I want to use BASIC.

```
.LOGIN
JOB 11 BENTLEY COLLEGE 602/14 TTY45
%LGNNOC No operator coverage.
#7100,1344
[LGNPWE This PPN will expire on 31-Jan-77]
Password:
1258    21-Nov-76        Sun

.R BASIC

READY, FOR HELP TYPE HELP.
```

NEW

Once you have signed onto the computer, it is desirable (in some computers necessary) to assign a name to the program you want to write. When you type NEW, the computer re-

```
NEW
NEW FILE NAME--EASY1

READY
10 A = 37
20 B = 52
30 C = 45
40 D = A + B + C
50 PRINT A, B, C, D
60 END
```

267

LIST

The use of LIST merely repeats back to you the program you have entered. However, instructions will have been placed in line number order, and any duplicate line numbers will have automatically wiped out any previous statements with that same number.

```
LIST

EASY1            12:44            21-NOV-76


10 A = 37
20 B = 52
30 C = 45
40 D = A + B + C
50 PRINT A, B, C, D
60 END

READY
```

RUN

Typing RUN causes the computer to either run the program if there are no clerical errors in it, or to furnish a list of program errors if there are any errors that prevent the machine from executing.

```
RUN

EASY1            12:46            21-NOV-76


37               52               45               13

TIME:  0.04 SECS.

READY
```

LIST NH

The use of NH prevents the heading from printing when listing the program.

```
LIST NH
10 A = 37
20 B = 52
30 C = 45
40 D = A + B + C
50 PRINT A, B, C, D
60 END

READY
```

sponds with a request for you to enter the program name you want to use. There is a limit as to how many characters long the name can be (in my case, it is six).

I have assigned the name EASY1 and then proceeded to type in the program.

RUN NH

The use of NH prevents the heading from printing when running the program.

```
RUN NH

37              52              45              134

TIME:  0.05 SECS.
READY
```

SAVE

If you would like to store the program at the Computer Center so that you can use it later without the need to type it in again, type SAVE. In most cases the program is copied from working storage to a file under your account number. This step does not remove the program from working storage.

```
          SAVE
          READY
```

CAT

Whenever you want to see what programs are stored under your account number, type CAT (or CATALOG). In the example shown, BAS refers to a program written in the BASIC language, as opposed to some other language such as COBOL or FORTRAN.

```
          CAT
          EASY1  .BAS
          READY
```

DELETE

Any instruction can be deleted from working storage (but not from the file where it was SAVEd) by typing DELETE followed by the appropriate line number.

```
          DELETE 30
          READY
```

RENAME

Assume you have saved a program (copied it to the file) and then made changes to the version that is still in working storage. If you then try to save the new version, the computer will not let you do so. You can RENAME the program in working storage and SAVE that version.

```
SAVE
? DUPLICATE FILE NAME. REPLACE OR RENAME
READY

RENAME
FILE NAME--EASY2

READY
SAVE

READY
CAT

EASY1 .BAS
EASY2 .BAS

READY
```

OLD

Whenever you wish, either when first signing on or at anytime during a session of using the computer, you can recall a saved program from the file into working storage. This does nothing to the program in the file, other than to copy it.

```
OLD
OLD FILE NAME--EASY1

READY
LIST

EASY1          12:53          21-NOV-76


10 A = 37
20 B = 52
30 C = 45
40 D = A + B + C
50 PRINT A, B, C, D
60 END

READY
```

UNSAVE

A program that had been SAVEd on the file can be removed by the use of UNSAVE followed by the name by which it was saved.

```
UNSAVE EASY2

FILES UNSAVED:
EASY2

READY
CAT

EASY1 .BAS

READY
```

REPLACE

Assume there is a program that had been SAVEd on the file, and you are now making changes to that program in working storage. You cannot SAVE the new version. You have to either RENAME or REPLACE. The use of RE-PLACE replaces the file version with the one in working storage.

```
LIST

EASY1          13:05          21-NOV-76


10  A = 37
20  B = 52
30  C = 45
40  D = A + B + C
50  PRINT A, B, C, D
60  END

READY
DELETE 30

READY
SAVE

? DUPLICATE FILE NAME. REPLACE OR RENAME
READY
REPLACE

READY
```

SCRATCH

A program in working storage can be wiped out by the use of SCRATCH.

```
SCRATCH

READY
LIST

EASY1          13:06          21-NOV-76


READY
```

RESEQUENCE

If, for any reason, you would like to resequence the line numbers of your instructions without having to type the whole program over, just type RESEQUENCE. The result is that all instructions are renumbered with line numbers in increments of 10. Any line numbers involved in branching steps (IF and GO TO) are automatically handled.

```
OLD
OLD FILE NAME--EASY1

READY
LIST


EASY1            13:06           21-NOV-76


10 A = 37
20 B = 52
40 D = A + B + C
50 PRINT A, B, C, D
60 END

READY
RESEQUENCE

READY
LIST


EASY1            13:07           21-NOV-76


10 A = 37
20 B = 52
30 D = A + B + C
40 PRINT A, B, C, D
50 END

READY
```

BYE

The use of BYE signs you off the computer. A final message from the computer indicates the amount of time used and other appropriate information.

```
BYE
Job 20, User [7100,1344]  Logged off TTY45    1256  21-Nov-76
Saved all files (3 blocks)
Runtime 4.36 Sec, 64 Kilo-core-seconds
Connect Time 00:14:33
```

Matrix Operations
APPENDIX C

The topic of double-subscripted or two-dimensional arrays was introduced in Chapter 10. Such an arrangement of data is also often called a matrix.

The BASIC language contains several instructions that greatly simplify the handling of matrices. Each of the specific instructions uses the term MAT.

Figures 10-1 through 10-4 in Chapter 10 showed a variety of ways to read into and print out a matrix. Figure C-1 works with the same raw data as those four earlier programs did.

Note in Fig. C-1 that the matrix itself is defined in line number 10 (a regular two-dimensional array). The entire matrix was read in line number 20. The word MAT was followed by the word READ and the name assigned to the matrix (A).

```
5     REM FIG. C-1.
10 DIM A (3,4)
12    REM ONE LINE OF CODING
14    REM READS ENTIRE MATRIX.
20 MAT READ A
30 PRINT "Q1", "Q2", "Q3", "Q4"
35    REM ONE LINE OF CODING
36    REM PRINTS ENTIRE MATRIX.
40 MAT PRINT A
50 DATA 15, 18, 20, 28
60 DATA 17, 24, 22, 29
70 DATA 16, 23, 25, 28
80 END

READY
RUN NH
```

Q1	Q2	Q3	Q4
15	18	20	28
17	24	22	29
16	23	25	28

```
TIME:   0.14 SECS.

READY
```

Fig. C-1.   Use of MAT to read and print.

273

Also, the entire matrix was printed by line number 40, where the word MAT was followed by PRINT and the name of the matrix (A). Thus voluminous, detailed coding can be avoided through use of a MAT instruction.

There are several MAT instructions that permit arithmetic to be performed on the data in matrices. Assume matrix B represents sales by quarter for three years for Corporate Division 20 and that matrix C represents similar data for Corporate Division 30. The objective of a program is to add the respective data from the two matrices and print it out as one matrix. Such an operation is shown in Fig. C-2.

In that program the only new instruction appears in line number 50. Matrix C is added to matrix B and replaces the original matrix B. If it would have been necessary to add B and C in such a way that the original B was not to be replaced, the following steps would replace their counterparts in Fig. C-2.

$$20 \quad \text{DIM B (3, 4), C(3, 4), D (3, 4)}$$
$$50 \quad \text{MAT D} = \text{B} + \text{C}$$
$$60 \quad \text{MAT PRINT D}$$

```
10      REM FIG. C-2.
20 DIM B(3,4), C(3,4)
30 MAT READ B
40 MAT READ C
50 MAT B = B + C
60 MAT PRINT B
70 DATA 15, 18, 20, 28
80 DATA 17, 24, 22, 29
90 DATA 16, 23, 25, 28
100 DATA 12, 78, 34, 23
110 DATA 45, 45, 23, 9
120 DATA 36, 23, 54, 76
130 END

READY
RUN NH
```

27	96	54	51
62	69	45	38
52	46	79	104

```
TIME:   0.14 SECS.

READY
```

Fig. C-2.   Adding matrices.

274   APPENDIX C

Matrix subtraction is performed by proper use of the minus sign. For example, if you want to subtract matrix E from matrix F, you could code MAT F = F - E. If you want to subtract and retain matrix F in its original form, you could define matrix G in a DIM statement and code MAT G = F - E.

A matrix can be multiplied by another matrix. The product, however, cannot be placed in either matrix that was a factor in the multiplication. Thus MAT H = H * I is not valid whereas MAT J = H * I is valid.

It is also possible to multiply a matrix by constant. In Fig. C-3, all the values in matrix C are multiplied by 1.10 to show the effect of increas-

```
5    REM FIG. C-3.
10 DIM G(3,4), H(3,4)
20 MAT READ G
30 MAT READ H
40 MAT J = (1.1) * G
50 MAT K = (1.4) * H
55 PRINT "Q1", "Q2", "Q3", "Q4"
60 MAT PRINT J
70 MAT PRINT K
190 DATA 15, 18, 20, 28
200 DATA 17, 24, 22, 29
210 DATA 16, 23, 25, 28
220 DATA 12, 78, 34, 23
230 DATA 45, 45, 23, 9
240 DATA 36, 23, 54, 76
250 END

READY
RUN NH
```

Q1	Q2	Q3	Q4
16.5	19.8	22	30.8
18.7	26.4	24.2	31.9
17.6	25.3	27.5	30.8
16.8	109.2	47.6	32.2
63.	63.	32.2	12.6
50.4	32.2	75.6	106.4

```
TIME:   0.22 SECS.

READY
```

Fig. C-3. Matrix multiplication.

ing the original DATA values by 10%. Also, matrix H is multiplied to give the effect of an increase of 40%. Observe that the constant value in such multiplication must be enclosed in parentheses (1.1) and (1.4).

Another version of a MAT instruction involves the INPUT step. Its form is MAT INPUT M. The matrix named M would naturally have to be defined in a DIM statement. The INPUT statement would replace the READ and DATA statements just as we have seen previously.

An Alternative
Sorting Method
APPENDIX D

Over the years a number of different, logical approaches have been used to accomplish the function of sorting. The different approaches are influenced by the type of equipment available, the nature of the raw data, and the personal opinion of the applicable programmer.

Figure D-1 shows an approach that required .12 seconds to sort that particular data. That amount compares to .14 seconds required in Fig. 11-1, where the same raw data was sorted by a different logic.

Since most BASIC users do not become involved in the details surrounding the sorting process, these users may not necessarily adopt the most efficient methods. This problem can be overcome if computer center specialists will prescribe certain standards and then control the resulting practices.

```
5    REM FIG. D-1.
10     REM INPUT VALUES.
20 DIM D(12)
30 FOR I = 1 TO 12
40 READ D(I)
50 NEXT I
60     REM FIND ELEMENT OUT OF ORDER, STARTING WITH FIRST.
70 I = 1
80 IF I > 11 THEN 260
90 IF D(I) > D(I + 1) THEN 120
100 I = I + 1
110 GO TO 80
120    REM SAVE SMALL ELEMENT IN TEMPORARY.
130 T = D(I + 1)
140    REM FIND POSITION FOR SMALLER, MAKING SPACE FOR IT.
150 D(I + 1) = D(I)
160 J = I - 1
170 IF D(J) <= T THEN 220
180 D(J + 1) = D(J)
190 J = J - 1
200 IF J = 0 THEN 220
210 GO TO 170
220    REM INSERT SMALLER ELEMENT IN POSITION.
230 D(J + 1) = T
240    REM CONTINUE SEARCH FOR ELEMENTS OUT OF ORDER.
250 GO TO 100
260    REM SORTING COMPLETE; PRINT LIST.
270 FOR I = 1 TO 12
280 PRINT D(I)
290 NEXT I
300 DATA 74, 12, 19, 5, 83, 18
310 DATA 4, 21, 36, 44, 62, 50
320 END

READY
RUN NH


4
5
12
18
19
21
36
44
50
62
74
83



TIME:   0.12 SECS.

READY
```

Fig. D-1.   An alternative method of a numeric sort.

Summary of Other Built-In Functions
APPENDIX E

Function*	Function Value
ATN(X)	The arctangent of X in radians, that is, the angle whose tangent is X.
COS(X)	The cosine of X, where X is in radians.
EXP(X)	The exponential of X, that is, the value of the base of natural logarithms raised to the power X.
LOG(X)	The natural logarithm of X, where X must be greater than zero.
SGN(X)	The sign of X: -1 if $X < 0$; 0 if $X = 0$; and $+1$ if $X > 0$.
SIN(X)	The sine of X, where X is in radians.
TAN(X)	The tangent of X, where X is in radians.

*X stands for a numeric expression.

Selected
Bibliography
APPENDIX F

BASIC BOOKS

Harvey Deitel, *Introduction to Computer Programming*, Prentice-Hall, 1977.

John Kemeny and Thomas Kurtz, *BASIC Programming*, Second Edition, Wiley, 1971.

Carl Pegels, *BASIC, A Computer Programming Language*, Holden-Day, 1973.

C. J. Sass, *BASIC Programming & Applications*, Allyn and Bacon, 1976.

Bernard M. Singer, *Programming in BASIC, With Applications*, McGraw-Hill, 1973.

FINANCIAL BOOKS

Charles T. Horngren, *Accounting for Management Control*, Third Edition, Prentice-Hall, 1974.

Eric L. Kohler, *A Dictionary for Accountants*, Fifth Edition, Prentice-Hall, 1975.

Lawrence Lipkin et al, *Accountant's Handbook of Formulas and Tables*, Prentice-Hall, 1963.

C. Rollin Niswonger and Philip E. Fess, *Accounting Principles*, Twelfth Edition, South-Western Publishing Co., 1977.

J. Fred Weston and Eugene F. Brigham, *Essentials of Managerial Finance*, Third Edition, The Dryden Press, 1974.

INDEX

Semivariable costs, 211
Signal value, 93, 96
Skip a line, 32
Sorting, 147–153, 277
  alphabetic, 150
  nonnumeric, 150
Spacing, columnar, 29
  vertical, 29
SQR, 76
Square root, 76, 109
START, 48
STEP, 110, 112
Straight-line depreciation, 247, 251
String, character, 11
Subroutine, 117–132
Subscripts, 112, 116, 117, 137
Subtraction, 34
Sum-of-the-years-digits deprecia-
  tion, 247, 251
Switch, program, 197, 198
Symbols, flowchart, 47, 48
System commands, 32

TAB, 29
Table, 137, 142
Table lookup, 142
Tax, income, 251, 255, 257
Teletypewriter, 4, 5, 7, 21, 57
THEN, 14, 109, 110
Time-sharing, 3
Time-sharing service, 5
Truncate, 71, 73, 101

Unconditional branch, 15, 127
UNSAVE, 270

Value, dummy, 77
Variable budgets, 211
Variable costs, 211
Variable name, 7, 9, 11, 21, 37, 57,
  61, 96, 137
Variable name legend, 61
Verb, 21, 37
Vertical spacing, 29, 32

WHAT, 21
Whole number, 71, 72

Zeroes, 71
=, 8, 9, 40, 61, 92
+, 9, 11, 27, 57
−, 57, 60
*, 38, 57, 58
/, 40, 51, 57
,, 10, 23, 29, 78
;, 78
", 11
O (letter "oh"), 21
0 (zero), 21
?, 39, 41, 42
>, 14, 40, 92
<, 92
>=, 92
<=, 92
<>, 92
$, 96
( ), 58, 59, 73
←, 26
↑, 57
\, 25